Heartland Utopia

–HEARTLAND–
UTOPIA

WILLIAM ALLEN WHITE ON
THE IDEAL MIDWESTERN TOWN

Edited by

Charles Delgadillo and Jason Stacy

University Press of Kansas

Published by the University Press of Kansas (Lawrence, Kansas 66045), which was organized by the Kansas Board of Regents and is operated and funded by Emporia State University, Fort Hays State University, Kansas State University, Pittsburg State University, the University of Kansas, and Wichita State University.

Library of Congress Cataloging-in-Publication Data is available.

LCCN: 2025032650

ISBN (cloth): 9780700640287

ISBN (epub): 9780700640294

British Library Cataloguing-in-Publication Data is available.

Authorised Representative Details: Easy Access System Europe

Mustamäe tee 50, 10621 Tallinn, Estonia | gpsr.requests@easproject.com

Jacket design by Karl Janssen

Photographs: Buildings: Matt Oaks/Shutterstock.com.

Sky: shine.graphics/Shutterstock.com.

Contents

Introduction

"The American country town is not Utopia; for Utopia is the hay on the end of the
stick before the donkey's nose, moving forward as he strains under his load to get his
heart's desire. But the American country town is much like the Utopia of the mid-
Victorian dream."
William Allen White, "The Other Side of Main Street," 1921

William Allen White, the editor of *The Emporia Gazette,* passed away at the
age of seventy-five on January 29, 1944. One might expect that the passing of
a newspaper editor in a small town of approximately fifteen thousand people
would have attracted little more than local attention, but the truth was quite
the opposite. William Allen White was an American institution, and his passing was national news even at the height of the Second World War. Condo-
lences rolled in from important journalists, literary figures, and world leaders,
including President Franklin Delano Roosevelt. The president commented
that America had lost one of its "wisest and most beloved editors in the death
of William Allen White," a man who was unsurpassed as "a writer of terse,
forcible, and vigorous prose" and who had "ennobled the profession of journalism which he served with such unselfish devotion through more than two
score years." Roosevelt confessed that White's "passing brings a real sense of
personal loss, for we had been the best of friends for years."[1]

Many talented small-town figures leveraged national acclaim into a big
city career, including such Kansas luminaries as poet Walt Mason, author
Dorothy Canfield Fisher, and theatrical producer Brock Pemberton. White
bucked this pattern. Despite having achieved national fame and hobnobbing

1. Franklin D. Roosevelt to Sallie White, January 29, 1944, Franklin D. Roosevelt Papers,
FDR Presidential Library, Hyde Park, NY.

regularly with society's upper crust in America's leading cities, White stead-
fastly remained an Emporia resident for half a century. Leaving Emporia for
the big city would have been convenient for White, who maintained an active
travel schedule and interacted frequently with the nation's elite. Money was
not a problem, since he had several opportunities to sell the *Gazette* at a large
profit and then accept one of several generously compensated job offers as a
columnist for urban newspapers. Being his own boss gave White the social,
economic, and editorial independence that he craved, but he stayed in Emporia for hard-nosed, pragmatic reasons as well. White was a clever marketer
who understood the value of his unique brand as "the voice of Main Street,"
and he was well-positioned to preach his vision of the kind of nation the
United States ought to be from this pulpit. America could be an ideal small
town writ large: a prosperous, happy country built on equality, on opportunity, on free and fair competition, and on neighborly generosity. One where
everyone had a chance to excel, and no one would be abandoned or forgotten. White was not naive, and he understood that this vision of America was
a dream to strive toward rather than an existent reality. Nevertheless, White
saw himself as a pioneer sowing the seeds of a great harvest to come, and he
believed that the small-town civilization he venerated represented what was
best in America.[2]

A Commercial Enterprise and an Enterprising Kansan

Nostalgic memory has shaped our conception of the particular attributes of the
Midwestern small town: its main street of independently owned businesses, its
rows of nineteenth-century houses with neat lawns, its surrounding agricultural districts of independent farms. Actually, these circumstances developed
largely for economic reasons. The Northwest Ordinance of 1785 established a
six-by-six square mile pattern of townships, which allowed for more uniform
settlement patterns than had been in place previously in Kentucky and other

2. White was one among many Midwesterners who understood their state in these
terms. James H. Madison characterizes Indianans' self-conception during the early twentieth century in similar terms. See *The Indiana Way: A State History* (Indiana University
Press, 1986).

territories south of the Ohio River.[3] The township grid provided the organizational kernel for the settlers who moved west and established towns around a commercial district of artisans and merchants serving independent, semi-subsistence farmers. By contrast, seventeenth-century New England villages organized themselves around a village green and a community church, while towns in the Southern states were centered on the region's system of plantations and subsistence farms. The Ohio River afforded American settlers a natural route into the southern portions of the Northwest Territory, and the forced purge of Native peoples after the War of 1812 paved the way for the new states of Indiana and Illinois. Native peoples were likewise forcibly removed from the upper Midwest or forced onto reservations after the Blackhawk War (1832), paralleling the 1830s removal of nations in the Southeast during the Trail of Tears.

The Midwest was positioned for white settler communities that produced goods for national distribution by the early nineteenth century. Midwestern farmers therefore practiced subsistence farming only partially, connected as they were to an increasingly national trade network from the Mississippi River to the port of New Orleans. Eventually this network expanded via the Great Lakes and the Erie Canal to include cities in the Northeast and reaching the rest of the world through their ports. By midcentury, railroads connected many small Midwestern towns to each other and to large regional centers, especially Chicago. In this regard, residents of small towns depended upon a "main street" commercial center, which ultimately provided farmers in the surrounding countryside with supplies, services, and access to other markets. Agricultural goods from the hinterland flowed along a river of commerce via the local grain elevator and railroad tracks that passed through the heart of the community.[4] Midwestern towns, at their inception, were commercial enterprises.

Kansas occupied a peculiar place in nineteenth-century America: It was simultaneously on the frontier and at the center of American national conflict. Beyond the borders of the Northwest Territory that made up an older

3. Gregory H. Nobles, "Straight Lines and Stability: Mapping the Political Order of the Anglo-American Frontier," *Journal of American History* 80, no. 1 (1993): 34.

4. James E. Davis, *Frontier Illinois* (Indiana University Press, 1998), 93, 220–234, and William Cronon, *Nature's Metropolis: Chicago and the Great West* (W. W. Norton, 1991), 59–70.

portion of the Midwest, the land that became the state of Kansas was part of the vast Louisiana Purchase (1803). The Kansas Territory was established by the Kansas-Nebraska Act of 1854, which opened territory that had ostensibly been closed to enslaved labor since the Missouri Compromise of 1820. This unclear status led to conflict between pro- and anti-slavery white populations almost upon the territory's establishment. Eastern Kansas was a battleground between pro-slavery and anti-slavery free-soil forces throughout the late 1850s, with some of the best-remembered incidents led by abolitionist John Brown. William Allen White's Emporia was founded in 1857 at the height of this miniature civil war, known as "Bleeding Kansas," that presaged the violence of the Civil War four years later. Territorial status also ignited conflict with the Native peoples who had been forcibly settled there during the 1830s, as well as nations who were native to the region. The Iowa, Kaw, Kickapoo, Potawatomi, Sac, and Fox nations, among others, were constricted to ever smaller reservations during the 1850s. Meanwhile, the territory's southern border was disputed by the Osage and Cherokee nations, a conflict that was only resolved after the Civil War with a cession of Cherokee land.[5]

Emporia was still very much a frontier town when White was born on February 10, 1868, and the town's settlement reflected the rush to profit common in previously settled Midwestern states. White's parents, Allen and Mary Ann White, were entrepreneurs who tried their hands at a variety of businesses, including a farm, a hotel, and a drug store. Allen White was a local Democratic Party leader, and it seemed likely that son would follow father into the party until Allen White passed away suddenly on October 4, 1882. Mary Ann White, a staunch Republican who had attended one of the Lincoln-Douglas debates as a young college student, ultimately molded her son in her own political image. Pragmatism also played a role in White's decision to become a Republican. In a state that was dominated by the GOP, anyone who wanted to play a defining role in Kansas politics had to be a Republican.

White graduated from high school in 1884 and his mother saw to it that he attended Emporia College, but he was a poor student who found academic life uninteresting compared to the allure of a newspaper career. White made

5. See H. Craig Miner and William E. Unrau, *The End of Indian Kansas: A Study in Cultural Revolution 1854–1871* (University Press of Kansas, 1990).

his entrée to the newspaper business during his college years by working as a printer's devil, a typesetter, a cub reporter, and a business manager on several small-town newspapers. Taking the advice of a friend, White transferred to the University of Kansas in Lawrence for the fall 1886 semester. KU offered White ample social opportunities and he eagerly embraced student life, but his failure to pass a required geometry course meant he would never graduate. Instead, White dropped out of KU in December 1889 to take a job managing the *El Dorado Republican*. His duties included selling advertising, supervising the staff, ordering supplies, contributing copy, and doing anything else that was necessary to see to the newspaper's successful publication. Occasionally his copy was picked up and republished in other regional newspapers, including *The Kansas City Star*.

Jon Lauck reminds us that local newspapers flourished throughout the Midwest during this period, and many prominent figures found their start in local journalism. Williams Jennings Bryan edited a paper in Omaha, Nebraska, before his rise to fame as the Democratic (and sometime Populist) standard-bearer in the presidential elections of 1896, 1900, and 1908. Arthur Vandenburg, senator from Michigan and motivating force behind support for the creation of the United Nations, edited the *Grand Rapids Herald* for a time. Illinois Senators Adlai Stevenson and Paul Simon both got their start in the newspaper business.[6] In the late nineteenth century, a local newspaper was a reasonable place from which to launch a public career.

Kansas in the 1890s was at the height of the Populist revolt, which was primarily an uprising of farmers against the elites they accused of limiting access to credit, of taking an inordinate share of the profit from their labor, and of abusing their political control. The value of staple crops fell after the Civil War when production outstripped demand, and Midwestern farmers accused bankers, railroads, and financiers of benefiting from their economic plight. As crop prices fell, farmers faced mounting debts and shrinking profits. The Populists' appeal to the free coinage of silver was part of a larger fight against economic interests that shaped a farmer's destiny, such as banks that held their mortgages, railroads that controlled the transportation networks, and investors who set prices in faraway stock exchanges. According to the Populists,

6. Jon Lauck, "The Shredding of Midwestern Newspapers," *Middle West Review* 9, no. 2 (2023): 6.

these nefarious forces left farmers at the mercy of their debts by controlling the national market for agricultural staples.[7]

White understood the economic logic behind the Populist movement, but he strongly identified with the town's political, business, and social elite, and he could not stomach the Populists' rural and lower-class character. The *El Dorado Republican* gave him a perch from which he could hurl vicious barbs at the Populists, and White's assaults eventually earned him a job as the Kansas political reporter for *The Kansas City Journal.* The *Journal* was a Republican machine newspaper that slavishly toed the party line, but the job put White into contact with Kansas political leaders and shepherded him into the inner sanctum of Midwestern machine politics. White soon outgrew the *Journal* and found work at *The Kansas City Star*, a first-rate newspaper that mentored his development as a professional journalist. By the spring of 1895, White was ready to strike out on his own and began casting about for a suitable newspaper.

White purchased a failing Populist newspaper, *The Emporia Gazette*, on June 1, 1895. The purchase was funded largely by loans from leading Kansas Republican machine figures, and White immediately deployed the *Gazette* against the state's Populists. Although White's fusillades made him popular among the town's elite and the Republican political establishment, they also opened him up to a daily stream of harassment from local Populists as he made his way through town. Such was the case on the morning of August 13, 1896. The weather was hot, the presidential election was underway, and White was in a hurry to depart for his annual summer vacation when he was cornered by several Populists seeking a political argument. White evaded his antagonists and returned to the *Gazette*'s office, where he dashed off a prickly editorial mocking the Populists as a pack of fools, lunatics, and failures. The piece, entitled "What's the Matter with Kansas?" blamed the Populists themselves for the state's economic stagnation. The Populists were men "who hate prosperity," wanted to "give the prosperous man the dickens," and "legislate the thriftless man into ease," and White blamed them entirely for driving both capital and potential residents away from Kansas. After turning in his editorial copy, White promptly departed for his summer vacation in Colorado.

The piece spread like wildfire in Republican newspapers, and the

---

7. See Charles Postel, *The Populist Vision* (Oxford University Press, 2007) and Michael Kazin, *The Populist Persuasion: An American History* (Cornell University Press, 1998).

presidential campaign of Republican William McKinley soon distributed it by the millions. White returned from Colorado to find that he was famous. McKinley defeated Bryan in the 1896 presidential election and White was offered a patronage job as a reward for his role in the campaign, which he declined. Nevertheless, "What's the Matter with Kansas?" made White a national figure, and with fame came material rewards. White received contracts to publish several well-received short stories about Kansas life, and the exposure eventually earned him lucrative contracts to write articles and short stories for national publications such as *McClure's Magazine*. The short stories White penned also led to his friendship with Theodore Roosevelt, then assistant secretary of the Navy, who had enjoyed them and wanted to meet the author. White was inspired by Roosevelt's vision of national greatness and was enthralled after Roosevelt earned national acclaim through his "Rough Rider" exploits in the Spanish-American War (1898). The two men became close friends, and Roosevelt became a guiding light that drew White inexorably into the Progressive reform movement. Meanwhile, Populism withered when prosperity returned after the 1896 presidential election, and White's fame attracted advertising from national corporations that made the *Gazette* financially profitable. By 1900 White felt sufficiently confident about both his and Emporia's success to declare that his dream, a transformed "Emporia . . . from the country village, to the energetic, enterprising town," had come to fruition.[8]

Heartland Utopia: William Allen White on the Ideal Midwestern Town does not seek to be a comprehensive review of White's writing. Instead, it includes a selection of work that spans nearly twenty-five years of White's writing with a focus on his idealized Midwestern community. For White, the ideal Midwestern community was a utopia that lay somewhere between the settler dreams of the mid-nineteenth century and the first twenty years of the twentieth. The structure of this edition is chronological, and divided into two eras.

The first, between 1896 to 1919, reflects White's rising national popularity. White's writings for both the *Gazette* and national outlets positioned him as the voice of the Midwestern small town, an increasingly representative place

8. "Street Fair Notes," October 5, 1899, *Emporia Weekly Gazette*.

for popular audiences during this period.[9] Our selections from these years trace White's ongoing effort to translate his romanticized Emporia into what he perceived to be essential American traits, including a pragmatic egalitarianism based on independent households and businesses, social mobility, and a broad neighborliness that fostered gradual social progress. Needless to say, White's utopian ideal left out whole populations and conflicts, and while it proved to be compelling for many Americans, a romanticized Midwestern town became increasingly untenable over the course of the twentieth century in the face of economic flux, political change, world wars, social shocks, and cultural conflict.

The second half of *Heartland Utopia* includes selections of writings between 1921 and 1931, which track White's reaction to a mounting set of challenges to this ideal that included nascent modernism, a resurgent Ku Klux Klan, the growing influence of urban culture, the reappearance of isolationist and nativist policies, and the disappearance of Progressive politics within the Republican Party. During these years, as White was faced with political disappointment and personal tragedy, his writing grew increasingly dismayed by challenges to the ideals he took to be both practical and universal.

These two periods of William Allen White's writing offer insights for modern readers. Between 1896 and 1931, White established an early version of a recurring idealized region. Later called the "heartland," this was a land of small towns, friendly neighbors, and stable national "values," where local sports, civic institutions, and "neighborliness" shaped a community.[10] White's works during this period also engaged critiques of this romantic ideal, and so they hint at the contours of the United States' recurring culture wars between the rural and urban, the retrograde, the progressive, the nostalgic, and the new. In this regard, White's writings offer a primary source for our own times too.

9. See Jason Stacy, *Spoon River America: Edgar Lee Masters and the Myth of the American Small Town* (University of Illinois Press, 2021).

10. True, "heartland" did not become a common term for the Midwest until the middle of the twentieth century. For example, the National Geographic Society first used the term to characterize the Midwest in 1952. Andrew R. L. Cayton, Richard Sisson, Chris Zacher, eds., *The American Midwest, an Interpretive Encyclopedia* (Indiana University Press, 2007), 72.

Rearguard Reformer

White established himself as an author of small-town short stories with *The Real Issue: A Book of Kansas Stories* (1896) and *The Court of Boyville* (1899), while his editorials in national publications increasingly solidified his profile as the voice of rural common sense. It is during this period that White's portrayal of Emporia as representative arose in tandem with trends that framed the Midwest as normative. *Heartland Utopia* begins with three short stories from *The Real Issue* that trace White's understanding of the Midwestern town as it matured from frontier enterprise to middle-class community. The first, "The City of Aqua Pura," depicts a failed pioneering town, which drew inspiration from more sophisticated stories of Midwestern hardship by authors like Hamlin Garland (1891). In the town of Aqua Pura, the settler Barringer and his daughter remain too long in an untenable environment and ultimately find themselves deserted by neighbors and destroyed by nature. While the East Coast settlers of Aqua Pura built a civil society in western Kansas that reflected the ideals of the old Northeast, their unwillingness to adapt to the environment augured their doom, culminating in a flood that washed the town away after years of drought. "The Home-coming of Colonel Hucks," on the other hand, offers a foil to "The City of Aqua Pura" by describing the "homecoming" of a farmer and his wife, who expectantly visit their native Ohio after a life on a Kansas homestead, only to realize that the Kansas they helped build had become a land with "lower taxes, better schools, and more advantages in every way." In these two stories, White exhibited a long-standing mythology of Midwestern settlement. Instead of a historical Kansas of Native removal and conflict over enslaved labor, White's Kansas Territory elided social conflict by pitting nature against white settlers, who meet the environment's resistance with common sense, thrift, and steady accumulation. Colonel and Mrs. Hucks's rewards grow from their hard work and modesty, positioning them as rightful inheritors of their happiness.

The settler generation's thrift and hard work came to fruition in the generation after settlement, represented in this edition by "The King of Boyville," which drew from humorous, boy-centric stories exemplified by Mark Twain's *The Adventures of Tom Sawyer* (1876).[11] Here, Piggy Pennington symbolizes

11. The late nineteenth and early twentieth centuries saw many versions of this kind

the generation after a Midwestern community's founding, where a mature town grows from its frontier roots into an ostensibly egalitarian community. In Piggy's Boyville, all boys "are born . . . free and equal" since "in a small town, every boy, good or bad, rich or poor, stands . . . on his own merits." Despite White's egalitarian claims for Boyville, Piggy represents the rising economic status of Main Street, as his father "kept a grocery store," positioning him within a growing middle-class economy of independent businesses and discrete households. Here are the small town's tree-lined streets of popular portrayals during the twentieth century. Piggy's hijinks, as he pursues a crush on an unnamed classmate, take place within a stable economy built by level-headed forebears. Ultimately, Piggy captures the attention of the young girl and embarks on "the soil of an unknown country," namely, the reproduction of a middle-class family for the next generation. Piggy might inherit his father's store, purchase a family home, and thereby perpetuate the "neighborliness" that White eulogized in later writings. In these three stories, then, White traced the trajectory of Midwestern towns from settlement communities to towns of normative middle-class households, a naturalized progression of the American republic manifested on the Kansas prairie.

In this regard, White's version of Midwestern settlement echoed contemporary conceptions of the region's origins and maturation. Only a few years before the publication of *The Real Issue*, the University of Wisconsin historian Frederick Jackson Turner characterized the Midwest as the first truly American region, unencumbered by the vestiges of European culture. For Turner,

> [the history of the frontier] begins with the Indian and the hunter; it goes on to tell of the disintegration of savagery by the entrance of the trader, the pathfinder of civilization; we read the annals of the pastoral stage in ranch life; the exploitation of the soil . . . of corn and wheat in sparsely settled farming communities; the intensive culture of the denser farm settlement; and finally the manufacturing organization with city and factory system.[12]

---

of coming-of-age story by prominent figures. Consider, for example, attorney Clarence Darrow's *Farmington* (1903).

12. Frederick Jackson Turner, "The Significance of the Frontier in American History," *Annual Report of the American Historical Association* (1894): 119–227.

And by implication,

> The Middle region was less English than the other sections. It had . . . a varied society, the mixed town and county system of local government, a varied economic life, many religious sects.[13]

Turner's sequence of settlement echoed long-standing myths of the frontier traced by Henry Nash Smith, where pioneering supposedly "fostered economic equality . . . [and] made for an increase of democracy."[14] According to this myth, the region's maturation allowed it to subsume the Northeast as the seat of American identity. In his earliest writings, White tapped into these broader tropes of the American frontier and its first fruits in the American Midwest. His essay, "Emporia and New York," for the *American Magazine* (1907), which is included in this edition, compared Emporia to New York City and found the latter wanting in important ways: "One may say that in Emporia there is that equality of opportunity for the youth—equality of education, of financial backing, of social standing—which guarantees a democratic community." The Midwestern town, though settled later than the Northeast, represented the culmination of the Founding through the actualization of the nation's founding ideals: "Country-dwelling American men and women are instinctively democratic." And while White generously sought to draw common American traits from the comparison—"We are of one blood—city and country—in America; our differences are superficial—the "social sympathy . . . among neighbors" that bound Emporians to each other offered a naturally-arising ethos in contrast to hurly-burly New York City, where space was limited, neighbors were strangers, and opportunities for economic prosperity were curtailed. Here, then, lay an early conception of the Midwest as essential to the American enterprise, a region newer than the Northeast in terms of settlement but fundamental in light of the nation's promise.

"Emporia and New York" exemplifies a latent truism in White's writings on small towns: His intended readers were not likely residents of rural communities. In these pieces, White adopted the tone of a knowledgeable resident

13. Turner, "Significance of the Frontier."
14. Henry Nash Smith, *Virgin Land: The American West as Symbol and Myth* (Harvard University Press, 1950), 252, 253.

who introduced a reader to a town's peculiar ways. And so, White's essays read like a tour guide's boosterism, encouraging readers to come away with an upbeat impression that reinforces a visitor's expectations with local color and charming anecdotes. White was popular in national publications like the *American Magazine, The Atlantic,* and *McClure's* because he reassured readers that there was a place, somewhere in the interior, where long-standing American bromides about equality, opportunity, familiarity and neighborliness abided in the face of economic change and social flux. By the first decade of the twentieth century, the United States had seen a generation of boom-and-bust economic cycles, rapid and destabilizing industrial and urban growth, and violent labor unrest.[15] The same year White's "Emporia and New York" appeared in the *American Magazine,* the New York Stock Exchange fell by nearly half, and the US economy was stabilized only with an infusion of cash by the investment banker J. P. Morgan.[16] Utopian visions reflect anxieties of the audiences to which they appeal, and White's Midwestern town assured readers that their version of a normative community abided somewhere in the center of the country. In this way, the popularity of White's portrayals revealed contemporary apprehensions about the state of the nation at large.

While White never sought to characterize the ethics of the Midwestern town in a systematic fashion, some broad attributes can be gleaned from a review of his writings before 1920. Significantly, in a nation of economic turbulence, White's small town incubated egalitarianism and social mobility. For example, "A Typical Kansas Community," published in *The Atlantic Monthly* in 1897 (one year after William Jennings Bryan's defeat in the presidential election), characterized the small town as an "intense social democracy," where a fluid social structure made the difference between "old rich" and "new rich" "meaningless." Instead, the pragmatism and hard labor that settled the frontier fostered a civil society that eschewed class and cultural hierarchies of the old Northeast. In "typical" Kansas communities, opportunity and social uplift abided. In "a family containing several grown-up children" for example, "one daughter attends lodge socials . . . [while] . . . the eldest daughter attends the

---

15. For an overview of this period, see T. J. Jackson Lears, *Rebirth of a Nation: The Making of Modern America, 1877–1920* (Harper Perennial, 2010).

16. See Robert F. Bruner, Sean D. Carr, *The Panic of 1907: Lessons Learned from the Market's Perfect Storm* (John Wiley & Sons, 2009).

meeting of the Browning Circle [a literary society]." And, if she is "bored for an hour or two; she probably comes home with a married couple who live on her street." A son may go "across the railroad track" to a "noisy quadrille on a bare kitchen floor" while his parents "may be present at the weekly meeting of the Bon Ton Whist Club, where the evening may start with an "elaborate . . . supper." These public-private organizations "indicate the utter absence . . . of what in older communities . . . [are] called class lines" and so "wealth plays a minor part in the appraisal of people" since "no one knows anybody's grandfather's previous condition" and therefore "young people find their own places." Local town gatherings—"football games, baseball games, political meetings"—round out this civil society and "play a more important part than the opera-house" since they are "not manacled by decorum:" "the girls join in the college yells, talk across the ropes to the players . . . surge up and down the line with the boys, and no one sneers." A similarly naturalized sorting process takes place in the public high school. There, "an ambitious mother, living on the wrong side of the railroad, is glad to find that her daughter has passed above the 'surprise party crowd' . . . and planted herself firmly among the 'entre-nous.'" This ascent allows the daughter opportunity to "marry into the 'young whist crowd,'" but even if unsuccessful, "in a few years she will begin to cultivate her mind, and . . . drift naturally into the Browning Circle."

The easy mixing of classes and interests, according to White, was maintained through "neighborliness," a natural trait that grew from the town's unaffected egalitarianism. In "Patriotism and Things" (1905) from *The Emporia Gazette*, White claimed that "love for those outside the family is a trait found only . . . in man," thereby establishing good social relations as a natural human state, and the small town as naturally representative. Accordingly, the true patriot, which White saw as a status in which one's loyalty grew in concentric circles out from one's community, "is public spirited, . . . [and] sinks his own comforts, . . . for consideration of the public good." Here, for example, was the Emporia railroad brakeman, who risked himself daily for the good of the community; in fact "any avocation from the ditch to the desk . . . does . . . his community honor by the life he lives." And, therefore, "we should honor our neighbors more" by "lend[ing] a hand where you can." In this regard, White's concept of neighborliness was socially engaged, but its engagement went no further than the town's extremities. Economically, the town's connections to the rest of the nation were incidental and neighborliness proved to be a universal ethos practiced on behalf of the people down the street. While railroads situated Midwestern towns within a national network of production and consumption, the train tracks for White only represented the porous dividing line of a fluid social structure. This gave White's Midwestern utopia both an insular and universal nature: It was both self-contained and, through its manifestation of American ideals, universally significant.

And yet there were threats to this natural order. When a town grew too large, familiarity between neighbors collapsed. Thereafter, businesses and political interest groups pursued power against the common interests of the community, as in White's story "The Man on Horseback" from *Stratagems and Spoils* (1899). Here, a Midwestern town grown city-sized saw its social structures ossify, and avarice and personal interest overcame the public good. Growth, then, undermined neighborliness, as if a larger purview distracted townspeople from their obligations to each other. Likewise, outsiders could throw a community into humorous confusion, as when the effete and pretentious Beverly Amidon came to town in "The Coming of the Leisure Class" (*Saturday Evening Post*, 1905) and "introduced ping-pong," rode "around the country bareheaded with two or three girls when honest men were at work," acquired "a fine leather-colored tan," and tried to organize a "polo club." And while White presented Amidon's comings and goings as an opportunity to explore the humorous incongruity of the fashionable newcomer in simple Emporia, he noted that, after his departure, Amidon fell on hard times: "He had to go to work. . . . so he went to Kansas City. He did not seem to 'make it' socially there, for he wrote to the girls that Kansas City was cold and distant and that everything was ruled by money." In effect, through the character Beverly Amidon, White made national readers spectators to the clash between the simple-rural and the cosmopolitan-urbane, and explicitly guided their sympathies toward the former. Ultimately, "in time our social life will resume its old estate" and the "caste lines set by the advent of [the] leisure class will be obliterated" so that it "will be no longer bad form for the dry-goods clerk to dance with the grocer clerk's wife at the Charity Ball." And while White's review of Amidon's visit was more light-hearted than his dark tale of greed and hypocrisy in "The Man on Horseback," the underlying message was the same: The town's best attributes were found when it remained small, its influences local, and its pretentions not much farther than the county line.

White claimed that town newspapers maintained localism and neighborly familiarity. In this regard, he wrote himself into his own utopia, and characterized the newspaper as the means by which the town knew itself. In "Scribes and Pharisees" (*Saturday Evening Post*, 1905), White let his middle-brow audience in on a secret: "In our little newspaper office . . . we know many intimate things about our people which we do not print." White then printed these intimate things: "We know . . . what wives will not let their husbands indorse other men's notes at the bank," "we know about the row the Baptists are having to get rid of the bass singer in the choir," "we know that the Methodists are having the same trouble with their soprano . . . ," "we know the politician who gets five dollars a day for his 'services' at the polls, and the man who takes three, and the man who will work for the good of the cause in the precious hope of a blessed reward at some future county convention." This tabulation of "secrets" served two purposes and exemplified White's sense of the role of the newspaper in the small town. First, it offered a set of anecdotes that reduced a Midwestern town's secrets to a size as charming as the town itself: manageable things, common human foibles, that likely elicited a nostalgic reaction from more urbane readers. Second, these anecdotes positioned White on the side of his intended audience: middle-class readers who likely did not live in small towns, or if they did, were fed a version of themselves that left more dire secrets unexposed. White, then, confirmed for readers that somewhere in the heartland a good and simple life existed. There, "a family vernacular has grown up in our paper which our people understand" though it is "Greek to those outside the circle." White provided his readers with translations both charming and reassuring.

White's role as small town guide also allowed him to frame his hesitant relationship with social and economic reform in humble terms: impatient activism lay outside the boundaries of "neighborliness." In this way, White situated himself within the progressive wing of the Republican party. White served as a convenient representative for moderate reformers who appealed to middle-class dismay over the industrial economy of the early twentieth century, while at the same time soothing their anxieties over more radical reform programs. Theodore Roosevelt's ascension to the White House after President McKinley's assassination in 1901, and his election outright in 1904, inaugurated a period of federal legislation like the Pure Food and Drug Act (1906) that appealed directly to middle-class consumers. White characterized reforms like this as growing naturally from common sense. For example, in a 1907 editorial from the *Gazette*, "A Slow Process," White promoted Roosevelt's "Square Deal" as necessarily working "from below upwards" since "the Lord is in no hurry" and "Legislation that tries to pull men ahead of their own instincts is often ineffective." Instead, change came "by every man uhselfishly paring off his own faults, and trusting to time to take care of his neighbor." Activists are "good for us. But they are sorely trying sometimes" since they run "ahead of the battle line . . . and grow irritable . . . because the line does not advance." Nevertheless, "all is evened up someway" since "honesty is not a set thing. It grows." White thereby traced structural reform to an ever-advancing horizon, appreciated only in hindsight and in increments. In this way, he situated his innate suspicion of radical politics within a framework of small-town pragmatics, and it was no wonder that White's ideal of consensual and measured reform proved appealing to moderate reformers like Roosevelt.

Other fields of social reform that shaped the twentieth century are largely absent from White's writings, particularly race and gender. Black Midwesterners are largely invisible in White's utopia, in contrast to the historical descendants of Exodusters who fled Southern states for opportunities on the Kansas prairie after the Civil War.[17] Black people occasionally appear on the margins. Colonel Hucks jokes after his excited dog celebrates his return, "Now lookie at that dog—come tearin' up here like he never saw white folks before!" In "The Coming of the Leisure Class," "black boys . . . loaf on the south side of the bank building through the long afternoons." And, later, in "A Look Ahead" from *The Old Order Changeth: A View of American Democracy* (1910), White dabbled in the Aryan racial theories popular among the reading classes during this period:[18] "But this blood will remain a clean Aryan blood, because there are no hordes of inferior races about us to sweep over us and debase our stock." Rare nods to the nation's racial complexity such as these belie another attribute of White's small-town utopia: by perpetuating a whitewashed trope that subsumed a troubled history, White perpetuated a myth of white homogeneity of Midwestern towns for the nation at large.[19]

17. For the seminal work on these migrants, see Nell Irvin Painter, *Exodusters: Black Migration to Kansas After Reconstruction* (W. W. Norton, 1986).

18. See, for example, Peter Gay, *The Cultivation of Hatred: The Bourgeois Experience Victoria to Freud* (W. W. Norton, 1993), 74–90.

19. For a history of the Great Migration and rural Midwestern towns, see Jennifer

White's Midwestern town also upheld traditional gender roles in the midst of a long-standing women's suffrage movement and challenges to the status quo.[20] His Kansas was "governed by petticoats" since "women shape public sentiment" in the state. Instead of dram-shops, town corners were "occupied by banks," and "a bookstore." Young men met in the latter, read books and magazines, and discussed recent sporting events and politics while "there is not one [there] whose name has been stained with scandal." In this way, White preserved the comforting notion for many readers that women remained confidently in their position as moral arbiters somewhere in the republic, outside of the realm of policy decision-making, but with a strong influence through their role as the sentimental core of the middle-class home. "The Court of Boyville" prepared Piggy's unnamed object of affection for this maternal role. Beverly Amidon, the stranger-to-town in "The Coming of the Leisure Class," contrasted a common-sense masculinity in White's utopia and was feminized as a result. When Amidon visited the newspaper office, a young staffer jokingly calls him the "Queen of the Handholders," a double-entendre that characterized Amidon's wooing as both lecherous and feminine. Later, after Amidon described his efforts to create "living pictures" using some of the young people in town, the staffer asked whether Amidon played "Psyche at the Pool . . . or a Breakfast Food baby," highlighting the stranger's feminine, or at least soft, features. In these cases, Amidon proved to be an aberration not only because of his pretense but also because of his challenges to masculine norms. White's townspeople mocked the newcomer for both muddying social norms and traversing gender traits. Readers are invited to laugh along with them.

By the end of the first decade of the twentieth century, White had become increasingly engaged by the moderate reform ideology of Theodore Roosevelt and other Republican progressives. He completed his first novel in 1908,

---

Sdunzik, *The Geography of Hate: The Great Migration Through Small-Town America* (University of Illinois Press, 2023).

20. See Eleanor Flexner, and Ellen F Fitzpatrick, *Century of Struggle: The Woman's Rights Movement in the United States* (Harvard University Press, 1996). For a survey of the fight for political, social, and sexual rights for women during the late nineteenth century, see Barbara Goldsmith, *Other Powers: The Age of Suffrage, Spiritualism, and the Scandalous Victoria Woodhull* (A. A. Knopf, 1998).

entitled *A Certain Rich Man*, which dramatized laissez-faire capitalism's effect on small-town America. There, according to White, a "prodigal son of predatory power and wealth" discovered "that he can do more good by personal service . . . than he can by getting money greedily and trying to do good with that." In this regard, White's protagonist served as a proxy for his arc from conservative to progressive: a conceited, materialistic young man who believed that he was better than the world and who slowly awakened to the middle-class reform ideology of Theodore Roosevelt's progressive Republicans.

A Certain Rich Man had no hero, according to White. The book reflected his belief that "human nature runs some good and some bad. There seems to be a regression which brings us all to the same moral average." Politically, *A Certain Rich Man* was a parable about the nineteenth century's unrestrained capitalism and crass materialism. The work sold thirty thousand copies in its first four months on the market, aided by its relevance to the ongoing progressive movement and by critical acclaim from the likes of Mark Twain. In praising the book, the progressive journal *La Follette's Magazine* asked how a democratic nation could allow a man like the book's main character to wreak such havoc without running afoul of the law. Theodore Roosevelt, then on safari in Africa, praised it as "a real, and very effective, tract for the times" that would help to advance "the cause of righteousness in our country." *A Certain Rich Man* was White's most successful novel by far, selling over a quarter of a million copies over the next two decades.[21]

White's first novel was such a success that he gave serious consideration to selling the *Gazette* and becoming a full-time novelist in the spring of 1911. Accordingly, he questioned his work as a journalist overall. He wondered whether he was "wrapping [his] one little old talent in a napkin" by neglecting his literary work in favor of politics and journalism, and he believed that he could preach the moderate progressive gospel more effectively through fiction. To this end, White courted potential buyers among his newspaper friends and by contacting a New York–based newspaper broker. Nothing came of the idea, however, and the family left Kansas in late August so that White could spend three or four months in Colorado "dead to the world," working on his new novel, *In the Heart of a Fool.*

21. Theodore Roosevelt to White, December 10, 1909, William Allen White Papers, Manuscript Division, Library of Congress, Washington, DC (hereafter WAW Papers).

White completed his rough draft in short order, summarizing its thesis as "there really are spiritual rewards for spiritual service and spiritual punishments for spiritual transgressions." The plot revolved around the tension between a Midwestern town's business-minded middle-class and its working-class, culminating in a labor strike. A union organizer's murder at the hands of vigilantes spurred both sides to find the grounds for cooperation, and White ended his book on an optimistic note. Unfortunately, it took him the next seven years to revise the novel for publication, and his progressive morality tale was badly suited for the cynical, postwar climate it encountered upon its publication in the fall of 1918. As White conceded, the First World War had changed the world so much as to make the story an anachronism, and he later called it "a real disappointment."[22] By late 1919 White resigned himself to work in nonfiction, and by midyear he was optimistically boosting the newly founded League of Nations by comparing its squabbling members to the pioneering stage of the Midwestern prairie, destined to eventual neighborliness.

Mid-Victorian Modern

The literary, social, and political culture of the early 1920s was considerably different from that which White had hitherto known. The Progressive Era had been marked by a spirit of optimism and reform, led by iconic figures such as Theodore Roosevelt and Woodrow Wilson. Both men departed the national stage in 1919, with Woodrow Wilson suffering a debilitating stroke and Theodore Roosevelt's unexpected death at the age of sixty. Neither the Democratic nor the Republican Parties fielded a leader of comparable stature. Worse, the nation was in the grips of the Red Scare, which White described as the "crazy notion to hunt 'em down and shoot 'em, and see red." The 1920 Republican presidential nomination went to a machine politician, Warren G. Harding, and the Democrats nominated conservative Ohio Governor James

22. White to Fred Trigg, May 29, 1911, WAW Papers; White to Murdock, August 20, 1911, WAW Papers; White to Roosevelt, October 16, 1911, WAW Papers; Richard W. Resh, "A Vision in Emporia: William Allen White's Search for Community," *Midcontinent American Studies* 10, no. 2 (1969): 20–22; White to Helen Mahin, October 7, 1929, WAW Papers.

M. Cox, who White summed as merely "Harding in Democrat terms." By the mid-1920s, in light of the unrealized dreams of the League of Nations and the United States' ability to make the world "safe for democracy," an isolationist and nativist temper soured the national mood.[23] White was left "heart broken about politics," and his hopes that the nation's dour outlook would be short-lived proved unfounded.[24]

The pain of national politics paled in comparison to the soul-crushing torment White suffered after the death of his sixteen-year-old daughter, Mary, in a horse-riding accident on May 13, 1921. Mary was a vivacious teenager who shared her father's impish streak along with his poor academic record, and she was both a handful and a joy to her parents. In contrast, White's twenty-year-old son, Bill Jr., studied at Harvard University, inheriting both his mother's serious demeanor and his father's writing talent. White loved his daughter as dearly as he loved his son, but he had a special place in his heart for Mary. Her death left both parents devastated, and White proposed taking his wife, Sallie, to Colorado for a vacation in the Rocky Mountains as a balm for their grief. Vacations in the Rockies had helped both of the Whites through many periods of mental and physical difficulty, but Sallie was too emotionally distraught to make the trip. The pain of Mary's death lingered, and White confessed seven months later that the couple still spoke about their daughter often, mixing tears with smiles. As White explained to his friend Herbert Hoover, Mary had been "an exceptional child. Full of gaiety and joy and quip and persiflage, and of wisdom far beyond her years."[25] White returned to something approaching normality within six months of Mary's death, but Sallie remained distraught for many more years.

White was always happiest when he was active, and one way that he recovered after his daughter's death was by throwing himself back into the effort to advance his vision of a neighborly American republic. The 1920s, unfortunately, were an infertile time for the kind of reform White envisioned.

23. As Woodrow Wilson justified US entry into the First World War in his war address, April 2, 1917.

24. White to Leonard Wood, August 7, 1919, WAW Papers; Borah to White, April 3, 1922, WAW Papers; "Be a Sport," *Emporia Gazette*, June 24, 1920; White to Rodney Elward, June 15, 1920, WAW Papers.

25. White to Herbert Hoover, August 16, 1921, WAW Papers; White to Victor Murdock, September 23, 1921, WAW Papers.

INTRODUCTION21

Furthering this dynamic was the fact that both political parties were heavily fragmented, with the Democrats divided between the North's ethnically diverse cities and the segregationist South, and the Republicans divided between the business-oriented Northeast and the more rural Midwest. But for White, the politics of fragmentation meant that common sense and an approach grounded in good faith, a kind of national neighborliness, could sooth national ills.

Few causes were more unpopular than that of organized labor in the aftermath of the Red Scare of 1919–1920, but White courageously voiced his support for striking railroad workers during the Great Railroad Strike of 1922, represented in this volume with the editorial "Emporia and the Strike." Carrying over his ideal of neighborliness from before the First World War, White reminded readers that the strikers were their "neighbors and friends," and that resolution required that citizens "keep our heads cool and our hearts always kind." Emporia was home to important railroad repair facilities and White hung a placard in his office window expressing support for the strike on the grounds that the workers had been treated unfairly. Despite their close friendship, Kansas Governor Henry J. Allen ordered White's arrest for violating a state anti-picketing law. The charge was eventually dismissed by the court, but White won the 1923 Pulitzer Prize for Editorial Writing for his piece "To an Anxious Friend," in which he explained to the governor that "you say that freedom of utterance is not for time of stress, and I reply with the sad truth that only in time of stress is freedom of utterance in danger." The editorial was widely reprinted, and White garnered support from major newspapers, from national groups such as the American Civil Liberties Union, and from Harvard Law Professor Felix Frankfurter, who wrote to White exclaiming "thank God we've got some people left with old fashioned guts!"[26]

Foreign policy was a second area where White sought to influence policy during the 1920s. The Senate's rejection of the Treaty of Versailles had not changed the fact that America was more involved in world affairs than ever, and White remained a strong internationalist. As he had at the inception of the League of Nations, he likened the world to a small-town American

26. "Free Speech in Kansas," *Emporia Gazette*, August 5, 1922, August 12, 1922, August 15, 1922; Felix Frankfurter to White, July 1922, WAW Papers; White to Roger Baldwin, September 13, 1922, WAW Papers.

neighborhood, with each "nation [a]s somewhat like a family." Each family in the neighborhood naturally saw itself as the best on the block, but each also had to accept the goodness of other families if it wanted to function as part of the community. Although White felt that America ought to "develop according to our own customs, our own blood, our own traditions," America could not treat other nations as if "we have the only customs, the only blood, the only traditions worthy of being preserved."[27]

The 1920s proved hostile to White's literary aspirations, as trends shifted to what critics now term "modernism," a movement that eschewed the reform-minded and sentimental literature of the first twenty years of the twentieth century. White looked back on the late 1890s and early 1900s, the era of his first professional success, with admiration for the earlier generation of writers who had "let themselves go; they believed in emotions," as he said in "For Those About to Die" (*The New Republic*, 1921). Such writers had "seen the physical miracle which populated the Mississippi valley . . . [and] . . . marveled at it; they frankly admired it." And while they "revolted at the materialism of the times," writers of the previous generation wrote books where "the heroes . . . were the people, or the embodied courage and faith and devotion of the people to the American spirit of progress." In this regard, White's wistful recollections characterized his own frustrated literary hopes. White critiqued 1920s writers who he alleged "psycho-analyze our subjects in fiction . . . [and] . . . the Silent Tear which once glittered upon the pages of American fiction is going dry . . . under some sort of literary Volstead act." Edgar Lee Masters was "dry surgery." Sherwood Anderson "gets away with every sort of cruelty" and "performs every sort of literary malpractice upon his heroines." F. Scott Fitzgerald "pin[s] up . . . the suppressed sex emanations of kids without releasing a temperature." Zona Gale "peddles a secret sorrow." Floyd Dell "is bone dry." The lot of them are "literary bootleggers," who "slip emotional hootch to us in queer packages."

Sinclair Lewis's breakthrough novel *Main Street* (1920) exemplified this dismaying trend. Lewis's novel revolved around an idealistic young woman from St. Paul, Minnesota, who moved to the small town of Gopher Prairie after marrying a local doctor. The woman soon discovered that Gopher Prairie was a drab and listless provincial village, and her efforts to reform the town proved futile. *Main Street* was written during the 1910s, but it resonated with

27. White to W. S. Dickey, April 29, 1920, WAW Papers.

the 1920s conflict between America's rising cosmopolitan society and its waning rural civilization. White liked the work, partly because it "makes us see our uglinesses, which are obvious, but often because they are so obvious, are overlooked." He wrote Lewis admitting that the Midwest had plenty of dull towns (typically those with fewer than five thousand residents), but he also claimed that one could find communities with "some civic spirit" that were "striving consciously to be just and beautiful."[28] White expanded this argument in his review of *Main Street*, entitled "The Other Side of Main Street" (*Collier's*, 1921), also included in this volume. There, White noted that Lewis "omit[ed] the facts about the pleasant . . . side of the street. . . . [Lewis's] facts fall short of the truth." Warming up to his argument, White chided Lewis for overlooking the fundamentals that made towns thriving communities, [w]ater, light, communication, heat, books, grass plots, sanitation, clean streets, [and] transportation are distributed equitably, almost equally. The telephone, the library, electric lights, running water in houses, schools, colleges, sewers. . . . [B]ehold the uplift." These simple, modern conveniences supported a civic life absent from Lewis's portrayals: the Chamber of Commerce, the Rotarians, "the Masons, the Knights of Columbus, the Red Men, the Elks, and the Moose, whose chief reason for being is fellowship. . . . [H]e is a rather measly citizen who is not a member of one of these bodies. . . . [H]e must be a cast-iron man who resists the infection of neighborliness that saturates them all." For White, neighborliness "marked the American small town" and "[m]en feel the strength of it, take courage from it, give themselves to it . . . and thus grow in stature by what they give." Ultimately, neighborliness, in the face of skepticism and half-blind cynicism like Sinclair Lewis's, defined the nation, "this belief that if you are good to somebody, somebody will be good to you . . . distinguishes Americans from the rest of mankind." Neighborliness as a distinguishing American quality was, for White, "not a product of our great cities, and not primarily is it a farm product. It is made in our country towns."

Like many Midwesterners, White saw the Midwest as the heart of American civilization, and he felt that it was under attack by outside forces. To

28. Jon Lauck, *From Warm Center to Ragged Edge: The Erosion of Midwestern Literary and Historical Regionalism, 1920–1965* (University of Iowa Press, 2017), 29–33; White to M. F. Amrine, January 22, 1926, WAW Papers; White to Herbert Croley, December 9, 1920, WAW Papers; White to Sinclair Lewis, November 23, 1920, WAW Papers.

White, Kansas seemed particularly important as the home of American reform. The state had been a laboratory for Progressive Era experiments in active government, including state-owned enterprises, regulations on freight and utility rates, pioneering labor laws, and a public university system that guaranteed admission to all high school graduates. White was proud of these innovations, which he attributed to the same Midwestern "country values" and "neighborliness" that he argued constituted the foundation of American progress. To White, American liberalism itself was merely "the application of a neighborly, village-minded aspiration to our national life."[29]

Yet cultural chauvinism was the dark side of White's faith in the supremacy of Midwestern civilization, especially his belief in Theodore Roosevelt's idea that race was an important component in national identity. The crime, corruption, and moral failings associated with America's large cities outraged White, who penned a 1922 article warning that Southern and Eastern European immigrants "from the low breeds of Europe" posed a dire cultural threat to American democracy. The article, entitled "What's the Matter with America?" (*Collier's*, 1922), included here, claimed that urban disorder was the product of the new immigrants' defective cultures, which lacked "Anglo-Saxon political taboos" against selfishness, corruption, and graft. He likened millions of urban immigrants to rapidly reproducing "political bacilli . . . tearing down the tissue of our institutions" with their alien culture. In contrast, White claimed that rural society had avoided the problems afflicting the nation's cities because country children were taught proper American values in the home, around town, and in church. White spoke volumes when he pronounced all other national issues "subsidiary to [the] fundamental clash of ideals" between those of rural America and those of the new immigrants, which he suggested might be genetically ingrained. The only hope for the survival of liberal democracy in America was to try to teach the new immigrants that "our ideals are better than theirs, or their ideals will overcome ours."[30]

29. James Shortridge, *The Middle West: Its Meaning in American Culture* (University Press of Kansas, 1989), 54–60; White, "The Blood of the Conquerors," *Collier's*, March 10, 1923, 5–6; Craig Miner, *Kansas: The History of the Sunflower State, 1854–2000* (University Press of Kansas, 2002), 190–220, 246–269.

30. William Allen White, "What's the Matter with America?" *Colliers*, July 1, 1922. See Gary Gerstle, *American Crucible: Race and Nation in the Twentieth Century* (Princeton University Press, 2001).

White proposed education as a remedy for the cultural infection he saw menacing American democracy, but many of his Midwestern neighbors preferred culture war. The Ku Klux Klan enjoyed a resurgence during the early 1920s as an organization that defended "traditional" values against urban elites, immigrants, religious minorities, and labor activists. While the Klan thrived in small towns dominated by native-born white Protestants, and its members were often middle-class professionals, historians like Leonard Moore have also connected the Klan in the 1920s to the recurring populist strain of American politics.[31] Kansas neatly fit these demographic profiles and political traditions, and while White was blind to the fact that his own rhetoric of native born, white, Protestant cultural superiority paralleled that of the Klan, he also likely sensed the populist current that drove the Klan of this era and reengaged his former misgivings about populist politics from late in the last century. By 1923 the Klan claimed approximately forty thousand members in Kansas, and Emporia had a Klan mayor, Klansmen infested the town's police department, and the *Gazette*'s exposés of Klan activities were met with a campaign of intimidation.[32]

The issue came to a head in 1924, when pro-Klan candidates won the Kansas gubernatorial nominations in both the Democratic and Republican parties. Outraged, White threw his own hat into the ring as an independent, declaring that he would defend American culture, small-town values, and the Constitution against the Klan. The K.K.K. was a "hooded gang of masked fanatics, ignorant and tyrannical in their ruthless oppression" of Catholics, Jews, African Americans, and immigrants. The group's doctrine of intolerance was an assault on the Constitution, which White called a "charter of freedom, under which men may live with one another under the rule of fraternity and neighborly consideration." He asserted that the Klan subverted the Anglo-Saxon notion of the rule of law by aiming to impose a shadow government that employed

31. Leonard J. Moore, *Citizen Klansmen: The Ku Klux Klan in Indiana, 1921–1928* (University of North Carolina, 1990), 2–3.

32. Rory McVeigh, *The Rise of the Ku Klux Klan: Right Wing Movements and National Politics* (University of Minnesota Press, 2009), 4–31, 55–75; Jack Wayne Traylor, "William Allen White's 1924 Gubernatorial Campaign," *Kansas Historical Quarterly* 42, no. 2 (1976): 180–191; White to H. B. Swope, September 17, 1921, WAW Papers,; Miner, *Kansas*, 252–257; Nancy MacLean, *Behind the Mask of Chivalry: The Making of the Second Ku Klux Klan* (Oxford University Press, 1994), xii–xiii, 10–32, 54–73, 99, 158.

"force instead of reason, terror instead of due process of law"; the Klan "undermines all that our fathers have fought for since free government has been established." White cast his candidacy as an opportunity for Kansans to defend the American political tradition and neighborly tolerance by voting for a "Governor to free Kansas from the disgrace of the Ku Klux Klan."[33] White ran a close third on election day with 150,000 votes, an impressive result considering that he had campaigned for less than six weeks, as an independent, and on a shoestring budget of just $476.60. Although White failed to win the governorship, his high-profile candidacy proved that the Republican victor could not afford to ignore anti-Klan Kansans. Furthermore, it helped to elect a slate of downballot, anti-Klan candidates who proved instrumental in the Klan's ouster as a corporation illegally operating without a state-issued charter.

The same Midwestern ideas of neighborliness and orderly government that had inspired White's anti-Klan campaign in 1924 motivated him against Al Smith, the Democratic presidential candidate in 1928, and he obliged Hoover's request to join the Republican campaign in October. White had been writing about Smith since at least 1926, as the Democratic governor of New York rose in national prominence. White's characterization of Smith, "Al Smith, City Feller" (*Collier's*, 1926) is included in this volume. Although White never mentioned Smith's Catholicism in his campaign speeches, he did not need to because his rhetoric about Tammany Hall and Prohibition played into widespread cultural biases against Catholics. White declared that "Tammany is like the Ku Klux Klan in robbing a man of his individuality and deadening his conscience," which resembled the slurs many flung against the Catholic Church. Speaking requests poured in, and White focused his energies on a Southern tour attacking Smith as the enemy of rural neighborliness and America's founding principles. White's stump speech acknowledged that both candidates were exceptional men, but he claimed that Hoover was "a farm boy" with "the American mind" and Smith was imbued with "the Tammany Mind," thereby presaging a century of political campaigning where candidates framed themselves as "real Americans" against their opponents. According to White, Hoover guaranteed "orderly, moral, healthy, neighborly, kindly,

---

33. "White Announces," *Emporia Gazette*, September 20, 1924; "Klanism vs Americanism," *Emporia Gazette*, September 26, 1924; "The Governorship," *Emporia Gazette*, September 16, 1924.

. . . just and equitable relations between all citizens rich or poor." Likewise, Hoover was best suited to preserve the nation's electoral integrity as well as its cultural "ideals of probity, of neighborly kindness."[34]

White also connected the Smith campaign to attempts to repeal Prohibition. Tammany rejected Prohibition because it represented "a conscience in politics, the rule of the majority, the obedience of the minority, [and] fundamental rights" without favor. White reasserted that Smith had consistently stood alongside Tammany in favor of saloons in the New York legislature, straining credulity by claiming that he meant to show "how Tammany perverts its followers," not to "pretend that any moral turpitude lurked in these votes." Smith would "stand in the White House as he has stood in Albany," and White begged his rural audiences to "save the America of our constitution, a free unbought, unbossed America," from the "gang of Tammany hoodlums" that would ride Smith's coattails into the White House.[35]

Though Hoover won the 1928 election, the stock market crash less than a year after his inauguration and the ensuing, decadelong Great Depression mired Hoover's presidency in emergency measures, public outcry, and social dislocation. Our edition ends in 1931, on the cusp of the election of Franklin Delano Roosevelt to the presidency and the ensuing transformation of the American economy through government fiat and world war. The last piece in this collection, "If I Were a Dictator" (*The Nation*, 1931) sees White humorously evoke his now well-worn neighborly ideal through a fantasy of an Emporian autocracy, where White establishes his idealized republic through dictatorial powers. Through the piece's ironic jocularity, some cynicism seeped into White's faith in the small utopia that he imagined as the nation's ideal a generation before. While White's editorials throughout the 1930s and early 1940s continued to attract readers, a utopian version of the Midwestern small town no longer fit so easily with the times.

34. "White Links Smith to Tammany 'Evils,'" October 20, 1928, *New York Times*; White Speech at Independence, KS, October 19, 1928, WAW Papers; "'Retracted Nothing,' White Says at Home," *New York Times*, October 2, 1928; "A Personal Word," *Emporia Gazette*, October 2, 1928.

35. White at Independence, KS, October 19, 1928, WAW Papers; "A Very Personal Matter," *Emporia Gazette*, November 5, 1928.

Depression and War

White supported Herbert Hoover in 1932 partly out of friendship and party loyalty, and partly because he was suspicious of Roosevelt's commitment to reform. Roosevelt's actions during the First Hundred Days restored the American people's morale, and White was pleased to admit that he had been wrong about the president. White still had plenty of disagreements with President Roosevelt, largely stemming from his irritation at FDR's political tactics, but he had long since made his peace with New Deal liberalism as policy. The Great Depression proved to White that his idealized vision of an America led by a middle-class business elite was gone forever, if it had ever existed. The reality was that middle-class business owners had long shirked their duty to treat workers fairly, forcing the federal government to take responsibility for the working class's economic security. Still, White rejected any suggestion of joining the Democratic Party, on the grounds that the Democrats could never be a real home for liberals with the South as one of its key constituencies. As long as this remained the case, conservative Southerners could sabotage liberalism by whipping up their poor, white electorate against it using the race issue. In the final analysis, White saw the New Deal as a profound revolution in American political thought, and when one thought of Roosevelt, one thought, "Here is a hero."[36]

Foreign policy returned to the fore in the late 1930s as the world careened toward war, and White once again inserted himself as one of America's leading internationalist voices. For years, White had described the world as being like a small town or neighborhood, with each nation being akin to a family in town. Naturally, each family saw its own ways as superior to those of every other family, but each family also had to respect its neighbors' ways if it wanted to be accepted as part of the community. Such sentiments made White a natural leader for a campaign to persuade the public to support American aid to the Allies after war broke out in September 1939. With Roosevelt's tacit encouragement, White chaired a committee advocating revisions to American neutrality law that facilitated Allied arms purchases in late 1939. The German

---

36. White, "The Challenge to the Middle Class," ca. 1938, WAW Papers; Ickes to White, September 23, 1938, WAW Papers; White to Harold Ickes, September 26, 1938, WAW Papers; White to Oswald Garrison Villard, January 28, 1939, WAW Papers.

blitzkrieg of the West in the spring of 1940 spurred him to accept the chairmanship of the Committee to Defend America by Aiding the Allies (CDAAA) that May. The CDAAA worked hand in glove with the Roosevelt administration to build public support for aid to the Allies, to fight appeasement, and to educate Americans about the fascist threat. The group was well-organized and professional, utilizing celebrity opinion leaders, opinion polling, volunteer telephone banks, a press service, and specialized divisions targeting women, labor, African Americans, and young people. White was an active chairman of what was known colloquially as the "White Committee," giving speeches, developing policy, raising funds, and privately consulting with Roosevelt on the group's overall strategy. Slowly but steadily, the group helped move public opinion towards aid to the Allies in the year before Pearl Harbor.

The United States joined the war after the Japanese attack on Pearl Harbor, and White began pondering the era that would follow. He hoped that the American people would accept their duty to help lead a substantial international organization to secure the world's peace after the war. Future conflicts, White believed, would be fought over raw materials and markets, and he understood that the United States had a direct interest in shaping the postwar economic order as the world's leading industrial powerhouse.

The alternatives to American leadership in the world were too terrible to countenance. One possibility was that the cycle of periodic world wars would continue until civilization itself collapsed. Another possibility was that other nations would exploit the power vacuum created by an isolationist United States to establish a world order friendly to their interests and inimical to ours. To White, it was evident that America had to embrace internationalism while maintaining its national sovereignty, avoiding the twin dangers of isolationism and military imperialism. America's role was to help "rehabilitate most of Europe to save it for capitalism which means to save it for American trade."[37] Ultimately, White's vision of the United States as an unabashedly capitalist

37. See Victoria de Grazia, *Irresistible Empire: America's Advance Through Twentieth-Century Europe* (Harvard University Press, 2006); White to Arthur Capper, February 4, 1942, WAW Papers; White to Capper, July 11, 1942, WAW Papers; White to Ed Rees, September 29, 1943, WAW Papers; White to Herbert Hoover, December 5, 1942, William Allen White Papers, Special Collections and Archives, Emporia State University, Emporia, Kansas.

and internationalist superpower presaged the course American policymakers
adopted after the Second World War.

The Last Chapter

William Allen White would not learn whether his hopes for the postwar world
were to be realized. He suffered from a number of maladies in his life, particularly diabetes beginning in the 1930s and a persistent, uncomfortable digestive
issue in the early 1940s. Despite his health problems, White found time to write
a remarkable series of editorials in February 1943 denouncing what he saw as
the Republican Party's dangerous flirtation with right-wing demagoguery. In
particular, White was outraged that his friend and former presidential candidate Alf Landon had referred to the "Nazi New Deal" in his comments on
February 12. Such extreme rhetoric was dangerous, White argued, because "in
rallying the boys in the pool hall, those cheap morons who are easily excited
by specious issues, the Republican party may be the center of a fascist movement."[38] In this regard, White remained true to his early and consistent suspicions of American populism. At the same time, White feared that President
Roosevelt was sitting atop a dangerously unstable political coalition of urban
liberals, the working class, and the conservative South. White saw Indiana
liberal Republican Wendell Willkie as the man best positioned to keep these
forces at bay, and he was only beginning to organize Kansas's delegation on
the latter's behalf in October 1943 when he was diagnosed with terminal colon
cancer. William Allen White passed away on January 29, 1944, less than two
weeks shy of his seventy-sixth birthday.

38. White to Capper, March 16, 1942, WAW Papers; White, "Out and Around," February 25–27, 1943, Wendell Willkie Papers, Lilly Library, Indiana University, Bloomington;
"Landon Assails 'Nazi New Dealers'," *New York Times*, February 13, 1943.

PART I

REARGUARD REFORMER

The City of Aqua Pura

(From *The Real Issue: A Book of Kansas Stories*, 1896)

People who write about Kansas, as a rule, write ignorantly, and speak of the state as a finished product. Kansas, like Gaul of old, is divided into three parts, differing as widely, each from the other, as any three countries in the same latitude upon the globe. It would be as untrue to classify together the Egyptian, the Indian and the Central American, as to speak of the Kansas man without distinguishing between the Eastern Kansan, the Central Kansan, and the Western Kansan. Eastern Kansas is a finished community like New York or Pennsylvania. Central Kansas is finished, but not quite paid for; and Western Kansas, the only place where there is any suffering from drouth or crop failures, is a new country—old only in a pluck which is slowly conquering the desert.[1]

Aqua Pura is a western Kansas town, set high up, far out on the prairie. It was founded nine years ago, at the beginning of the boom, not by cow-boys [*sic*] and ruffians, but by honest, ambitious men and women. Of the six men who staked out the town site, two—Johnson and Barringer—were Harvard men, one, Nickols, was from Princeton; and the other three, Bemis, Bradley and Hicks, had come from inland state universities. When their wives came west there was a Vassar reunion, and the first mail that arrived after the post office had been established brought New York magazines. The town was like dozens of others that sprang up far out in the treacherous wilderness in that fresh, green spring of 1886.

They called it Aqua Pura, choosing a Latin name to proclaim to the world that it was not a rowdy town. The new yellow pine of the little village gleamed in the clear sunlight. It could be seen for miles on a clear, on warm days it stood upon a rise of ground; and over in Maize, six miles away, the electric lights of Aqua Pura, which flashed out in the evening before the town was six months old, could be seen distinctly. A school house that cost twenty thousand dollars

1. Drouth: drought.

was built before the town had seen its first winter; and the first Christmas ball in Aqua Pura was held in an opera house that cost ten thousand. Money was plentiful; two and three story buildings rose on each side of the main street of the little place. The farmers who had taken homesteads in the country around the town had prospered. The sod had yielded handsomely from the first breaking. Those who had come too late to put in crops found it easy to borrow money. There was an epidemic of hope in the air. Everyone breathed the contagion. The public library association raised a thousand dollars for books during the winter, and in the spring a syndicate was formed to erect a library building. Aqua Pura could not afford to be behind other towns, and the railroad train that passed the place threw off packages of the newest books as fast as mails could come from New York. The sheet-iron tower of the Aqua Pura waterworks rose early in the spring of '87, and far out in the high grass the hydrants were scattered. Living water came bountifully from the wells that were sunk from fifty to one hundred feet in the ground.

Barringer was elected mayor at the municipal election in the spring of '87, and he platted out Barringer's Addition, and built a house there with borrowed money in June. There were two thousand people in Aqua Pura then. Hacks rolled prosperously over the smooth, hard, prairie streets; two banks opened; and the newspaper, which was printed the day the town was laid off, became a daily.[2] Society grew gay, and people from all corners of the globe met in the booming village.

There was no lawless element. There was not a saloon in the town. A billiard hall, and a dark room, wherein cards might be played surreptitiously, were the only institutions which made the people of Aqua Pura blush, when they took the innumerable "eastern capitalists" over the town who visited Western Kansas that year. These "capitalists" were entertained at a three-story brick hotel, equipped with electricity and modern plumbing in order to excel Maize, where the hotel was an indifferent affair. There were throngs of well-dressed people on the streets, and sleek fat horses were hitched in front of the stores wherein the farmers traded.

This is the story of the rise. Barringer has told it a thousand times. Barringer believed in the town to the last. When the terrible drouth of 1887, with its furnace-like breath, singed the town and the farms in Fountain County,

2. Hack: a carriage for hire.

Barringer led the majority which proudly claimed that the country was all right; and as chairman of the board of county commissioners, he sent a scathing message to the Governor, refusing aid. Barringer's own bank loaned money on land, whereon the crop had failed, to tide the farmers over the winter. Barringer's signature guaranteed loans from the east upon everything negotiable, and Aqua Pura thrived for a time upon promises. Here and there, in the spring of 1888, there was an empty building. One room of the opera house block was vacant. Barringer started a man in business, selling notions, who occupied the room. Barringer went east and pleaded with the men who had invested in the town to be easy on their debtors. Then came the hot winds of July, blowing out of the southwest, scorching the grass, shriveling the grain, and drying up the streams that had filled the spring. During the fall of that year the hotel, which had been open only in the lower story, closed. The opera house began to be used for "aid" meetings, and when the winter wind blew dust-blackened snow through the desolate streets of the little town, it rattled a hundred windows in vacant houses, and sometimes blew sun-warped boards from the high sidewalk that led across the gully to the big red grade of the unfinished "Chicago Air Line."

Barringer did not go east that year. He could not. But he wrote—wrote regularly and bravely to the eastern capitalists who were concerned in his bank and loan company; and they grew colder and colder as the winter deepened and the interest on defaulted loans came not. Barringer's failure was announced in the spring of '89. Nickols had left. Johnson had left. The other founders of Aqua Pura had died in '87–'88, and their families had gone, and with them went the culture and the ambition of the town. But Barringer held on and lived, rent free, in two front rooms of the barn of a hotel. His daughter, Mary, frail, tanned, hollow-eyed, and withered by the drouths, lived with him.

In 1890 the hot winds came again in the summer, and long and steadily they blew, blighting everything. There were only five hundred people in Fountain County that year, and they lived on the taxes from the railroad that crossed the county. Families were put on the poor list without disgrace—it was almost a mark of political distinction—and in the little town many devices were in vogue to distribute the county funds during the winter.

There was no rain that winter and the snow was hard and dry. Cattle on the range suffered for water and died by the thousands. A procession from the little town started eastward early in the spring. White-canopied wagons, and wagons covered with oil table-cloths of various hues, or clad in path-work quilts, sought the rising sun.

Barringer grew thin, unkempt and gray. Every evening, when the wind rattled in the deserted rooms of the old hotel, and made the faded signs up and down the dreary street creak, the old man and his daughter went over their books, balancing, accounting interest, figuring on mythical problems that the world had long since forgotten.

Christmas Eve, 1891, the entire village, fifteen souls in all, assembled at Barringer's house. He was hopeful, even cheerful, and talking blithely of what "one good crop" would do for the country; although there were no famers left to plant it, even if nature had been harboring a smile for the dreary land. The year that followed that Christmas promised much. There were spring rains, and in May, the brown grass and the scattered patches of wheat grew green and fair to see. Barringer freshened up perceptibly. He sent an account of his indebtedness—on home-ruled manilla paper—to his creditors in the east and faithfully assured them that he would remit all he owed in the fall. A few wanderers straggled into Fountain County, lured by the green fields and running brooks. The gray prairie wolf gave up the dug-out to human occupants. Lights in the prairie cabins twinkled back hope to the stars. Before June there were a thousand people in Fountain County. Aqua Pura's business-houses seemed to liven up. There was a Fourth-of-July celebration in town. But the rain that spoiled the advertised "fire works in the evening" was the last that fell until winter. A car load of aid from Central Kansas saved a hundred lives in Fountain County that year.

When the spring of 1893 opened, Barringer looked ten years older than he looked the spring before. The grass on the range was sere, and great cracks were in the earth. The winter had been dry. The spring opened dry, with high winds blowing through May. There were but five people on the townsite that summer, Barringer, his daughter, and the postmaster's family. Supplies came overland from Maize. A bloody county-seat war had given the rival town the prize in 1890. Barringer had plenty of money to buy food, for the county commissioners distributed the taxes which the railroad paid.

It was his habit to sit on the front porch of the deserted hotel and look across the prairies to the southwest and watch the breaking clouds scatter into the blue of the twilight. He could see the empty water tower silhouetted against the sky. The frame buildings that rose in the boom days had all been moved away, the line of the horizon was guarded at regular intervals by the iron hydrants far out on the prairie, that stood like sentinels hemming in the past. The dying wind seethed through the short, brown grass. Heat lightening winked devilishly in the distance, and the dissolving clouds that gathered every afternoon laughed in derisive thunder at the hopes of the worn old man sitting on the warped boards of the hotel porch. Night after night he sat there, waiting, with his daughter by his side. There had been a time when he was too proud to go to the east, where his name was a by-word. Now he was too poor in purse and in spirit. So he sat and waited, hoping fondly for the realization of a dream which he feared could never come true.

There were days when the postmaster's four-year-old child sat with him. The old man and the child sat thus one evening when the old man sighed: "If it would only rain, there would be half a crop yet! If it would only rain!" The child heard him and sighed imitatively: "Yes, if it would only rain—what is rain, Mr. Barringer?" He looked at the child blankly and sat for a long time in silence. When he arose he did not even have a pretense of hope. He grew despondent from that hour, and a sort of hypochondria seized him. It was his fancy to exaggerate the phenomena of the drouth.

That fall when the winds piled the sand in the railroad "cuts" and the prairie was as hard and barren as the ground around a cabin door, Barringer's daughter died of fever. The old man seemed little moved by sorrow. But as he rode back from the bleak grave-yard, through the sand cloud, in the carriage with the dry, rattling spokes, he could only mutter to sympathizing friends who had come from Maize to mourn with him, "And we laid her in the hot and dusty tomb." He recalled an old song which fitted these words, and for days kept crooning: "Oh, we laid her in the hot and dusty tomb."

That winter the postmaster left. The office was discontinued. The county commissioners tried to get Barringer to leave. He would not be persuaded to go. The county commissioners were not insistent. It gave one of them an excuse for drawing four dollars a day from the county treasury; he rode from Maize to Aqua Pura every day with supplies for Barringer.

The old man cooked, ate, and slept in the office of the hotel. Day after day he put on his overcoat in the winter and made the rounds of the vacant store buildings. He walked up and down in the little paths through the brown weeds in the deserted streets, all day long, talking to himself. At night, when the prairie wind rattled through the empty building, blowing snow and sand down the halls, and in little drifts upon the broken stairs, the old man's lamp was seen by straggling travelers burning far into the night. He told his daily visitor that he was keeping his books.

Thus the winter passed. The grass came with the light mist of March. By May it had lost its color. By June it was brown and the hot winds came again in August, curving the warped boards a little deeper on the floor of the hotel porch. Herders and travelers, straggling back to Green County, saw him sitting there at twilight, looking toward the southwest—a grizzled, unkempt old man, with a shifting light in his eye. To such as spoke to him he always made the same speech: "Yes, it looks like rain, but it can't rain. The rain has gone dry out here. They say it rained in Hutchinson,—maybe so, I doubt it. There is no God west of Newton. He dried up in '90. They talk of irrigation. That's an old story in hell. Where's Johnson? Not here! Where's Nickols? Not here! Bemis? Not here! Bradley? Not here! Hicks? Not here! Where's handsome Dick Barringer, Hon. Richard Barringer? Here! Here he is, holding down a hot brick in a cooling room of hell! Yes, it does look like rain, doesn't it?"

Then he would go over it all again, and finally cross the trembling threshold of the hotel, slamming the crooked, sun-steamed door behind him. There he stayed, summer and winter, looking out across the burned horizon, peering at the long, low, black line of clouds in the southwest, longing for the never-coming rain.

Cattle roamed the streets in the early spring, but the stumbling of the animals upon the broken walks did not disturb him, and the winds and the drouth soon drove them away. The messenger with provisions came every morning. The summer, with its awful heat, began to glow. The lightening and the thunder joked insolently in the distance at noon; and the stars in the deep, dry blue looked down and mocked the old man's prayers as he sat, at night, on his rickety sentry box. He tottered through the deserted stores calling his roll. Night after night he walked to the red clay grade of the uncompleted "Air Line" and looked over the dead level stretches of prairie. He would have gone away, but something held him to the town. Here he had risked all. Here, perhaps, in his warped fancy, he hoped to regain all. He had written so often, "Times will be better in the spring," that it was part of his confession of faith—that and "One good crop will bring the country around all right." This was written with red clay in the old man's nervous hand on the side of the hotel, on the faded signs, on the deserted inner walls of the stores,—in fact, everywhere in Aqua Pura.

The wind told on him, it withered him, sapped his energy, and hobbled his feet.

One morning he awoke and a strange sound greeted his ears. There was a gentle tapping in the building and a roar that was not the guffaw of the wind. He rushed for the door. He saw the rain and bareheaded he ran to the middle of the streets where it was pouring down. The messenger from Maize with the day's supplies found him standing there, vacantly, almost thoughtfully, looking up, the rain dropping from his grizzled head, and rivulets of water trickling about his shoes.

"Hello, Uncle Dick," said the messenger. "Enjoying the prospect? River's risin'; better come back with me."

But the old man only answered, "Johnson? Not here! Nickols? Not here! Bemis? Not here! Bradley? Not here! Hicks? Not here! And Barringer? Here! And now God's moved the rain belt west. Moved it so far west that there's hope for Lazarus to get irrigation from Abraham."

And with this the old man went into the house. There, when the five days' rain had ceased, and when the great river that flooded the barren plain had shrunk, the rescuing party, coming from Maize, found him. Beside his bed were his balanced books and his legal papers. In his dead eyes were a thousand dreams.

The Home-Coming of Colonel Hucks

(From *The Real Issue: A Book of Kansas Stories*, 1896)

A generation ago, a wagon covered with white canvas turned to the right on the California road and took a northerly course toward a prairie stream that nestled just under a long, low bluff. When the white pilgrim, jolting over the rough, unbroken ground through the tall "blue stem" grass, reached a broad bend in the stream, it stopped.[1] A man and a woman emerged from under the canvas, and stood for a moment facing the wild, green meadow and the distant hills. The man was young, lithe, and graceful, but despite his boyish figure the woman felt his unconscious strength as he put his arm about her waist. She was aglow with health; her fine, strong, intelligent eyes burned with hope, and her firm jaw was good to behold. They stood gazing at the virgin field a moment in silence. There were tears in the woman's eyes as she looked up after the kiss and said:

"And this is the end of our wedding journey; and—and—the honey-moon—the only one we can ever have in all the world—is over."

The horses, moving uneasily in their sweaty harness, cut short the man's reply. When he returned, his wife was getting the cooking utensils from under the wagon, and life—stern, troublous—had begun for them.

It was thus that young Colonel William Hucks brought his wife to Kansas. They were young, strong, hearty people and they conquered the wilderness. A home sprang up in the elbow of the stream. In the fall, long rows of corn shocks trailed what had been the meadow. In the summer the field stood horse-high with corn. From the bluff, as the years flew by, the spectator might see the checkerboard of the farm, clean cut, well kept, smiling in the sun. Little children frolicked in the king row, and hurried to school down the green lines of the lanes where the hedges grow. Once, a slow procession, headed

---

1. White pilgrim: a reference to the white canvas top of a wagon and its similarity to a traditional, Anglo-American bonnet of the seventeenth century.

by a spring wagon with a little black box in it, might have been seen filing between the rows of the half-grown poplar trees and out across the brown, stubble-covered prairie to the desolate hill and the graveyard. Now, neighbors from miles around may be heard coming in rattling wagons across vale and plain, laden with tin presents, after which the little home is seen ablaze with lights while the fiddle vies with the mirth of the rollicking party dancing with the wanton echoes on the bluff across the stream.

There were years when the light in the kitchen burned far into the night, when two heads bent over the table, figuring to make ends meet. In these years the girlish figure became bent and the light faded in the woman's eyes, while the lithe figure of the man was gnarled by the rigors of the struggle. There were days—not years, thank God—when lips forgot their tenderness; and, as fate tugged fiercely at the curbed bit, there were times when souls rebelled and cried out in bitterness and despair at the roughness of the path.

In this wise went Colonel William Hucks and his wife, through youth into maturity, and in this wise they faced towards the sunset.

He was tall, with a stoop; grizzled, brawny, perhaps uncouth in mien. She was stout, unshapely, rugged; yet her face was kind and motherly. There was a boyish twinkle left in her husband's eyes and a quaint, quizzing, one-sided smile often stumbled across his care-furrowed countenance. As the years passed, Mrs. Hucks noticed that her husband's foot fell heavily when he walked by her side, and the pang she felt when she first observed his plodding step was too deep for tears. It was in these days that the minds of the Huckses unconsciously reverted to old times. It became their wont, in these latter days, to sit in the silent house whence the children had gone out to try issue with the world, and, of evenings, to talk of the old faces and of the old places in the home of their youth. Theirs had been a pinched and busy life. They had never returned to visit their old Ohio home. The Colonel's father and mother were gone. His wife's relatives were not there. Yet each felt the longing to go back. For years they had talked of the charms of the home of their childhood. Their children had been brought up to believe that the place was little less than heaven. The Kansas grass seemed short, and barren of beauty to them beside the picture of the luxury of Ohio's fields. For them, the Kansas streams did not ripple and dimple so merrily in the sun as the Ohio brooks that romped through dewy pastures in their memories. The bleak Kansas plain, in winter and in fall, seemed to the Colonel and his wife to be ugly and gaunt when they remembered the brow of the hill under which their first kiss was shaded from the moon while the world grew dim under a sleigh that bounded over the turnpike. The old people did not give voice to their musings. But in the woman's heart there gnawed a yearning for the beauty of the old scenes. It was almost a physical hunger.

After their last child, a girl, had married and had gone down the lane toward the lights of the village, Mrs. Hucks began to watch with a greedy eye the dollars mount toward a substantial bank account. She hoped that she and her husband might afford a holiday.

Last year, Providence blessed the Huckses with plenty. It was the woman who revived the friendship of youth in her husband's cousin, who lives in the old township in Ohio. It was Mrs. Hucks who secured from that cousin an invitation to spend a few weeks in the Ohio homestead. It was Mrs. Hucks, again, who made her husband happy by putting him into a tailor's suit—the first he had bought since his wedding—for the great occasion. Colonel Hucks needed no persuasion to take the trip. Indeed, it was his wife's economy which had kept him from being a spendthrift, and from borrowing money with which to go on a dozen different occasions.

The day which Colonel and Mrs. William Hucks set apart for starting upon their journey was one of those perfect Kansas days in early October. The rain had washed the summer's dust from the air, clearing it, and stenciling the lights and shades very sharply. The woods along the little stream which flowed through the farm had not been greener at any time during the season. The second crop of grass on the hillside almost sheened in vividness. The yellow of the stubble in the grain fields was all but a glittering golden. The sky was a deep, glorious blue, and the big, downy clouds which lumbered lazily here and there in the depths of it, appeared near and palpable.

As Mrs. Hucks "did up" the breakfast dishes for the last time before leaving for the town to take the cars, she began to feel that the old house would be lonesome without her. The silence that was about to come seemed to her to be seeping in, and it made her feel creepy. In her fancy, she petted the furniture as she "set it to rights," saying mentally, that it would be a long time before the house would have her care again. To Mrs. Hucks every bit of furniture brought up its separate recollection, and there was a hatchet-scarred chair in the kitchen which had come with her in the wagon from Ohio. Mrs. Hucks felt that she could not leave that chair. All the while she was singing softly as she went about her simple tasks. Her husband was puttering around the barn-yard, with the dog under his feet. He was repeating, for the twentieth time, the instructions to a neighbor about the care of the stock, when it occurred to him to go into the house and dress. After this was accomplished, the old couple paused outside the front door while Colonel Hucks fumbled with the key. "Think of it, Father," said Mrs. Hucks as she turned to descend from the porch. "Thirty years ago—and you and I have been fighting so hard out here—since you let me out of your arms to look after the horses. Think of what has come—and—and—gone, Father, and here we are alone, after it all."

"Now, Mother, I—" but the woman broke in again with,

"Do you mind how I looked that day? O, William, you were so fine and so handsome then! What's become of my boy—my young—sweet—strong—glorious boy?"

Mrs. Hucks's eyes were wet, and her voice broke at the end of the sentence.

"Mother," said the Colonel, as he went around the corner of the house, "just wait a minute till I see if this kitchen door is fastened."

When he came back, he screwed up the corner of his mouth into a droll, one-sided smile and said, with a twinkle in his eyes, to the woman emerging from her handkerchief:

"Mother, for a woman of your age, I should say you had a mighty close call to being kissed just then. That kitchen door was all that saved you."

"Now, Pa, don't be silly, " was all that Mrs. Hucks had the courage to at-tempt as she climbed into the buggy.

Colonel Hucks and his wife went down the road, each loath to go and leave the homeplace without their care. Their ragged, uneven flow of talk was filled with more anxiety about the place which they were leaving, than it was with the joys anticipated at their journey's end. The glories of Ohio and the wonderful green of its hills and the cool of its meadows, veined with purl-ing brooks, was a picture that seemed to fade in the mental vision of this old pair when they turned the corner that hid their Kansas home from view. Mrs. Hucks kept reverting in her mind to her recollection of the bedroom, which she had left in disorder. The parlor and the kitchen formed a mental picture in the housewife's fancy which did not leave place for speculations about the glo-ries into which she was about to come. In the cars, Colonel Hucks found him-self leaning across the aisle, bragging mildly about Kansas for the benefit of a traveling man from Cincinnati. When the Colonel and his wife spread their supper on their knees in the Kansas City Union Depot, the recollection that it was the little buff Cochin pullet which they were eating made Mrs. Hucks very homesick.[2] The Colonel, on being reminded of this, was meditative also.

They arrived at their destination in the night. Mrs. Hucks and the women of the homestead refreshed old acquaintance in the bedroom and in the kitchen, while the Colonel and the men sat stiffly in the parlor and called the roll of the dead and absent. In the morning, while he was waiting for his breakfast, Colonel Hucks went for a prowl down in the cow lot. It seemed to him that the creek which ran through the lot was dry and ugly. He found a stone upon which, as a boy, he had stood and fished. He remembered it as a huge boulder and he had told his children wonderful tales about its great size. It seemed to him that it had worn away one half in thirty years. The moss on the river bank was faded and old, and the beauty for which he had looked was marred by a thousand irregularities which he did not recall in the picture of the place that he had carried in his memory since he left it.

Colonel Hucks trudged up the bank from the stream with his hands clasped behind him, whistling "O, Lord, Remember Me," and trying to reconcile the things he had seen with those he had expected to find. At breakfast he said nothing of his puzzle, but as Mrs. Hucks and the Colonel sat in the parlor alone, during the morning while their cousins were arranging to take the Kansas people over the neighborhood in the buggy, Mrs. Hucks said:

"Father, I've been lookin' out the window and I see they've had such a dreadful drouth here.[3] See that grass there, it's as short and dry—and the ground looks burneder and crackeder than it does in Kansas."

"Uhm, yes," replied the Colonel. "I had noticed that myself. Yet crops seem a pretty fair yield this year."

As the buggy in which the two families were riding rumbled over the bridge, the Colonel, who was sitting in the front seat, turned to the woman in the back seat and said:

"Lookie there Mother, they've got a new mill—smaller'n the old mill, too."

To which his cousin responded, "Bill Hucks, what's got into you, anyway? That's the same old mill where me and you used to steal pigeons."

The Colonel looked close and drawled out, "Well, I'll be doggoned! What

2. Cochin is a breed of chicken; a pullet is a hen.
3. Drouth: drought.

makes it look so small? Ain't it smaller, Mother?" he asked, as they crossed the millrace, that seemed to the Colonel to be a diminutive affair compared with the roaring millrace in which as a boy he had caught minnows.

The party rode on thus for half an hour, chatting leisurely, when Mrs. Hucks, who had been keenly watching the scenery for five minutes, pinched her husband and cried enthusiastically as the buggy was descending a little knell: "Here 't is, Father! This is the place!"

"What place?" asked the Colonel, who was head over heels in the tariff.

"Don't you know, William?" replied his wife with a tremble in her voice, which the woman beside her noticed.

Everyone in the buggy was listening. The Colonel looked about him; then, turning to the woman beside his wife on the back seat, he said:

"This is the place where I mighty nigh got tipped over trying to drive two horses to a sleigh, with the lines between my knees. Mother and me have remembered it, someway, ever since." And the old man stroked his grizzled beard and tried to smile on the wrong side of his face, that the women might see his joke. They exchanged meaning glances when the Colonel turned away, and Mrs. Hucks was proudly happy. Even the dullness of the color on the grass, which she had remembered as a luscious green, did not sadden her for half an hour. When the two Kansas people were alone that night, the Colonel asked:

"Don't it seem kind of dwarfed here—to what you expected it would be? Seems to me like it's all shriveled and worn out and old. Everything's got dust on it. The grass by the roads is dusty. The trees that used to seem so tall and black with shade are just nothing like what they used to be. The hills I've thought of as young mountains don't seem to be so big as our bluff back— back home."

Kansas was "home" to them now. For thirty years the struggling couple on the prairie had kept the phrase "back home" sacred to Ohio. Each felt a thrill at the household blasphemy and both were glad that the Colonel had said "back home," and that it meant Kansas.

"Are you sorry you come, Father?" said Mrs. Hucks, as the Colonel was about to fall into a doze.

"I don't know, are you?" he asked.

"Well, yes, I guess I am. I haven't no heart for this, the way it is, and I've some way lost the picture I had fixed in my mind of the way it was. I don't care for this and yet it seems like I do, too. Oh, I wish I hadn't come to find everything so washed out—like it is!"

And so they looked at pictures of youth through the eyes of age. How the colors were faded! What a tragic difference there is between the light which springs from the dawn, and the glow which falls from the sunset.

After that first day Colonel Hucks did not restrain his bragging about Kansas. And Mrs. Hucks gave rein to her pride when she heard him. Before that day she had reserved a secret contempt for a Kansas boaster and had ever wished that he might see what Ohio could do in the particular line which he was praising. But now Mrs. Hucks caught herself saying to her hostess, "What small ears of corn you raise here!"

The day after this concession Mrs. Hucks began to grow homesick. At first, she worried about the stock; the Colonel's chief care was about the dog. The fifth day's visit was their last. As they were driving to the town to take the train for Kansas, Mrs. Hucks overheard her husband discoursing something after this fashion:

"I tell you, Jim, before I'd slave my life out on an 'eighty' the way you're doin,' I'd go out takin' in whitewashin.' It's just like this—a man in Kansas has lower taxes, better schools, and more advantages in every way than you've got here. And as for grasshoppers! Why, Jim West, sech talk makes me tired! My boy Bill's been always born and raised in Kansas and now he's in the legislature, and in all his life, since he can remember, he never seen a hopper. Wouldn't know one from a sacred ibex if he met it in the road."

While the women were sitting in the buggy at the depot waiting for the train, Mrs. Hucks found herself saying:

"And as for fruit—why, we fed apples to the hogs this fall. I sold the cherries, all but what was on one tree near the house, and I put up sixteen quarts from just two sides of that tree, and never stepped my foot off the ground to pick 'em."

When they were comfortably seated on the homeward-bound train, Mrs. Hucks said to her husband:

"How do you suppose they live here in this country, anyway, Father? Don't any one here seem to own any of the land joinin' them, and they'd no more think of puttin' in water tanks and windmills around their farms than they'd think of flyin.' I just wish Mary could come out and see my new kitchen sink with the hot and cold water in it. Why, she almost fainted when I told her how to fix a dreen for her dishwater and things." Then after a sigh she added, "But they are so un-progressive here, now-a-days."[4]

That was the music which the Colonel loved and he took up the strain and carried the tune for a few miles. Then it became a duet, and the two old souls were very happy.

They were overjoyed at being bound for Kansas. They hungered for kindred spirits. At Peoria, in the early morning, they awakened from their chair-car naps to hear a strident female voice saying:

"Well, sir, when the rain did finally come, Mr. Morris he just didn't think there was a thing left worth cutting on the place, but lo, and behold, we got over forty bushel to the acre off of that field, as it was."

The Colonel was thoroughly awake in an instant, and he nudged his wife, as the voice went on:

"Mr. Morris he was so afraid the wheat was winter killed; all the papers said it was; and then come the late frost, which everyone said had ruined it— but law me—."

Mrs. Hucks could stand it no longer. With her husband's cane she reached the owner of the voice, and said:

"Excuse me, ma'am, but what part of Kansas are you from?"

It seemed like a meeting with a dear relative. The rest of the journey to Kansas City was a hallelujah chorus wherein the Colonel sang a powerful and telling bass. When he crossed the Kansas state line, Colonel Hucks began, indeed, to glory in his state. He pointed out the schoolhouses that rose in every village, and he asked his fellow passenger to note that the schoolhouse is the most important piece of architecture in every group of buildings. He told the history of every rod of ground along the Kaw to Topeka. He dilated eloquently, and at length, upon the coal mines in Osage county, and he pointed with pride to the varied resources of his state.[5] Every prospect was pleasing to Colonel Hucks as he rode home that beautiful October day, and his wife was more radiantly happy than she had been for many years.

4. Un-progressive: Mrs. Hucks likely means "retrograde" in the social, economic, and technological sense. Compare to Col. Hucks's claim about taxes and education in Kansas, marks of "progress."

5. Compare to the Hucks's celebrations of "progressive" in terms related to economic, social, and technological "progress" above.

As the train pulled into the little town of Willow Creek that afternoon the Colonel craned his neck at the car window to catch the first glimpse of the big, red standpipe, and of the big stone schoolhouse on the hill. When the whistle blew for the station, the Colonel said:

"What is it that fool Riley feller says about 'Grigsby's Station, where we used to be so happy and so pore'?"[6]

As the Colonel and his wife passed out of the town into the quiet country, where the shadows were growing long and black and where the gentle blue haze was hanging over the distant hills that undulated the horizon, a silence fell upon the two hearts. Each mind sped back over a lifetime to the evening when they had turned out of the main road in which they were traveling. A dog barking in the meadow behind the hedge from them did not startle their reveries; restless cattle wandering down the hillside toward the bars made a natural complement to the picture which they loved.

"It is almost sunset, Father," said the wife as she put her hand upon her husband's arm.

Her touch and the voice in which she had spoken tightened some cord at his throat. The Colonel could only repeat, as he avoided her gaze:

"Yes, almost sunset, Mother, almost sunset."

"It's has been a long day, William, but you have been good to me. Has it been a happy day for you, Father?"

The Colonel turned his head away. He was afraid to trust himself to speech. He clucked to the horses and drove down the lane. As they came into the yard, the Colonel put an arm about his wife and pressed his cheek against her face. Then he said drolly:

"Now lookie at that dog—come tearin' up here like he never saw white folks before!"[7]

---

6. The poem "Griggsby's Station" by the Indiana poet James Whitcomb Riley (1849–1916), celebrates the simplicity of rural life when compared to the affluence of upper-class urban life with the opening stanza, "Pap's got his patent right, and rich as all creation; / But where's the peace and comfort that we all had before? / Le's go a-visitin' back to Griggsby's Station— / Back where we ust to be so happy and so pore!"

7. White's connotation is difficult to glean here. Black Americans settled in Kansas throughout the nineteenth century, especially in the late 1870s and 1880s. See Charlotte Hinger, "'The Colored People Hold the Key': Abram Thompson Hall, Jr.'s Campaign to Organize Graham County," *Kansas History* 31, no. 1 (2008): 32–47.

And so Colonel William Hucks brought his wife back to Kansas. Here their youth is woven into the very soil they love; here every tree around their home has its sacred history; here every sky above them recalls some day of trial and of hope.

Here in the gleaming tonight stands an old man, bent and grizzled. His eyes are dimmed with tears, which he would not acknowledge for the world, and he is dreaming strange dreams while he listens to a little, cracked voice in the kitchen, half humming and half singing:

> "Home again, home again,
> From a foreign shore."[8]

---

8. First line from the tune "Heavenly Home, Heavenly Home, Precious Name to Me" (1850), by Marshall S. Pike, mostly popularly sung by the Harmoneons, a minstrel group popular during the 1840s and 1850s.

The King of Boyville

(From *The Real Issue: A Book of Kansas Stories*, 1896)

Boys who are born in a small town are born free and equal. In the big city it may be different; there are doubtless good little boys who disdain bad little boys, and poor little boys who are never to be noticed under any circumstances. But in a small town, every boy, good or bad, rich or poor, stands among boys on his own merits. The son of the banker who owns a turning-pole in the back yard does homage to the baker's boy who can sit on the bar and drop and catch by his legs; while the good little boy who is kept in wide collars and cuffs by a mistaken mother gazes through the white paling of his father's fence at the troop headed for the swimming hole and pays all the reverence which his dwarfed nature can muster to the sign of the two fingers. In the social order of boys who live in country towns, a boy is measured by what he can do, and not by what his father is. And so, Winfield Hancock Pennington, whose boy name was Piggy Pennington, was the King of Boyville. For Piggy could walk on his hands, curling one foot gracefully over his back, and pointing the other straight in the air; he could hang by his heels on a flying trapeze; he could chin a pole so many times that no one could count the number; he could turn a somersault in the air from the level ground, both backwards and forwards; he could "tread" water and "lay" his hair; he could hit any marble in any ring from "taws" and "knucks down,"—and better than all, he could cut his initials in the ice on skates, and whirl around and around so many times that he looked like an animated shadow, when he would dart away up the stream, his red "comfort" flapping behind him like a laugh of defiance.[1] In the story books such a boy would be the son of a widowed mother, and turn out very good or very bad, but Piggy was not a story book boy, and his father kept a grocery store, from which Piggy used to steal so many dates that the boys said his father must have cut up the almanac to supply him. As he never gave the goodies to

1. Taws and knucks down: two games played with marbles.

the other boys, but kept them for his own use, his name of "Piggy" was his by all the rights of Boyville.

There was one thing Piggy Pennington could not do, and it was the one of all things which he most wished he could do; he could not under any circumstances say three consecutive and coherent words to any girl under fifteen and over nine. He was invited with nearly all of the boys of his age in town, to children's parties. And while any other boy, whose only accomplishment was turning a cart wheel, or skinning the cat backwards, or, at most, hanging by one leg and turning a handspring, could boldly ask a girl if he could see her home, Piggy had to get his hat and sneak out of the house when the company broke up. He would comfort himself by walking along on the opposite side of the street from some couple, while he talked in monosyllables about a joke which he and the boy knew, but which was always a secret to the girl. Even after school Piggy could not join the select coterie of boys who followed the girls down through town to the post office. He could not tease the girls about absent boys at such times and make up rhymes like

> "First the cat and then her tail;
> Jimmy Sears and Maggie Hale,"

and shout them out for the crowd to hear. Instead of joining this courtly troupe Piggy Pennington went off with the boys who really didn't care for such things, and fought, or played "tracks up," or wrestled his way leisurely home in time to get in his "night wood." But his heart was not in these pastimes; it was with a red shawl of a peculiar shade, that was wending its way to the post office and back to a home in one of the few two-story houses in the little town. Time and again had Piggy tried to make some sign to let his feelings be known, but every time he had failed. Lying in wait for her at corners, and suddenly breaking upon her with a glory of backward and forward somersaults did not convey the state of his heart. Hanging by his heels from an apple tree limb over the sidewalk in front of her, unexpectedly, did not tell the tender tale for which his lips could find no words. And the nearest he could come to an expression of the longing in his breast was to cut her initials in the ice beside his own when she came weaving and wobbling past on some other boy's arm. But she would not look at the initials, and the chirography of his skates was so indistinct that it required a key; and everything put together, poor Piggy was no nearer a declaration at the end of the winter than he had been at the beginning of autumn. So only one heart beat with but a single thought, and the other took motto candy and valentines and red apples and picture cards and other tokens of esteem from other boys, and beat on with any number of thoughts, entirely immaterial to the uses of this narrative. But Piggy Pennington did not take to the enchantment of corn silk cigarettes and rattan and grape vine cigars; he tried to sing, and wailed dismal ballads about the "Gypsy's Warning," and "The Child in the Grave with Its Mother," and "She's a Daisy, She's a Darling, She's a Dumpling, She's a Lamb," whenever he was in hearing distance of his Heart's Desire, in the hope of conveying to her some hint of the state of his affections; but it was useless.[2] Even when he tried to whistle plaintively as he passed her house in the gleaming, his notes brought forth no responsive echo.

One morning in the late spring, he spent half an hour before breakfast among his mother's roses, which were just in first bloom. He had taken out there all the wire from an old broom, and all his kite string. His mother had to call three times before he would leave his work. The youngster was the first to leave the table, and by eight o'clock he was at his task again. Before the first school bell had rung, Piggy Pennington was bound for the school house with a strange looking parcel under his arm. He tried to put his coat over it, but it stuck out and the newspaper that was wrapped around it, bulged into so many corners, that it looked like a home-tied bundle of laundry.

"What you got?" asked the freckle-faced boy, who was learning at Piggy's feet how to do the "muscle grind" on the turning-pole. But Piggy Pennington was the King of Boyville, and he had a right to look straight ahead of him, as if he did not hear the question, and say: "Lookie here, Mealy, I wish you would go and tell Abe I want him to hurry up, for I want to see him."

"Abe" was Piggy's nearest friend. His other name was Carpenter. Piggy only wished to be rid of the freckle-faced boy. But the freckle-faced boy was not used to royalty and its ways, so he pushed his inquiry.

"Say, Piggy, have you got your red ballpants in that bundle!"

There was no reply. The freckle-faced boy grew tired of tattooing with a

---

2. "Gypsy's Warning": D. S. Holmes, "The Gypsy's Warning," 1864; "The Child in the Grave with Its Mother": likely T. Paine, "The Old Cabin Home" (1858), also referenced in Mark Twain's *Roughing It* (1872); "She's a Daisy": J. F. McArdle, "She's a Daisy, She's a Darling. She's a Dumpling. She's a Lamb," 1881.

stick, as they walked beside a paling fence, so he began touching every tree on the other side of the path with his fingers. They had gone a block when the freckle-faced boy could stand it no longer and said: "Say Piggy, you needn't be so smart about your old bundle; now honest, Piggy, what have you got in that bundle?"

"Aw—soft soap, take a bite—good fer yer appetite," said the King, as he faced about and drew up his left cheek and lower eyelid pugnaciously. The freckle-faced boy saw he would have to fight if he stayed, so he turned to go, and said, as though nothing had happened, "Where do you suppose old Abe is, anyhow!"

Just before school was called Piggy Pennington was playing "scrub" with all his might, and a little girl—his Heart's Desire—was taking out of her desk a wreath of roses, tied to a shaky wire frame. There was a crowd of girls around her admiring it, and speculating about the possible author of the gift; but to these she did not show the patent medicine card, on which was scrawled, over the druggist's advertisement: "Yours truly, W. H. P."

When the last bell rang, Piggy Pennington was the last boy in, and he did not look toward the desk, where he had put the flowers, until after the singing. Then he stole a sidewise glance that way, and his Heart's Desire was deep in her geography. It was an age before she filed past him with the "B" class in geography, and took a seat directly in front of him where he could look at her all the time, unobserved by her. Once she squirmed in her place and looked toward him, but Piggy Pennington was head over heels in the "Iser rolling rapidly."[3] When their eyes did at last meet, just as Piggy, leading the marching around the room, was at the door to go out for recess, the thrill amounted to a shock that sent him whirling in a pin wheel of handsprings toward the ball ground, shouting "scrub—first bat, first bat, first bat" from sheer, bubbling joy. Piggy made four tallies that recess, and the other boys couldn't have put him out, if they had a hand-grenade or a Babcock fire extinguisher.

He received four distinct shots that day from the eyes of his Heart's Desire, and the last one sent him home on the run, tripping up every primary urchin, whom he found tagging along by the way, and whooping at the top of his voice. When his friends met in his barn, some fifteen minutes later, Piggy tried to turn a double somersault from his spring board, to the admiration

3. From the poem "Hohenlinden," by Thomas Campbell (1777–1844).

of the crowd, and was only calmed by falling with his full weight on his head and shoulders at the edge of the hay, with the life nearly jolted out of his little body.

The next morning, Piggy Pennington astonished his friends by bringing a big armful of red and yellow and pink and white roses to school. He had never done this before, and when he had run the gauntlet of the big boys, who were not afraid to steal them from him, he made straight for his schoolroom, and stood holding them in his hands while the girls gathered about him teasing for the beauties. It was nearly time for the last bell to ring, and Piggy knew that his Heart's Desire would be in the room by the time he got there. He was not mistaken. But Heart's Desire did not clamor with the other girls for one of the roses. Piggy stood off their pleadings as long as he could with "Naw," "Why naw, of course I won't," "Naw, what I want to give you one for," and "Go way from here I tell you," and still Heart's Desire did not ask for her flowers. There were but a few moments left before school would be called to order, and in desperation Piggy gave one rose away. It was not a very pretty rose, but he hoped she would see that the others were to be given away, and ask for one. But she—his Heart's Desire—stood near a window, talking to the freckle-faced boy. Then Piggy gave away one rose after another. As the last bell began to ring he gave them to the boys, as the girls were all supplied. And still she came not. There was one rose left, the most beautiful of all. She went to her desk, and as the teacher came in, bell in hand, Piggy surprised himself, the teacher, and the school by laying the beautiful flower, without a word on the teacher's desk. That day was a dark day. When a new boy, who didn't belong to the school, came up at recess to play, Piggy shuffled over to him and asked gruffly: "What's your name!"

"Puddin' 'n' tame, ast me agin an' I'll tell you the same," said the new boy, and then there was a fight. It didn't sooth Piggy's feelings one bit that he whipped the new boy, for the new boy was smaller than Piggy. And he dared not turn his hushed face towards his Heart's Desire. It was almost four o'clock when Piggy Pennington walked to the master's desk to get him to work out a problem, and as he passed the desk of Heart's Desire he dropped a note in her lap. It read: "Are you mad?"

But he dared not look for the answer, as they marched out that night so he contented himself with punching the boy ahead of him with a pin, and stepping on his heel, when they were in the back part of the room, where the teacher would not see him. The King of Boyville walked home alone that eve-ning. The courtiers saw plainly that his majesty was troubled.

So his lonely way was strewn with broken stick-horses, which he took from the little boys, and was marked by trees adorned with the string, which he took from other youngsters, who ran across his pathway playing horse. In his barn he sat listlessly on a nail keg, while Abe and the freckle-faced boy did their deeds of daring, on the rings, and the trapeze. Only when the new boy came in, did Piggy arouse himself to mount the dying bar, and, swinging in it to the very rafters, drop and hang by his knees and again drop from his knees, catch-ing his ankle in the angle of the rope where it meets the swinging bar. That was to awe the new boy.

After this feat the King was quiet.

At dusk, when the evening chores were done, Piggy Pennington walked past the home of his Heart's Desire and howled out a doleful ballad which began:

> "You ask what makes this darkey wee-eep,
> Why he like others am not gay."[4]

But a man on the sidewalk passing said, "Well son, that's pretty good, but wouldn't you just as lief sing as to make that noise." So the King went to bed with a heavy heart.

He took that heart to school with him, the next morning, and dragged it over the school ground, playing crack the whip and "stinkbase." But when he saw Heart's Desire wearing in her hair one of the white roses from his moth-er's garden—the Penningtons had the only white roses in the little town—he knew it was from the wreath which he had given her, and so light was his boy-ish heart, that it was with an effort that he kept it out of his throat. There were smiles and smiles that day. During the singing they began, and every time she came past him from a class, and every time he could pry his eyes behind her geography, or her grammar, a flood of gladness swept over his soul. That night

---

4. "Kitty Wells," likely by Thomas Bingham Bishop 1835–1905), was published in the 1860s. The lyrics here imply that the tune was intended for a minstrel repertoire. However, a version from 1861 begins "You ask what makes me sad and weep, / And why like others I'm not gay."

Piggy Pennington followed the girls from the schoolhouse to the post office, and in a burst of enthusiasm, he walked on his hands in front of the crowd, for nearly half a block. When his Heart's Desire said: "O ain't you afraid you'll hurt yourself, doing that?" Piggy pretended not to hear her, and said to the boys: "Aw, that ain't nothin'; come down to my barn, an' I'll do somepin that'll make yer head swim."

He was too exuberant to contain himself, and when he left the girls he started to run after a stray chicken, that happened along, and ran till he was out of breath. He did not mean to run in the direction his Heart's Desire had taken, but he turned a corner, and came up with her suddenly. Her eyes beamed upon him, and he could not run away, as he wished. She made room for him on the sidewalk, and he could do nothing but walk beside her. For a block they were so embarrassed that neither spoke.

It was Piggy who broke the silence. His words came from his heart. He had not yet learned to speak otherwise.

"Where's your rose?" he asked, not seeing it.

"What rose?" said the girl, as though she had never in her short life heard of such an absurd thing as a rose.

"Oh, you know," returned the boy, stepping irregularly, to make the tips of his toes come on the cracks in the sidewalk. There was another pause, during which Piggy picked up a pebble, and threw it at a bird in a tree. His heart was sinking rapidly.

"O, that rose!" said his Heart's Desire, turning full upon him with the enchantment of her childish eyes. "Why, here it is in my grammar. I'm taking it to keep with the others. Why?"

"O, nuthin' much," replied the boy. "I bet you can't do this," he added, as he glowed up into her eyes from an impulsive handspring.

And thus the King of Boyville first set his light, little foot upon the soil of an unknown country.

A Typical Kansas Community

(*The Atlantic Monthly*, August 1897)

Forty years ago there were on the map of Kansas a few red spots indicating the location of forts, and here and there along the streams near the State's eastern border were little circles indicating towns. Many of the names upon that early map remain, and designate hopeless villages, the scenes of brave deeds and patriotic efforts; and a few of the towns of a generation ago survive, fulfilling in some small measure the bright dreams of their founders. But most of the old names, once familiar to the whole nation, are forgotten. Could some ghost of those stirring times come back to call the roll, how many such towns would fail to respond! Quidaro? Gone! Mariposa? Gone! Sumner? Gone! Tecumseh? Gone! Minneola? Gone!

From 1870, for several years eastern and central Kansas was a battle-ground between man and nature. In those years the desert was finally subdued. During the succeeding decade, men devoted themselves to the occupation of running up and down the newly made garden with surveyors' chains, making squares and parallelograms, and selling them to one another, or to such strangers as were drawn into the game by the enticement of speculation. Fictitious values prevailed. There was a very plague of financial delusions. Men from all parts of the world were victims of the disease, and came to Kansas to satisfy their longing to behave unwisely. Cities sprang up in a month. Men ceased to be business men, and became gamblers, with land as the stakes. Then, nine years ago, the crash came. Since that time, the face of the Kansas town, and the heart of it too, have changed. One might reasonably call the present an era of home-making. The gambler has gone. The speculator finds his market unresponsive. Another generation is reaching maturity. This generation, which is not native to the State, is trying to make home more attractive; indeed the word "home" has been generally applied to Kansas for the first time during the last five years. The present residents of the State mean to remain. They are no in camp. No one now talks of going "back home" when his fortune is made. To mention this condition as remarkable may amuse the outside world, but the experience is a new and delightful one for Kansas.

Chiefly by reason of its newness and of a certain cosmopolitan aspect, the Kansas town differs from villages elsewhere in the United States, and presents a few interesting variations from the common type. The largest town in the commonwealth has hardly forty thousand inhabitants. Most of the county-seats in the eastern half of the State, where the rainfall is copious and where crops are bountiful and regular, contain about three thousand persons each. The county-seat is in the strictest sense a country town. The people live almost entirely upon the tributary country. There are no factories. The money that the farmers of the county spend for food, clothing, fuel, and the comforts of the farm home is the cash capital upon which the town does its business. This capital is passed from the grocers to the clothing merchants, to the druggists, to the furniture dealers, to the hardware sellers, and to the professional men. In the older communities of the Eastern and Middle States necessity has developed factories, which convert raw material into finished products, and money from the outside world comes in. But Kansas is yet hardly a generation old, and it has not entered the manufacturing era of industry.

In Kansas towns the streets run at right angles. The highways are as straight as the surveyor's chain could make them. Set back at regular distances from the sidewalks are the more pretentious residences, built in the obtrusive architectural style of the "boom" days, complacent in their sham magnificence. The paint has been washed from many of them, and their faded appearance is almost tragic. The story of these unpainted houses is written upon the town, and in the leafless season it depresses the stranger; but in the early spring, when the grass comes, nature covers up the barren aspect. The smaller houses of the village are less depressing. Perhaps they do not cover such bitter disappointment. They are like modest cottages the world over.

There is in these towns an intense social democracy, such as does not exist in older American States. Class lines are but indistinctly drawn. The term "family," as used to distinguish the old rich from the new rich, is meaningless. There are of course gradations, lines of difference, and distinction between cliques and coteries, in the polite society of any town. There are indeed the upper and the lower crusts in the social formation. But there is no "dead-line." In every Kansas community, society is graded something after this fashion: the "old whist crowd," the "young whist crowd," the "literary crowd," the "young dancing crowd," the "church social crowd," or "lodge crowd," and the "surprise party crowd."[1] It often happens, in a family containing several grown-up children, that one daughter attends lodge socials, where there are spelling-matches, and where she may enjoy what the reporter for the country paper calls "a literary and musical programme." Perhaps the eldest daughter attends the meeting of the Browning Circle, where she is bored for an hour or two; she probably comes home with a married couple who live on her street.[2] The son of the family goes across the railroad track, and dances a noisy quadrille on a bare kitchen floor, to the music of a cabinet organ and a fiddle.[3] It is possible that the parents may be present at the weekly meeting of the Bon Ton Whist Club, where the festivities begin with an elaborate seven o'clock supper.[4] At these stately functions, the awarding of the gilt-edged copy of *Ben-Hur* and the hand-painted smoking-set to the best players forms an important part of the evening's enjoyment.[5]

This fictitious but typical instance should not be taken too literally, though it is true enough to indicate the utter absence in Kansas society of what in older communities are called class lines. One may almost choose his own companions. Wealth plays a minor part in the appraisal of people. Indeed, the commercial rating of the "lodge crowd" is probably higher than that of the "old whist crowd," although the "lodge crowd" does reverence to the "old whist crowd" by referring to it sneeringly as "society." Since there are no old social standards, and since no one knows anybody's grandfather's previous condition, young people find their own places. The assorting occurs in the high school. An ambitious mother, living on the wrong side of the railroad, is glad to find that her daughter has passed above the "surprise party crowd," has gone around the "church socials," and at the end of her schooldays has planted herself firmly among the "entre-nous" girls.[6] There

1. Whist: a card game.
2. Browning Circle: named after poets Elizabeth Barrett Browning (1806–1861) and Robert Browning (1812–1889). A women's book club, usually for literary novels and poetry, which are discussed over tea.
3. Quadrille: a type of dance popular at the time.
4. Bon Ton refers to high society; an elite social club.
5. A novel by Lew Wallace (1827–1905), *Ben-Hur* (1880) tells the fictional story of Judah Ben Hur and his interaction with Jesus. It became a best-seller.
6. Entre-nous: "between us" in French. Can refer to a private group.

the young lawyer's wife and the old cattleman's daughter meet. A young woman in this group finds an opportunity to marry into the "young whist crowd." After the children are in school she may be graduated easily into the Bon Ton Whist Club. But if she does not improve the opportunities offered at the "entre-nous" gatherings, in a few years she will begin to cultivate her mind, and will drift naturally into the Browning Circle. Then she will appear occasionally at the quarterly town dances, when the most exclusive women of the village wear their second-best gowns as a rebuke to the men for inviting such a mixed company.

Generally the church members do not view these semi-public dances with alarm. The Methodists are the strictest of the popular sects in nearly every Kansas community. When the State was safely Republican by enthusiastic majorities, it used to be said that the Methodist church was the Republican church. In the old days of the boom, the Baptist church was often called the Democratic church. Even now the Baptists find their congregations somewhat smaller than those of the Presbyterians. In nearly every town there is a struggling Episcopal church, and in its folds gather the society leaders, and the wives of the traveling men who make their homes there. On the outskirts of every important village are to be found the humble meeting-houses of worshipers after the old fashion—the Friends, the Free Methodists, the United Brethren, and the Dunkards. These churches gather their congregations from the one-story houses of the town and from the farms nearby. Frequently waves of intense religious feeling sweep over these flocks. In winter they hold "protracted meetings," and glow with a fervor all unknown to the dwellers in the upper streets. In summer these simple worshipers hold camp-meetings in the groves along the creeks, and members of the more fashionable churches drive from town in the cool of the evening, and from their buggies watch them with patronizing interest.

It is the occupants of the buggies who give the town whatever intellectual reputation it may have in the State. They are the buyers and the readers of books. Nothing else indicates the exact grade of a town's intelligence so clearly as the books which the people read. The town in which I write is a fair example of Kansas communities; and here all the most interesting new books in popular literature and the best periodicals have a good market. Yet our kinspeople in the Eastern States carefully save their year-old magazines and books to send to us. In every Kansas town there is a group of men and women who read the best books, and who go regularly to Chicago or to St. Louis every year to hear the best music.

During the days of the boom innumerable "real estate" colleges sprang up. They indicated the presence of men and women whose ideals were high, and who, when money was abundant, immediately began to surround themselves with those influences that would soften the hard environments of the Western life, and make "reason and the will of God" prevail. Their zeal led these promoters beyond the limits of sound judgement, but it is to their credit that their intentions were good. The colleges survive, and they are the best things that have outlived the boom. Only here and there has one been abandoned; on the other hand, in many a Kansas town, the little, debt-ridden college that has survived, after a struggle against great odds, is the nucleus around which gathers whatever light the community may have. The children of the adjacent country are sent to these schools; for though they are not the best possible, they are the best now obtainable. One finds, for instance, their instructors on the school boards and in the city councils. They appear as delegates to the state political conventions, indicating by their presence that the voters in the towns bear no grudge against a man for being careful of his "seens" and "saws," whatever men in the country may think of such refinements of speech.

The best manifestation of the influence of the college is found in the security and growth of the town public library. It is worth a ward politician's political life to talk about cutting down library expenses. Generally a public library contains from one thousand to four thousand books. The schoolchildren, black and white, spend their odd moments in the reading-room. Women from every social circle use the books. E. P. Roe is still the favorite author, as he is the favorite author of the frequenters of libraries in some of the Eastern States.[7] On the other hand, in one public library in Kansas the copy of Emerson's *Frist* [sic] *Series of Essays* has been rebound four times.[8] In this village no bookseller finds it profitable to keep the old-fashioned dime novels, so popular among boys ten years ago.

When Kansas goes to the theatre, however, it drops back into the dark ages.

7. Edward Payson Roe (1838–1888): A popular author during this period, he wrote agrarian- and Christian-themed books.

8. Ralph Waldo Emerson (1803–1882); White refers to his series of essays on transcendentalism, first published in 1841.

Doubtless there are worse theatrical companies than those that visit Kansas, but no one has ever described them. The best people leave the theatre to those who like to hear the galleries echo with merriment when the supernumeraries walk before the curtain to light the gas footlights. The opera-house is not a town gathering-place, except when the graduation exercises of the high school are held there, and when the townspeople come together to hear the terrible annual concert of the silver cornet band. On these occasions one observes the absence of the chaperon, and here, as elsewhere in the town, young men and women meet upon terms of equality.

There are three out-of-doors town gatherings—football games, baseball games, and political meetings—where-at men play a more important part than they play in the opera-house, for they are not manacled by decorum. At the political meetings the men predominate; but at the town games it is the women—the younger women—who give the scene the appearance which may have made ancient tournaments so glorious. Here there is a homely familiarity. When one pounds whoever sits beside him on the bench, at the climax of the game, it is with the assurance that one is pounding an old friend. The men take off their coats, but the crowd is decorous. There is no drinking. A drunken boy at a Kansas game would cause nearly as much comment as a drunken girl. The girls join in the college yells, talk across the ropes to the players in the field, surge up and down the line with the boys, and no one sneers.

There are no rich men in these Kansas towns. The men who own a million dollars' worth of property number less than half a score in the whole State. Those who control half a million dollars' worth of property might ride together in a sleeping-car, with an upper berth or two to spare. Every town has its rich man, measured by a local standard, who is frequently a retired farmer turned banker; not one in five of these is rated at $100,000, but each is the autocrat of his county, if he cares to be. The mainspring that moves the town's daily machinery may be found in the back room of the bank. There it is decided whether or not the bonds shall be voted. There it is often determined whether there shall be eight or nine months of school. There the village chronicles are spread upon the great ledgers every day. The town banker supplies the money for every contest. If he is wise, he watches his little corner of the world as a spider watches from its web. The great trust which he keeps requires a knowledge of the details of the game that men are playing around him. Yet with all his power this town banker would be counted a poor man in the city.

Seldom is his annual income as much as $10,000. But he lives in the best house in the town. The butcher saves his best cuts for him, the grocer puts aside his best vegetables, and the whole town waits to do his bidding.

Next to the banker in economic importance is the best lawyer. If the town is a thriving one, the lawyer makes perhaps $4000 a year. But he does not receive all his income in cash. Some of it he takes in trade: from the farmer butter and eggs, from the storekeeper his wares, from the editor printing. There are from three to five lawyers, in each good county town in Kansas, who earn more than $1500 a year. When a lawyer gets in debt to a respectable minority of the influential people, he may be elected county attorney, and during his term of office he is expected to pay his debts. If he fulfills the public expectation, he has another season of waiting, and at the end of it he is made district judge, when the balance-sheet with the town is supposed again to be made up. A district judge, upon retirement, can generally make a living. The town doctor knows so many things about so many people, and so many people owe him money, that he too is always considered a safe man to put on a local county ticket. Be it said to his credit he makes an efficient officer; there is no man in better standing than he.

In a community where there is no large source of outside revenue, where no factory pours its wages into the local commerce, much of the business is done on credit. The storekeepers do so much bartering that they have established a system of currency of their own. A merchant will issue sets of coupons, in one dollar and five dollar books. The coupons are of various decimal denominations, and they read, "This coupon is good for cents in trade at Witherspoon's grocery." When the cash in the drawer is low, and when the creditor will accept them, these coupons pass over the counter for cash. They pass from one hand to another, and are usually accepted at face value. The merchant invests his earnings in local bank-stock, farms, or farm mortgages, and after a while he may retire from business to lend his money; then he is on the way to the presidency of the bank. The real estate agent and insurance broker who lends money in a small way is also in the line of promotion to the banker's desk. But before he reaches the goal he lives many a shabby day, which he hopes the grocer and the coal dealer have forgotten.

The real estate agent's money comes in lumps, and he lacks the peace of mind which the storekeeper's clerk enjoys, whose wages may be $20 or $40 or even $80 a month; for his wages come regularly, and there is always the reasonable hope that someday he may be a partner in the business or have a store of his own. In addition to this hope, the clerk's social position may be as good as anybody's. His wife and daughter may find friends among the most desirable people in the community. If the clerk and his son do not meet their employer at the whist club, it may be only because it is their night "off" and his night "on" at the store. Prices of real estate are so low that many a man earning $50 a month builds a cottage by the aid of the Home Building and Loan Company which flourishes in every town. Instead of paying rent, he pays interest and a few dollars of the principal every month. On his own lot he may grow flowers for the annual sweet-pea contest, and fortune may send him such a bounty of bloom as will give him the right to assume a tolerant air when discussing floriculture with the man who holds his note.

The tenement-house and the flat are unknown in Kansas. Wages are not high, but opportunities for saving are many. The man who, rated by his wages, in another State would be called a poor man, in Kansas is fairly well-to-do. A printer's wages, for instance, are rarely more than eight dollars a week, yet many a printer has made a start in life, and has even bought the paper which employed him. There is a tradition that the Kansas country editor is poor. The truth is, he earns from $1200 to $3000 a year. He lives well; and being a politician, he frequently shares the party loaves and fishes.[9] He is respected and his credit is good at the bank, where he is able, and generally willing, to give the one good turn which deserves another. It may be said in the editor's favor that he is the only regular employer of skilled labor in the community. The mason and the carpenter work at odd times. The village cobbler does repairing only. There are no great factories that employ hundreds of laborers. Here and there is a town favored with a railroad-shop, where a few score men find irregular work repairing damaged cars. But the dinner-pail is hardly seen in Kansas.

A well-known writer of Western stories, half a decade ago, drew a picture of the hopeless faces of the women who rode in a parade of the Kansas Farmer's Alliance.[10] The type in the story was interesting, but the real Kansas

9. Matthew 14:17–19.

10. In the late nineteenth century farmers formed local political alliances to achieve economic security. White here refers to the Kansas Farmers Alliance, which often worked with the Republican party. For a history of populism see Charles Postel, *The Populist Vision* (Oxford University Press, 2007).

women who rode in the Alliance parade saved it from becoming a clumsy and stupid affair. By their very presence they made it a cheering, good-natured, color-flecked pageant. They rode on hay-racks covered with patriotic bunting, and they were dressed in white and in yellow at the ratio of sixteen to one, to symbolize their financial creed. In all the parades of any political party the women are an important feature. But their participation in politics practically ends with the parades. They vote only in municipal and school elections. Now and then, at a municipal election in a very small town, it happens that, half in a jocose spirit, the men elect a women's ticket, when there is absolutely nothing for the women elected to do.[11] The incident is a neighborhood joke, at which the women laugh; and the thrifty correspondents of Eastern journals sell to their papers "stories" about the "great fight between the men and the women of Kansas, which ended in the overthrow of the men." Women are often elected to clerical position in the county and in the city. A woman was once successful as an assistant attorney-general of the State. When the Kansas woman becomes a bread-winner, her social position is not affected. There is no social circle that the working woman finds it impossible to enter. The stenographer, with her $50 a month, may snub the banker's daughter. The schoolteacher finds no door closed to her social advancement.

Yet it is said that Kansas is governed by petticoats.[12] If by this it be meant that women shape the public sentiment of the Kansas town, the saying is true. In most towns in other States, the corners of the principal streets are occupied by dram-shops.[13] In this town where this paper is written, the influence of women has been exerted so forcibly that three of the four corners where the two main streets cross are occupied by banks. Instead of Hogan's Retreat on the fourth corner stands a bookstore. There the boys and the young men of the town find a meeting-place. There they make their appointments. There they browse through the weekly illustrated papers and the magazines, and look through new books. In this bookstore the football games are bulletined, the baseball games are talked over, and politics finds its forum. Among all the men and boys who frequent this resort there is no habitual drinker; there is not one whose name has been stained with scandal. These young fellows are

11. Jocose spirit: to be in a playful and or humorous mood.
12. A petticoat is a type of skirt worn by women.
13. Dram-shop: a place where alcohol is sold or served.

business men, clerks, professional men, real estate brokers, and college students. They are clean, shrewd, active young men, who have been brought up
in a town where the women make public sentiment—in a town of petticoat
government, wherein a woman has never held an administrative municipal
office. It is a town of eight thousand inhabitants, without a saloon, without a
strange woman, without a town drunkard.

Sloping down from a gentle hill toward a creek, the Kansas town shows
at a distance its pointed steeples, its great iron water-tower, and its massive
schoolhouse, which stands above the elms and cottonwoods and maples. No
smokestack pours its blackening flood over the natural beauty of grass and
trees. At night, the farmer across the valley sees the town as a garden of lights.
At such a time, one does not recall the geometrically exact angles of the streets
and the gray dust upon the unpainted houses; the night softens the garish rem-
nants of the boom. Then the sunburned Kansas town has a touch of romance.

Patriotism and Things

(*The Emporia Gazette*, August 25, 1899)

In what the esteemed Populist platform in and for Lyon County calls "these days of uncertain peace," there is much loose and vain-glorious talk about the excellent virtue called patriotism. Naturally enough the word patriotism is associated with the fife and drum and "the pride, pomp and circumstance of glorious war." This association of ideas may have brought some confusion and it is therefore in order to consider what this fine thing is we call patriotism.

Self-love is the first instinct of animate life.

Love of family belongs to the higher orders of animals, and many a man who is good to his family is a forty-horse-power devil to his neighbors.

Love for those outside the family is a trait found only in a few social animals, and in man. "Love thy neighbor" was the eleventh commandment and the sum of them all.[1] "Greater love hath no man than this, that he lay down his life for his friends"—not for himself—for self-preservation is the first law of nature; not for his child or his mate—animals and savages do this, but for his friend.[2] The patriot is he who obeys the eleventh commandment, who rules his conduct for others, who is public spirited, who sinks his comforts, his own pleasures, his own happiness, his own life if need be, out of consideration for the public good. The unselfish man is a patriot. The generous man is a patriot. The soldier is a patriot. The citizen who votes against his own class interests for the good of the state, that man is just as surely a patriot as the man who stands up to be shot at.

Yesterday a runaway team was tearing down Commercial Street.[3] A child wheeling a baby buggy was directly in the path of the mad horses. An unknown man jumped in the wagon over the endgate, stopped the team, and

---

1. Matthew 22:34–40.
2. John 15:13.
3. Runaway team: Refers to a horse team pulling something.

saved the lives of two children whom he had never seen before. He risked "his life for his friend," for in that man's heart every human creature in peril or in need is a friend. That man was as truly a patriot as though he had charged San Juan Hill or had marched with Sherman to the sea.[4] He had obeyed the summons to duty, had risked his life, had realized the highest joy God gives to man—the joy of doing his full service well. He did what he did without the challenge of the drum, without allurement of popular hero worship. He did what he did as simply and unostentatiously as he would do any natural act in the ordinary course of life. The Catholic sisters who nursed the smallpox in Emporia did a brave thing as Roosevelt did in Cuba or as Funston in Manila.[5] They deserve monuments they will never get.

All over the old world these quiet, unadvertised heroes are doing their deeds of courageous self-sacrifice. All the patriotism is not displayed before guns. The brakeman who pulls out of Emporia on a stock extra, is a hero and a patriot. He takes risks for society and for his fellow men in danger, just as hazardous as the soldiers who charge across the open. Heroes fall unsaluted in the railroad yards of America by the hundreds of thousands and no articles appear in the papers about what kind of food they have, or what kind of attention they get in hospitals. These railroad boys are patriotic. The man who does his duty in the fear of God and the respect of man in any avocation from the ditch to the desk does mankind a service and his country honor by the life he lives.

Therefore we should honor our neighbors more. Therefore we should be more friendly with the world. Don't arrogate all the virtues of this world to yourself, you grouchy man. Look the world in the face and smile. Your poor friend is as important to God as you are. It is not money but heart that counts in this world. The greatest novel in the world exalts "Mr. Great Heart."[6] Take notice.

---

4. San Juan Hill: famous battle fought at San Juan Heights in Cuba on July 1, 1898, during the Spanish-American War (1898) where American soldiers charged Spanish positions. Sherman: General William Tecumseh Sherman (1820–1891) led a campaign through several Southern states, including Georgia and the Carolinas, during the American Civil War.

5. Roosevelt in Cuba: Refers to Theodore Roosevelt (1858–1919) when he led the Rough Riders in the Spanish-American War. Fuston: Frederick Funston (1865–1917) was an American general who led US forces in the Philippines during the Spanish-American War.

6. Character in the novel *The Pilgrim's Progress* (1678) by John Bunyan (1626–1688).

This is a good world full of good people. So don't sour on the world. Brace up and don't take things too seriously. To whistle a gay tune is better than to frown. A merry heart maketh a glad countenance. Be merry and lend a hand where you can. That is patriotism. That is the way to final peace.

The Meaning of the Fair

(*Emporia Weekly Gazette*, October 5, 1899)

Never before in the history of Emporia was there such a crowd as gathered here last week. It was a peaceful crowd, and it conducted itself decently and in order. There were no fakirs to rob the people and their money, and so the merchants had a good steady trade.[1]

For the first time in the history of the town, six excursion trains dumped their multitudes into the streets. These people came from a territory within a circle of a radius of one hundred miles from Emporia. This is Emporia's commercial territory. Of this country, Emporia is the commercial capital. The people came after a good time and their visit was a festival. Business was not the main object of their visit, nor of their entertainment.

The real meaning of the fair was not a festival, and had its serious side.

Emporia has changed. It has not come in a night—this change—from the country village, to the energetic, enterprising town; but it has been a matter of slow, steady perseverance. The manifestation last week was the only sudden thing about it.

The old town of cliques and factions and rings and gangs and crowds is gone; the new town of energy and unity of spirit and ambition for Emporia has replaced it. This is what the Fair means. This is its promise, the promise of a better town, of an awakened industry, of new prosperity.

The fact that the merchants of Emporia could make such a beautiful spectacle as that on Commercial Street during the Fair, could unite so unanimously in support of one proposition; could work so energetically for a common cause, is a much more important fact than that there were twenty thousand people on Commercial Street yesterday.

1. Fakir: a Muslim or Hindu monk who subsists by begging for alms. In this context, White uses the term *fakir* to contrast his ideal of the small town with men and women who value hard work. In their context, fakirs are considered holy through their detachment to the material world.

To no one man, nor to one set of men, does the success of this Fair or any portion of it belong. It was the people's Fair; everyone helped. It was the small efforts of everyone that made the great Fair so creditable. Everyone did his part; no one shirked. Emporia was at her best.

The Fair next year will be four times as big, because the accumulated energy of all the people for a year will be behind it.

The people have tried the motto, "Lend a hand, not a hammer," and they are going to stay with it.[2]

If there are any kickers no one has observed them.[3]

The Emporia Street Fair is worth more than any other thing that has happened to Emporia for many, many years; for it united the people and gave them faith in themselves.

That was the meaning of the Fair.

2. A common phrase used in the late nineteenth and early twentieth centuries, frequently used by White. The phrase means to assist directly instead of from afar.

3. Kicker: someone who objects or complains.

The Man on Horseback

(From *Stratagems and Spoils*, November 1899)

Beside the Missouri River there is a busy city. At the outskirts of the city there is a beautiful suburb called Brookdale Park. In Brookdale Park there is a wide lawn, shaded here and there by tall elm trees. Upon the wide lawn there is a sprawling gray stone castle. In the great castle there is a room, lined with leather and decorated with long rows of books, most of which stand in unbroken sets. In one of the books—a fat book bound in morocco—is the steel-engraved picture of a man with a scraggly, unkempt beard and keen dark eyes. The picture shows the man wearing a black string necktie and Prince Albert coat, after the exact fashion of the coats and ties in all the other pictures in the book.[1] Under the picture is a cramped facsimile of a signature written with a stub-pen, without a curve of flourish. On the opposite page is the title of the volume, "Makers of the Mighty West," and near it is the page number 988, and then follows this sketch:

Joab T. Barton—Financier.

Joab Teal Barton was born in Huron County, Ohio, in 1838, of poor but honest parents. He was educated in the country schools and spent a few months in Miami Academy before the breaking out of the war. He entered the 27th Regiment of Ohio Volunteers and served his country four years, taking part in the battles of the Wilderness and in the campaign that ended at Appomattox Court House. He came west at the close of the war, and 1866 found him at Hannibal, Missouri, where, being without employment and funds, he accepted a position as brakeman on the Hannibal and St. Joe Railroad. Promotions came rapidly, and three years later as a conductor Mr. Barton ran the first train into Denver. A year later he was made trainmaster, and in 1872 he was superintendent of the Missouri Valley Division of the Hannibal and St. Joe, and

1. Prince Albert coat: a double-breasted men's coat worn during the Victorian era.

in 1875 he became traffic manager of the Corn Belt system when it was known as the Leavenworth and Solomon Valley. The road at that time began at the Missouri River, and, as its directors used to say, "lost itself in the sage-brush" near what is now Abilene. Today, when Joab T. Barton, President and General Manager of the close corporation which controls this mighty national highway, issues a system pass, it is good from the Great Lakes to the Pacific, and from the Missouri River to the Gulf.

But the management of this vast enterprise consumes only a part of the man's energy. Being public spirited, he organized the company which was granted the franchise for the water-works system that his home city enjoys, and his efforts were instrumental in getting Eastern capital to put down the first street railway in the city in 1876. That street railway was operated by three mules, yet it was the beginning from which the magnificent transportation system known as the West Side Electric Railway sprang. This is one of the enterprises to which Mr. Barton gives much of his attention. He is also a large owner of the stock of the Missouri Valley Gas Heating and Electric Company, and his real estate holdings are found all over the city.

Personally the subject of this sketch is quiet and unassuming. He shrinks from publicity, and prefers the society of his intimate friends to the hubbub attendant upon a political career. He has fixed convictions, and cares nothing for the plaudits of the multitude. He is said to be a loyal ally and a sleepless enemy. In 1870 he married Miss Mary Stone at Denver, and one child, George M., born in 1872, is the fruit of this union.

Now it may be proved easily that Joab T. Barton owned this book, this room, this house, and this lawn. For all practical purposes he owned the soul of Brookdale Park, and there were five ably edited newspapers in the city which insisted that Joab T. Barton might as well have a warranty deed to the city, and there were two hundred thousand people who were supposed to go to bed at night in the belief that when they got up in the morning they might find that "Old Joab," as they called him, had dug up and carted away the Missouri River. For Barton was the town bogy-man.

People blamed him for every evil thing that happened in the community. If a bank failed, they said Old Joab wrecked it. If a street-car killed a man, Old Joab was committing his daily homicide. If men couldn't pay their bills at the end of the month, they laid their failures to Old Joab's extortionate charges for light and water. At different times he had been called an octopus, an incubus, a vampire, and a hydra-headed monster.

As for Mrs. Barton (she that was Mary Stone), she never read the papers, even though her husband bought one—type, presses, editor and all—that the family might enjoy the news of the day without wading through the columns filled with abuse of the head of the household. Under the circumstances, the purchase of the newspaper was a wanton waste of money, for young George M. Barton read all the other papers at the club and enjoyed the remarks about his father immensely. The young man did not take his father seriously. Young Barton played chess in the middle of the day and refused to go to meetings of directors where he didn't know the rules of the game, and often renigged [sic] and did other embarrassing things. He drank some hot, rebellious liquor, but not too much, and winked pleasantly at policemen who had been of service to him. He knew the names of the street-car conductors and elevator-boys with whom he rode, and if he went to the boiler-makers' ball, he didn't conceal it from the patronesses of the dances given by the Colonial Dames. He was rated as a good fellow by those who knew him, and by his father's friends he was accounted worthless, but not a spendthrift. The elder Barton seemed to be concealing an expression of unspeakable fatigue whenever the boy came into his office, or whenever the youth's name was mentioned there.

Joab T. Barton had long since ceased to be surprised at anything that his son might say or do; and yet when he saw his son wearing a Civic Federation button, and met his name in the list of members of the Committee of Safety, the father was irritated. For the Committee of Safety was at that time engaged in prosecuting, for election frauds, some gentlemen whom, for good and sufficient reasons, Joab T. Barton had seen fit to take into the employ of the West Side Electric Railway. Apparently the Civic Federation was organized under a charter to make Joab T. Barton's life a burden. When the boy went into it the Federation was giving life to a movement which demanded that Barton pay the city for the renewal of his expiring street railway franchise—a demand which Barton frankly called robbery; for he had already paid the election expenses of a majority of the councilmen and the mayor and the city counsellor, and he considered enough enough. Two bills were before the council for consideration at the time young Barton donned the Federation button; one, known as the Barton bill, merely extended a twenty years' franchise to the West Side Electric Railway. The other, known as the Federation bill, granted the extended franchise but required Barton to provide transfer privileges, three-cent fares to school-children, and to pay to the City Library Fund 1 percent of the company's earnings after the earnings reached 10 percent. Public feeling was at a boiling-point. Open charges of official corruption were being made. The newspapers were indulging in bitter editorials with nonpareil slugs between the lines. And George Barton suavely wore his blue and white Federation button and referred to his father jocularly as "the Oppressor of the Poor."

Young George Barton considered his membership in the Federation a joke. He found the Federation at his club, with the occasional cocktail and the billiard-cue, and took the Federation with the other things, because they were easier to embrace than to avoid. He gave it about as much thought as he gave to the affair with Mrs. Kelsey at Manitou. Mrs. Kelsey was a blondined lady, who drove bobtailed horses in silver-mounted harness hitched to outlandish rigs.[2] George had met her somewhat informally before she found Kelsey. At Manitou, with a maid and a nurse for her two overdressed children, Mrs. Kelsey was the queen of something like one hundred linear feet of veranda at the barny summer hotel. The affair between the youth and "our lady of the sawdust," as George was wont to call her, was really trivial. A handsome young man with unlimited credit is a decorative appurtenance to a high yellow and black English cart. And when the owner of the cart puts just a little too much padding—not much too much, but just a little too much—on her hips and at her bust, and lays one thin hair-line too much of black on her eyebrows and under her eyes—and when the lady after doing these things adds three unnecessary carats to the weight of her diamond earrings, she may ornament her equipage with a beautiful man a trifle too youthful and a trifle too careless of the amenities, even if she does have to pay the price.[3] But at a summer-resort the price of these things is not so high as it is elsewhere in the world; so Mrs. Kelsey paid it; and as for George Barton, he sent the account home to his parents. His father's estimate of the importance of the affair was gathered from the size of the florist's bill. It was under two hundred dollars, and the father was not disturbed. But when the Manitou gossip filtered into her home, George's mother went to bed and remained there a week in rage and humiliation. After that Mrs. Barton carried with her a hatred for Mrs. Kelsey

2. Blondined: blonde.
3. Equipage: horse-drawn carriage.

and a fear of her that distinguished Mrs. Kelsey from the throng of strangers
beyond the pale and brought her into the circle of Mrs. Barton's intimate enemies. Barton and Jim Kelsey had been friends for ten years. Kelsey had been
a section boss on the Corn Belt and had prospered after constructing two or
three branch lines for the system in the eighties. Later he had moved to the city
and had turned a more or less honest penny in cedar block paving; still later he
went into asphalt paving and kept in the State Senate and in the city council
half a dozen foremen, a superintendent, and friends innumerable who acted
with Barton's friends in the Legislature. If Barton's son wished to be pleasant
to Jim Kelsey's new wife and Tom Hubbard's children, Joab T. Barton saw no
reason for a demonstration of grief, if Jim did not complain. But Mrs. Barton
gave more importance than her husband to Mrs. Kelsey's social impossibil-
ity, and since George Barton's return from Manitou, Mrs. Barton had felt an
uneasiness lest the idle hours the boy spent with Mrs. Kelsey should affect the
family's status in society. Yet so long as Mrs. Barton had the gray stone castle
in Brookdale Park, the command of the income from a fortune that piled into
the teens among the millions, and so long as she had the advantage of having
entered the portals of the town's aristocracy, just before the boom widened the
threshold, she was firmly established. This fact of her absolute social security
was one of the many important things that Mrs. Barton did not know. Bright-
eyed, fluffy-haired Mrs. Kelsey, who had struggled bravely for several years
to keep the gentlemen of her acquaintance from saying "Hello" to her on the
street, was shrewd enough to know what Mrs. Joab Barton did not know—
that to land and to have money to bank up and keep the tide back was to have
her feet upon a rock. Mrs. Barton always harbored a fear that she would betray
the fact of her humble origin. Her mother once presided at the lunch-counter
in Sharon Springs, and her father used to work on the cinder-pit at the roundhouse; and although the family came up in the world so rapidly that the child
wore silk dresses before she was sixteen, her girlhood was spent in a family
where nothing was thought of leaving the soap in the water or of sweeping dirt
under the cupboard. So existence with Mrs. Barton was a constant struggle
against reversion to type. In her twenties and thirties she wore the longest possible seal-skins and the most dazzling jewels. In her forties she built the castle
in Brookdale Park and covered it with towers, swelling balconies, bulging windows, and ginger-bread confections of architecture, until the house seemed
inflated with sinful pride to the bursting-point.

The year before the Manitou incident ruffled her, Mrs. Barton had begun to find solace in severe simplicity. She came to worship austerity as madly and as abjectly as she had worshipped flash and show. Thereafter the foot-man went in black, the silver came off the harness, the front of the house was straightened. The towers were scraped away; the débris of bric-à-brac was swept out of the halls and reception-rooms, and life became a serious business to her. Yet eight years before she had beamed with joy when the newspapers printed her name among the patronesses of the Harvard Glee Club's annual entertainment. She had been reading the society columns of that paper every Sunday for years, familiarizing herself with the important names, and when she saw the excellent company she was in as a patroness, Mrs. Barton was sure for the first time that she had arrived. But she knew how thin her veneer was and she always feared it would crack and show the truth.

It was a vain house, an arrogant house, was this house of Barton. It stood amid the turmoil and the hubbub of a bitter contest with the people, when calamity fell and brought mourning with it. The news of George Barton's sud-den death appearing on the first page of the morning papers, under one of the four flash-heads that greeted the reader's eyes, brought a shock with it. For the very papers which contained the news of the death crowded the account of it down to half a column, in order to print fiery communications from lead-ing citizens and tax-payers, protesting against the passage of the Barton bill. The council was to cast its final vote in the matter on the evening of the next day. In their newspaper protests the citizens took for granted that the council would stand by Joab T. Barton in the street-railway matter, as the council had protected him in the water-works bond proposition, in his gas and electric lighting schemes, in his river-front right-of-way grab, and in all the matters wherein the welfare of the people and the interests of Joab T. Barton had stood in opposition.

Therefore the town did not mourn with the Bartons. When death came to them and smote them dumb, the town forgot them. The mourning in the town was for the young life that was cut off; for the smile that was chilled; for the boyish heart that was still; for the loss of the warm hand's clasp, and the eternal silence of a cheery voice. But for the living—for old Joab and his proud wife—the world forgot that they were coming through the great shadow, where the high and the lowly, the worldly and the righteous, the saints and those who are unclean, grope and stretch out their hands, and where all are

kith and kin in the Democracy of Despair. But over the great house in Brookdale Park there hung a dreadful silence. Now and again the creak of a door
would shatter it; the thud of a booted foot upon a heavy hall-rug told of the
florist's invasion. The daylight darted impertinently through the hush of the
darkened rooms; the master of the house, alone in the library, could feel rather
than hear the servants gliding by his door. The whispering of visitors in the
hall below sounded to Barton like an agitation in some cave of bats. He sat
in a leather chair for hours, staring at the frescoed pattern on the ceiling. By
mid-day his nerves had set him walking. For a time he paced the room; tiring
of it, he went down the stairs and slipped past the parlor, and the neighbors
saw the gray-clad human pendulum swing for two hours from end to end of
the long veranda. An instinct for work nagged at Joab Barton, and the instinct
brought the bitter knowledge that the incentive for work was gone. The day
before he would not have owned that all his labor was for his son; but as the
father walked his weary round that day there came a mighty press of grief
upon him and he was sick—sick in the very flesh—at the stress of it. In that
hour it was not the loss of one whom he loved that lashed his spirit; perhaps
it was pride, perhaps it was the uprooting of the unspoken hopes that nature
plants and nourishes in the breasts of fathers, though they know it not; perhaps it was the smarting of the blow that death deals to those near the swath
of the sickle; perhaps it was—God knows what. But some mighty force came
to the father there and he wrestled with a growing impulse which he put from
him, when it first came. But as the shadows lengthened upon the lawn, all his
sinews seemed to be pulling against his iron will. Time and again he passed
the closed door of the parlor and beat off the impulse to enter the silent room
and throw himself beside the body and let loose the throbbing tide of sorrow
that pulsed within him. His sense of loneliness had been growing as he faced
his future and realized its emptiness; and, as he looked back and measured the
brief span of years that had enclosed the boy's short life, this sense of loneliness grew deeper and deeper, tearing into the core of his soul. The sunlight of
the day in which he had been walking burned him like a fire, at the constantly
recurring thought that the boy had passed forever out of it and out of all that
was quickening in the world. Every sense lashed him to a madness, and when
the loneliness became utter, when from the abyss of his future a great black
cloud rose and enveloped him, Joab Barton entered the hall and tiptoed to
the parlor-door as one ashamed. He turned the knob of the door softly and

went in, his frame convulsing with grief. The stifling odor of the room choked him. He paused till his eyes adjusted themselves to the semi-darkness. He saw that the room was a veritable mass of lilies. Everywhere the whiteness of the flowers beat upon him and the artificiality of the place, the ostentation of the garish spectacle which money had made, mocked the anguish that had led him to the room. His eyes, revolting from the ghastly flowers, fell upon the dead boy's face. Barton lifted his arms high above his head in a spasm of anguish and groaned as he turned away—his sorrow unspent, his soul unsatisfied. The hatred of all the world and its affairs burned his vitals like an adder's sting. After the impotent spasm of his passion had gone, Barton stood in the darkened room a long time with his fingers locked behind him.

Again and again the sight and the odor of the flowers nauseated him. A loathing of everything his money had brought came upon him, and following that came a doubt that his own life had been spent wisely. He stood by the coffin for many minutes. And then he passed an hour walking beside the form among the flowers. In that hour the busy years of his life went by in review. A strange psychological disorder was upon him, and whatever period in his life he tried to recall, whatever deed he dwelt upon, whatever point of his career he examined, the lapping of waters—sweet and sybillant, upon a skiff-side—broke in upon his reverie and brought him back to the days of his youth—to the days when he lived out of doors and tramped in fields and through grassy meadows; when he was brother to all the gentle-folk of wood and stream. And so it fell out that by degrees Joab Barton's heart understood the heart of his son, and he saw the good that was in the life that had passed. With his widened understanding came a warm love for the boy, and then with the whisper of the water still in his ears, the father gave up a pride in his own achievements. He was inspired to do some fine act of charity to perpetuate the dead boy's name. It seemed to Barton that he was but doing for the boy that which death had robbed the boy of the time and opportunity to do for himself. This brought peace to the father, and he hugged the inspiration fondly. The waters ceased lapping then, and Barton walked out into the light of the waning day with a mellow heart, almost rejoicing as a strong man to run a race. His transformation seemed as wonderful to him as that which befell Aaron's rod.

He went to the library, and before he took his chair he saw Lawton, the attorney for his street railway system, coming up the curved stone path to his house. Barton guessed his mission. He felt that it concerned the matters pending in the city council. When Lawton came into the room Barton was sitting listlessly, looking at the floor. He did not rise. After a few formal words the attorney broke the ice.

"Mr. Barton, things are going to pieces downtown. The council's against us."

"I suppose so," returned Barton, not lifting his head.

"Jim Kelsey's flown the coop with his seven men, and that's got the mayor scared; and the fellows who are under obligations to us are getting panicky. They want some assurance that we're going to win, or they'll pull out. I don't know what to do?" There was a question in the last sentence. Barton answered it with a sigh as he put his head on his hand.

"Well, I don't, either."

Lawton was clearly absorbed in the fight. Yet he did not wish to intrude too grossly upon Barton's sorrow. There was a pause. When Lawton saw that Barton was not going to break it, the attorney ventured:

"Kelsey's the key; get him back and you're all right."

"What ails Jim?"

"I haven't the slightest idea, Mr. Barton; he's wearing a Federation button to-day, and the fellows say he's been consorting with the Truly Good and his gang for a month on the quiet. I had a talk with him this morning, but he began telling me about what the people demand, and the people's rights, and the need of your friends getting you down next to the grass roots. I asked him who'd put up for him and left him."

"Yes, I suppose so," replied Barton, turning his heavy eyes toward Lawton.

"Mr. Barton, suppose you have a talk with Jim, you understand him."

This closed a deep silence.

"I don't care what he does," sighed Barton.

But Lawton persisted, telling Barton that the fight had gone so far that many of Barton's friends had cast their fortunes with him for success, and urging him to make some effort in their behalf. The result of the conference was this: That Barton, weary of the persistence of his lawyer, and to be rid of the man for the hour, consented to see James Kelsey that evening.

Twilight was falling when Kelsey entered the Barton house. Kelsey was a large man. He bumped into the furniture of the lower hall, and his voice dropped into a whisper that penetrated the quiet rooms like the hiss of escaping steam. Ascending he thumped each foot twice on every stair, once with his heel, once with his toe. That was because he tried to walk slowly, out of respect for the family's sorrow. Barton, still sitting by his desk where the attorney had left him, heard Kelsey at the door, and querulously cried "Come in!"

Kelsey entered the room ready for a struggle with Barton. The contractor had deliberately broken a ten-years alliance. He was prepared to hear a number of disagreeable things. Barton turned his face from his old ally and said, with a long breath:

"Sit down, Jim."

From a seat by the window Kelsey, who had struck a match, began his charge with: "Don't object to smokin', do you?" This came from between teeth that were biting a cigar. Kelsey was leaning well back in a deep chair and added:

"I'm awfully sorry, Mr. Barton, about George. He was a terrible good boy. My wife was tellin' me to-day how good he was to her at Manitou last summer. She said he was the best-hearted boy she'd ever saw. Well, it's the way of the world, I guess."

Barton made no reply. He walked to a window. The mantel-clock ticked ten minutes before Barton came back to his desk and rested his head on his hand. He began jabbing his pen in a glass of shot, not looking at Kelsey. Kelsey wished to be polite. He waited the first five of the ten minutes to give Barton the advantage of opening the controversy. During the last three minutes Kelsey began to suspect that Barton was planning some vicious trick, and that the silence was a part of a plan to outwit him. He decided to take the bit in his teeth.

"Well, sir, they sent me out to see you—what is it?"

Barton kept on trifling with the pen and the shot-glass, apparently giving his undivided thought to it, and replied:

"So they sent you out, did they?"

"They said you wanted to talk over the West Side Franchise business with me."

"So that's what you came for, is it?"

"It is." Kelsey was braced for the crisis. He crossed his legs and clasped his hands over a knee. Barton put down his pen. He let his eyes wander idly over his desk and said: "All right then—talk!"

No word was emphasized.

"Well, what shall I say? Do you want to know what I think of this business?" Barton nodded a weary head. His eyes were not lifted. Kelsey rose, walked to a smouldering grate-fire and punched it. He faced Barton and spoke: "Lookee here, Barton, me and you's been together in a lot of things for ten years. I've been a friend of yours and I am now. See here—what you need is someone to tell you the truth. The fellows in your office slop over you and lie to you. I won't. You've got to get down to the grass roots. Excuse me for sayin' it at such a time as this—but what you want to do is to get right with the people. They say you're an old hog. They say you want the earth with a fence around it and the taxes paid. And this franchise proposition of yours has got 'em wild."

"Well let 'em get wild and stay wild," replied Barton. His tone was dead, but he lifted his eyes to his companion's.

"That's all right to say, Joab Barton, but the people are after you now in earnest. And they're goin' to get you. More than that, they're goin' to rip every man up the back who stands with you. They're out for blood, and you better pick your tree; I did. Had to. You wouldn't blame me if you knew how things are going down town this week."

Barton's eyes were staring keenly at Kelsey. Barton spoke mechanically. "Pull 'er wide open, old man. Straight track ahead."

"Now, I suppose you're mad. All right, get mad. But I'm right here to tell you it'll be the costliest thing you ever got. This franchise ordinance will be beaten. That's dead open and shut. And it's the first thing you've lost in ten years. If they down you now, the whole kit and boodle will quit you; and you won't amount to more'n a feather fan in a cyclone. The people want to look at the books of this county anyway; and if you don't meet 'em half way in this you're a busted community, politically—or I'm a goat."

Barton looked up quickly and prefaced his remarks with a little nervous cough that he used when about to enter an important discussion.

"Well, say, Jim, what do they want? How would you go at it to get them?"

After the answer came, Barton beat spiritedly on his table with his wiry fingers, and said:

"Well, Jim, you could just as well have the $100,000 that I lose in ten years on your compromise, yourself!"

"Oh, that's all right, Barton. But I'm like old Tom Wharton; I've got money enough to afford the luxury of being honest. But that ain't the point. I can't go into this thing—now honest. As I was tellin' my wife this mornin,' if a fellow amounts to anything in this man's town, he's got to get in with the best people. That's the point. And what's more, they really cut the ice."

Barton could see a small straw then. He grabbed it.

"Your wife agrees with you?"

"You're mighty right she agrees with me, and I'd take her judgment before I would any man's in this town." Kelsey knocked back the ashes from his cigar and put it back at a reflective angle in his mouth, and added, as he threw a leg over the arm of his chair: "I've got money enough now to put her right in the best society in this town. But she don't care a cent for it; throws 'em all down. What she's after is this cold-nosed Brookdale outfit; they make me hurt, but if she wants 'em they're hers. And she knows I know and you know, that it's Katy bar the door if Jim Kelsey isn't as straight as a string. And what's more, the people are with this outfit and it's the only way you can win. You can't beat the people; they've got the votes. And now's the time for you to get right, Joab T. Barton, or the devil will be to pay and the note past due." Kelsey's eyes twinkled as he finished speaking; for the Irish are never so merry as when they are dealing their hardest blows. There was no shadow of yielding in Kelsey's eyes.

Kelsey's words served only to awaken a fighting devil in Barton's heart that had held domain there for thirty years. It was a shrewd, merciless devil that loved a fight for the sake of winning, and it had been the motor that had pushed Joab T. Barton the whole way along his road to riches and power. This devil had been watching Kelsey from the moment he entered Barton's room, even when the stricken father loathed the world of affairs. This under-consciousness must have seen that Kelsey, who for years had been loyal to Barton, was moving by some new and unknown lever. Slowly as the habit of a lifetime took possession of Barton, his sub-conscious reasoning merged into the conscious, and he was as alert as a tiger. Barton's mind worked in vivid, heat-lightning flashes of intuition. In one of these illuminated seconds he suspected that Kelsey's new wife was his lever. The reply to his question about her agreement with her husband convinced Barton. When Kelsey had ceased speaking, Barton rose languidly, stretched himself, walked over to Kelsey, and began purring:

"Oh, well, Jim, don't take it so hard; you're all right. Go on down town and tell the fellows not to get too far away from me. I'll be decent enough, Jim. But I can't talk it over now." Barton said these last words intentionally, and even while he spoke a stunning blow fell upon him as his grief came back to him. He did not wince, but went on—"Women are pretty smart, Jim, smarter than we are at times. Your wife may be right—I don't know, I don't know."

He had managed, by that indescribable pantomime that one uses to dismiss a guest, to get Kelsey on his feet and near the door as the sentence closed. A few formal words ended the meeting.

Barton walked to the grate and jabbed the fire until it blazed. He stood in the flare of light for two or three minutes, with two perpendicular ridges cut in his brow. He was taking mental invoice of Mrs. Kelsey. He recalled mechanically how all the men in the office had sniffed the year before, when she had married Kelsey. Barton remembered that many intangible things had been left unsaid about her. He peered intently into the image of her face as he remembered seeing it upon the street. It occurred to him that he had never met her at an evening gathering; he saw that she was not in society, and deducing from Kelsey's words about her, he concluded that she was forcing Kelsey into the respectability of the Civic Federation to pave her way to social recognition. When Barton went over the ground again, and felt sure of his woman and of the force that was leading her, he stepped back to the telephone and asked her to come to his house that evening. It was Barton's habit to strike like a thunderbolt.

It was not anxiety lest she should fail him that set Barton tearing papers on his desk to bits, while he waited. It was the chilling sense of anguish which he was strangling. This racked his nerves, but as he sat before the sinking fire, his sorrow was numbed by the spirit of combat that was grappling him body and soul. And the hand that touched the electric-light button, at the sound of a woman's voice in the hall, was of iron. Mrs. Kelsey entered in a whirlwind of invisible silks. She fluttered across the room to Barton, and took his hand in both of hers and held it for nearly a second, sighing before she spoke.

"Oh, Mr. Barton, how do you do? Tell me, how is your wife? Poor, poor George!" Mrs. Kelsey caught her breath on something that might have been a sob. At the formal reply she continued: "You know, Mr. Barton, she never called on me, but, in times like this, neighbors can't stand on ceremony. I'm so glad you sent for me, I do hope I can do something." Barton found a chair for her. "Mr. Barton, I've been trying so hard to keep up and be brave all day. But you are his father and you will understand, when I tell you that George was the noblest boy I ever knew—like a benediction I used to think, and now—" A bediamonded hand held her lace handkerchief to her eyes a moment. She straightened up presently and said, in a calm voice: "You will pardon my weakness, I know, Mr. Barton. I came thinking I might help you; that I might do something. And here I am only making it harder for you."

Barton had been watching her out of eyes shaded by his hand. His features had not moved during her speech. He answered, "Not at all, Mrs. Kelsey, not at all." Then he cleared his throat and said:

"It was of another matter that I wished to speak, one that concerns me deeply. I want your help. It is in the West Side Franchise business that comes before the council to-morrow night." "Yes," returned Mrs. Kelsey with the sweetest imaginable bell-like voice, and with an enticing rising inflection.

Barton went on in a dry, dead intonation: "Yes, Mrs. Kelsey, Jim's against me, and I want your help."

"Why did you think I could help you, Mr. Barton? Mr. Kelsey never comes to me for advice in these matters, and he's not a member of the council, either." Barton caught her eye and held it till it dropped.

"Mrs. Kelsey, you are making a mistake. Jim can cat's-paw for those Civic Federation fellows all he pleases, but they will not admit him to fellowship with them, nor will their wives know you. You're on the wrong track. I can help you."

Mrs. Kelsey leaned forward, put her elbow on her chair-arm and her chin in her hand. She fixed Barton on the prongs of a questioning gaze. She was trying to probe him to see what truth was there. It is the habit of women who have been mistaken often.

"Can't we have an understanding?" asked Barton. "You can help me, and my wife and I can do more in two months to get you what you want, than the Civic Federation will do in a dozen years. Mrs. Kelsey, I'm a plain man. I always speak right out. Now then, [the little cough put the comma in here], if you'll see that Jim's friends in the council vote for my Franchise bill, I'll see that every house in Brookdale Park is open to you before snow falls. I give you my word."[4]

Mrs. Kelsey did not take her eyes from Barton's face. She was thinking. The thought uppermost in her mind was that the council would vote the following evening, and that it would be a year before Mrs. Barton could come out of mourning to fulfil the compact. Barton divined some obstacle like this and repeated:

"I give you my word, Mrs. Kelsey."

To Joab T. Barton that sentence was a solemn obligation. Even those

---

4. Bracketed text in the original. Perhaps an editing error.

who hated him, never claimed that he would break a promise or forget it. Mrs. Kelsey nodded absently and said, in a preoccupied tone, as she went on searching for some way to bind the bargain: "Yes, I know."

The answer revealed so much of the woman's past to Barton that he would have winced if he had been of flesh and blood. "Well?" he asked. The silence continued. But when Barton saw Mrs. Kelsey moisten her lips and heard her expel the faintest little sigh, he knew that some decision had been reached. He was too wise to put another interrogation. Mrs. Kelsey dropped her eyes, and put the ferrule of her umbrella on her glossy shoe-tip and began, in a mellow voice that had a show of pathos in it:

"Mr. Barton, I'm not the kind of a woman you have taken me for. I can't enter into a cold-blooded deal like that. I love to do things for my friends. It gives me pleasure to help them. I thought the world of George, Mr. Barton. I would have done anything in the world for him that a mother would do. He was just a boy. I want to be friends with his father and mother. If you come to me as a friend and ask this that you do, I'll help you. I don't want any re-ward—only to be considered your friend."

Barton could see whither she was drifting. The president of the West Side Electric Railway Company did not recoil at her audacity, and George Barton's father was dumb. The president of the West Side Railway Company saw only the great game that had been almost lost, now almost won. The lust to win tingled through his veins. He filled a pause with:

"I understand exactly."

"Do you?" she inquired. She was screwing her courage to the point. To be accepted as a friend of the Bartons in a great family crisis like this would put Mrs. Kelsey's social status beyond question. After that, she believed that she could take care of herself.

"I knew you would understand when I told you. George's father must have understood. And it is for George's sake that I want to be friends with you—you and his poor heart-broken mother. I want to comfort her. I want you to let me come to-morrow and help her through that terrible ordeal. I want to be here in the house, to receive the curious strangers, to shield her; to let her lean upon me for her boy's sake. It will comfort me—you don't know how much."

He did not answer. She feared she had moved too suddenly; that Barton, being unprepared, would refuse her request. Wishing to cinch the proposition, she spoke through her handkerchief:

"And don't—don't you think—Mr. Barton," a bubble of sobs broke the sentence, "that Jim Kelsey wouldn't brave the whole world for anyone who was that good to me. Oh, Jim is so good to me, Mr. Barton, so good."

It was not Mrs. Kelsey's grief that moved Barton. For he looked up at her quickly, and when he saw that her eyes were dry, he knew that he was facing a business proposition. Mrs. Kelsey did not meet his gaze, but her eyes fell, coyly enough perhaps, to have deceived a meaner judge of human nature into parleying and haggling for better terms. Joab Barton consumed one—two—three—four—five minutes in debate with the devil before Mrs. Kelsey got her answer. In that five minutes Barton looked at the naked facts in the case. He took into account his wife's hatred for Mrs. Kelsey. He saw clearly that he was trading his wife's peace of mind for votes to pass the Franchise bill. He knew that such a course would be abhorrent to his son. But the spirit of the fight was so big in him that he put by his wife's scruples as the whims of a foolish woman, and passed over what might have been his son's objections as the quibblings of a sentimental boy. As for his own high purposes of the earlier hours of the day, he saw in them only the vaporings of an unbalanced mind. Still it took time to settle these things, and while they were settling Mrs. Kelsey composed herself and waited her answer patiently. Barton had been drumming on his desk with the long thin blade of a paper-knife, and he did not lift his eyes from the tip of the blade as he said:

"Very well, Mrs. Kelsey, very well," and then added: "Will that be all?"

"No, I think not," replied Mrs. Kelsey, as if trying to recall the last article on a shopping list. "Mrs. Barton and I should have an understanding, and there will be no better time than now. I believe I would send for Mrs. Barton, if I were you."

Mrs. Barton came into the room, her large figure trembling, and her head, that was crowned with crimping-pins, nodding as in a palsy. The brown wrinkles in her face were drawn and deepened, and there was a pitiable abandonment to grief in her wrinkled clothes. If the stricken mother's heart was clutched by surprise or anger, when she recognized Mrs. Kelsey, her heavy face did not show it. She seemed to have reached a point where her body did not repeat the agonized writhings of her soul.

"Well, Joab, what is it?" was her greeting.

When she heard her husband's disagreeable prefatory cough she must have known that his words would be painful to her. But she seemed none the less ready to hear them.

"Mrs. Barton," began her husband, "you know Mrs. Kelsey." The wife made a trembling acknowledgment to Mrs. Kelsey's effusion. "Mrs. Kelsey," continued Barton, "is going to place us greatly in her debt. And in a way that nothing except a manifestation of our gratitude can repay her. I have had a talk with Mrs. Kelsey, and she tells me that she considers it important to be here to-morrow, to represent us during the morning and to be with us during the afternoon. I have pledged her your consent. Considering the debt we owe her I could do nothing else."

It was a long speech; but Barton had braced himself for it, and said it carefully and slowly, as though he were dictating it to his stenographer. Mrs. Barton, who had seated herself before the message started, seemed to be on the point of speaking once or twice during the recitation, but checked herself, and when her husband ceased talking she replied:

"It's just as you say, Joab."

Mrs. Kelsey, rising to go, said: "I'm so glad, Mrs. Barton, that you will let me do something to help you in your trouble."

Mrs. Kelsey approached the elder woman, and brought with her the odor of violets and the irritating rustle of silk. There was a creaking mechanism about her gestures and in her manner that rasped the nerves of the heart-broken mother. In a second she lost her self-control. Anger made her joints rigid as she stood before her husband; but her voice quavered and broke and she ran the gamut along its short register as she spoke:

"Joab Barton, do you know what that—that—that creature is?" She pointed to Mrs. Kelsey. "What she has done? That's the person that tagged after George in Manitou and tried to bring him to her level. Let her in the house? That woman—that—that—"

Barton did not stop drumming with his knife upon his desk. Mrs. Kelsey stood motionless near the grate. In the helplessness of her rage, the mother turned, as if to step toward the younger woman, and cried:

"How dare you come here! How dare you! Isn't it enough for you to hound my boy in life? Are you going to—" But Mrs. Barton did not finish the sentence. She lost voice in a burst of tears. And Mrs. Kelsey exclaimed, in the calmest and sweetest tone:

"My poor dear woman, you don't realize what you are saying and you cannot know what you are talking about. Why, I loved George like he was my own child."

The violet perfume from the handkerchief at Mrs. Kelsey's eyes stimulated the rage of the mother and she found speech.

"Don't I know what I'm talking about? Don't I?" Mrs. Barton trembled, not with the palsy of grief but with pent-up wrath, which passed away as she turned to her husband:

"For God's sake, Joab, are you going to do this? Don't, don't, Joab; please don't. Not now—any time but now."

Barton again spoke in his emotionless voice. "You don't understand. It is a matter of business—purely business. And I must have my way. What time in the morning shall Mrs. Kelsey call?"

Probably Mrs. Barton had met the look before that came into her husband's face. But she stood and stared at him hopelessly, and moaned:

"Oh, God! Business! Business!"

At the door, before she closed it behind her, the mother broke into tears. And they heard her heavy footsteps in the hall and on the stairs. Her cry came back to them:

"George! George! Oh, George!"

Through the stillness of the house came the click of the parlor-door, and after the two above stairs heard a wild, piteous burst of sorrow, the house grew quiet, and the clock-ticks came into the silence and startled them.

The *Morning Times*, which told of the pomp and splendor of George Barton's funeral, published, under the caption of "The Man on Horseback," a double-leaded editorial which Joab T. Barton did not read. Yet it contained much of interest to him and to all good citizens. The editorial ran thus:

Last night the city council passed Joab T. Barton's ordinance granting him a re-newal of his street railway franchises in this city for twenty years. The ordinance was passed just as it came from the law department of the West Side Electric

Railway Company, without an ink-scratch on the twenty-five handsome green type-written pages. It was passed by a majority of five, the exact majority that the West Side people boasted it would have six months ago. There was in it not one concession to the people. For three months the citizens of this town have made public sentiment against this nefarious measure so plain that no one has disputed it. If there had been the slightest remnant left of the institution of a government by the people, Joab T. Barton would have paid the city some adequate return for the great concession he has wrested from the people through chicanery and corruption.

But the vote last night has demonstrated that this town no longer enjoys popular government. This town, its citizens, its prosperity, real and personal, and the hereditaments thereunto appertaining, are the chattels of Joab T. Barton. He not only owns the executive and legislative branches of the civil government, but the judiciary is recruited from his law offices. He can give us water or not, at his will; he can furnish us with light or not, at his will. He can bid us walk, and there is no recourse from his edict. By a scratch of his pen he can increase freight-rates on his great railroad system, putting the necessaries of life out of the reach of one-third of the population in the city, and no State Legislature dare check his avarice. There has been much talk about the coming revolution that is to destroy property rights and overthrow free government. The talk is idle. A silent revolution has been accomplished. Our dictator is here. Napoleon's monarchy had only limited powers compared with those which Joab T. Barton controls. What a farce are these empty forms of popular government!

Out of the mad struggle for commercial supremacy—a struggle that has cost America a thousand times more lives, and better lives than the revolutionary guillotine took from France—has risen in every American city, and in many American States, some bloodless, greedy, brutal incarnation of the spirit of the times, like Joab T. Barton. He is the man on horseback.

The Greatest of These

(Emporia Gazette, May 12, 1900)

A man in this town has been living three years for the sole purpose of getting even with some other men. He fancies they downed him. What they really did was to stand by a friend. But this man, who is unusually bright, exceptionally active, and unusually courageous, is wasting these talents; he is literally throwing away the best years of his manhood and is letting a canker of hatred eat out the good red blood in his heart; vinegar and wormwood are beginning to course through his salivated veins. In ten years more, he will be an envious, mean, contentious old devil, who will rejoice in the downfall of others and gnash his teeth at his neighbor's good fortune.

And what's the use?

Why devote the golden hours of this beautiful world to sowing the seeds of dissent? No good comes from it. The world isn't pushed forward by pulling anyone backward, even a bad man. The world is helped, not by reforming and punishing one's enemies, but by reforming one's self. Vengeance is mine, saith the Lord.[1] Why in Heaven's name should a man desire to take away from the Lord his only unpleasant duty? There are so [many] good things undone that might be done, so many good words to plant that may grow into brave deeds, that a man is squandering God's patrimony when he sows dragon's teeth and plants the roots of woe.[2]

Here in Emporia we are all neighbors. We have to live close to one another; why should we not see one another's good points rather than spend our time contemplating the evil. No man or woman in this town is wholly bad. There are many good points in the worst. The Lord only knows what hereditary devil a man may have to fight or a woman have to strangle to be half way decent. And because the Lord only knows, vengeance is His. Let us, who have not been

---

1. Romans 12:19.
2. To sow dragon's teeth: to incite conflict.

found out, be charitable to those who have been caught. The greatest of these is charity.

Scribes and Pharisees

(*Saturday Evening Post*, September 9, 1905)

Ours is a little town in that part of the country called the West by those who live east of the Alleghenies and referred to lovingly as "back East" by those who dwell west of the Rockies. It is a country town where, as the song goes, "you know everybody and they all know you," and the country newspaper office is the social clearing house.[1]

When a man has published a paper in a country community for many years he knows his town and its people, their strength and their weakness, their joys and their sorrows, their failings and their prosperity—or if he does not know these things he is on the road to failure, for this knowledge must be the spirit of his paper. The country editor and his reporters sooner or later pass upon everything that interests their town. In our little newspaper office we are all re-porters, and we know many intimate things about our people which we do not print. We know, for instance, what wives will not let their husbands indorse [*sic*] other men's notes at the banks. We know about the row the Baptists are having to get rid of the bass singer in their choir, who has sung at funerals for thirty years until it has reached a point where all good Baptists dread death on account of his lugubrious profundo. Perhaps we should take this tragedy to heart, but we know that the Methodists are having the same trouble with their soprano who "flats"—and has flatted for ten years, and is too proud to quit the choir "under fire" as she calls it; and we remember what a time the Congregationalists had getting rid of their tenor. So that choirs' troubles are to us only a part of the grist that keeps the mill going.

As the merest incident of the daily grind, it came to the office that the

---

1. "You know everybody": a line from the 1896 song "There'll Be a Hot Time in the Old Town Tonight," composed by Theodore Metz (1848–1936) and Joe Hayden (1845–1916). Theodore Roosevelt (1858–1919) used it as a marching theme for his Rough Riders during the Spanish-American War, greatly increasing its popularity.

bank cashier, whose retirement we announced with half a column of regret, was caught $3500 short, after twenty years of faithful service, and that his wife sold the homestead to make his shortage good. We know the week that the widower sets out, and we hear with remarkable accuracy just when he has been refused by this particular widow or that, and when he begins on a school-teacher the whole office has candy and cigars and mince pies bet on the results, with the odds on the widower five to one. We know the woman who is always sent for when a baby comes to town, and who has laid more good people of the community in their shrouds than all the undertakers. We know the politician who gets five dollars a day for his "services" at the polls, and the man who takes three, and the man who will work for the good of the cause in the precious hope of a blessed reward at some future county convention. To know these things is not a matter of pride; it is not a source of annoyance or shame; it is part of the business.

Though our loathed but esteemed contemporary, the *Statesman*, speaks of our town as "this city," and calls the marshal "chief of police," we are none the less a country town.[2] Like hundreds of its kind, our little daily newspaper is equipped with typesetting machines and is about to be printed from a web perfecting press, yet it is only a country newspaper, and knowing this we refuse to put on city airs. Of course we print the afternoon Associated Press report on the first page, under formal heads and with some pretense at dignity, but that first page is the parlor of the paper, as it is of most of its contemporaries, and in the other pages they and we go around in our shirt sleeves, calling people by their first names; teasing the boys and girls good-naturedly; tickling the pompous members of the village family with straws from time to time, and letting out the family secrets of the community without much regard for the feelings of the supercilious.

Nine or ten thousand people in our town go to bed on this kind of mental pabulum, as do country town dwellers all over the United States, and although we do not claim that it is helpful, we do contend that it does not hurt them. Certainly by poking mild fun at the shams—the town pharisees—perhaps we make it more difficult to maintain the class lines which the pretenders would establish. Possibly by printing the news of everything that happens, suppressing

2. Probably referring to *The Kansas Statesman*, a populist weekly periodical that began publication from Atchison, Kansas, in 1901.

nothing "on account of the respectability of the parties concerned," we may prevent some evil-doers from going on with their plans, but this is mere conjecture and we do not set it down to our credit. What we maintain is that in printing our little country dailies, we, the scribes, from one end of the world to the other, get more than our share of fun out of life as we go along, and pass as much of it on to our neighbors as we can spare.

Because we live in country towns, where the only car-gongs we hear are on the baker's wagon, and where the horses in the fire department work on the streets, is no reason why city dwellers should assume that we are natives. We have no dialect worth recording—save that some of us Westerners burr our "r's" a little and drop an occasional final "g." But you will find all the things advertised in the backs of the magazines in our houses, and young men in our towns walking home at midnight, of a hot evening, with their coats over their arms, whistling the same popular airs that love-lorn boys are whistling in New York, Portland, San Francisco, or New Orleans that same fine evening. Our girls are those pretty, reliant, well-dressed young women whom you see at the summer resorts from Coronado Beach to Buzzard's Bay. In the fall and winter these girls fill the colleges of the East and the State universities of the West. Those wholesome, frank, good-natured people whom you met last winter at the Grand Canons, who told you of the funny performance of Uncle Tom's Cabin in Yiddish at the People's Theatre on the East Side in New York, and insisted that you see the totem pole in Seattle and take a cottage for a month at Catalina Island, and who gave you the tip about Abson's quaint little beefsteak chop-house up an alley in Chicago, and told you of the Irish woman who keeps a second-hand furniture shop in Charleston, where you can get real Colonial stuff dirt cheap—those people are our leading citizens, who either run the bank or the dry-goods store or the flour-mill. At our annual arts and crafts show we have an exhibition loot from the four corners of the earth, and the club woman who has not heard it whispered around in our art circles that Mr. Sargent is painting too many portraits lately, and that a certain long-legged model whose face is familiar in the weekly magazines is no better than she should be—a club woman in our town who does not know of these things is out of caste in clubdom, and women say of her that she is giving too much time to her church. [3]

---

3. John Singer Sargent (1856–1925) was an American painter known for his portraitures of wealthy upper-class Europeans and Americans in the Edwardian period.

We take all the beautiful garden magazines, and our terra-cotta works are turning out creditable vases—which we pronounce "vahzes" you may be sure—for formal gardens. And though we men for the most part run our own lawn-mowers, and personally look after the work of the college boy who takes care of the horse and the cow for his room, still there are a few of us proud and haughty creatures who have automobiles, and go snorting around the country scaring horses and tooting terror into the herds by the roadside. But the bright young reporters on our papers do not let an automobile come to town without printing an item stating its make and its cost, and whether or not it is a new one or a second-hand one, and what speed it can make. At the flower parade in our little town last October there were ten automobiles in line, decked with paper flowers and laden with pretty girls in lawns and dimities and linens—though as a matter of fact most of the linens were only "Indian head."[4] And our particular little country paper printed an item to the effect that the real social line of cleavage in the town lay not between the cut-glass set and the devotees of hand-painted china but between the real nobility who wore real linen and the base imitations who wore Indian head.

In some towns an item like that would make people mad, but we have our people trained to stand a good deal. They know that it costs them five cents a line for cards of thanks and resolutions of respect, so they never bring them in. They know that our paper never permits "one who was there" to report social functions, so that dear old correspondent has resigned; and be-cause we have insisted for years on making an item about the first tomatoes that are served in spring at any dinner or reception, together with the cost per pound of the tomatoes, the town has become used to our attitude and does not buzz with indignation because we poke a risible finger at the home-made costumes of the Plymouth Daughters when they present *The Mikado* to pay for the new pipe-organ.[5] Indeed, so used is the town to our ways that

4. Indian head: a type of fabric used in place of linen for clothing in the nineteenth and twentieth centuries.

5. The Plymouth Daughters was a women's society founded by members of the Empo-ria's First Congregationalist church in January 1904. The society hosted dinners, concerts, and other events within the community. *The Mikado* is a comic opera first performed at the Savoy Theatre in London in March 1885 that enjoyed widespread success. The music was composed by Arthur Sullivan (1842–1900) and the libretto was written by W. S. Gilbert (1836–1911).

when there was great talk last winter about Mrs. Frelingheysen for serving fresh strawberries over the ice cream at her luncheon in February, just after her husband had gone through bankruptcy, she called up Miss Larrabee, our society editor, on the telephone and asked her to make a little item saying that the strawberries served by Mrs. Frelinghuysen at her luncheon were not fresh but were sun-dried. This we did gladly and printed her recipe. So used is the town to our school-teachers resigning to get married that when one resigns for any other reason we make it a point to announce in the paper that it is not for the usual reason, and tell our readers exactly what the young woman is going to do.

So gradually, without our intending to establish it, a family vernacular has grown up in the paper which our people understand but which—like all other family vernaculars—are Greek to those outside the circle. Thus we say:

"Bill Parker is making his eighth biennial distribution of cigars to-day for a boy."

City papers would print it:

"Born to Mr. and Mrs. W. H. Parker, a baby boy."

Again we print this item:

"Mrs. Merriman is getting ready to lend her fern to the Nortons, June 15."

That doesn't mean anything unless you happen to know that Mrs. Merriman has the prettiest Boston sword fern in town, and that no bow-window is properly decorated at any wedding without that fern. In larger towns the same news item would appear thus:

"Cards are out announcing the wedding of Miss Cecil Norton and Mr. Collins R. Hatcher at the home of the bride's parents, Mr. and Mrs. T. J. Norton, 1022 High Street, June 15."

A plain drunk is generally referred to in our columns as a "guest of Marshal Furgeson's informal house-party," and when a group of drunk-and-disorderlies is brought in we feel free to say of their evening diversion that they "spent the happy hours, after refreshments, playing progressive hell." And this brings us to the consideration of the most important personage whom we have to deal with. In what we call "social circles," the most important personage is the woman who keeps two hired girls and can pay five dollars a week for them when the prevailing price is three; in financial circles the most important personage is the man who buys real-estate mortgages; in political circles the most important personage is the man who knows the railroad attorneys at the capital and can get passes for the county delegation to the State convention; in the railroad-yards the most important personage is the division superintendent, who smokes ten-cent cigars and has the only "room with a bath" at the Hotel Metropole. But with us, in the publication of our newspaper, the most important personage in town is Marshal Furgeson.

If you ever looked out of the car-window as you passed through town you undoubtedly saw him at the depot, walking nervously up and down the platform, peering into the faces of strangers. He is ever on the outlook for crooks, though nothing more violent has happened in our county for years than an assault and battery. But Marshal Furgeson never relinquishes his watch. In winter, clad in his blue uniform and campaign hat, he is a familiar figure on our streets, and in summer, without coat or vest, with his big silver star on which is stamped "chief of police," may be seen at any point where trouble is least likely to break out. He is the only man on the town site whom we are afraid to tease, because he is our chief source of news; for if we ruffle his temper he sees to it that our paper misses the details of the next chicken-raid that comes under his notice. He can bring us to time in short order.

When we desire to please him particularly we refer to him as "the authorities." If the Palace Grocery has been invaded through the back window and a box of plug tobacco stolen, Marshal Ferguson is delighted to read in the paper that "the authorities have an important clew [sic] and the arrest may be expected at any time." He is "the authorities." If "the authorities have their eyes on a certain barber-shop on South Main Street, which is supposed to be doing a back-door beer business," he again is "the authorities," and contends that the word strikes more terror into the hearts of evil-doers than the mere name, Marshal Furgeson.

Next in rank to "the authorities," in the diplomatic corps of the office, come our advertisers: the proprietors of the White Front Dry-Goods Store, the Golden Eagle Clothing Store, and the Bee Hive. These men can come nearer to dictating the paper's policy than the bankers and politicians, who are supposed to control country newspapers. Though we are charged with being the "organ" of any of half-a-dozen politicians whom we happen to speak of kindly at various times, we have little real use for politicians in our office, and a business man who brings in sixty or seventy dollars' worth of advertising every month has more influence with us than all the politicians in the county. This is the situation in most newspaper offices that succeed, and when any other situation prevails, when politicians control newspapers, the newspapers don't pay well, and sooner or later the politicians are bankrupt.

The only person in town whom all the merchants desire us to poke fun at is Mail-Order Petrie. Mail-Order Petrie is a miserly old codger who buys everything out of town that he can buy a penny cheaper than the home merchants sell it. He is a hard-working man, so far as that goes, and so stingy that he has been accused of going barefooted in the summertime to save shoes. When he is sick he sends out of town for patent medicines, and once he worked for ten years in his truck-garden, fighting floods and droughts and bugs and blight, and saved something like a hundred dollars, which he put in a mail-order bank in St. Louis. When it failed he grinned at the fellows who twitted him of his loss and said: "Oh, come easy, go easy!"

A few years ago he subscribed to a matrimonial paper, and one day he appeared at the probate judge's office with a mail-order wife, who, when they had been married a few years, went to an orphan asylum and got a mail-order baby. We have had considerable sport with Mail-Order Petrie, and he has become so used to it that he likes it. Sometimes on dull days he comes around to the office to tell us what a bargain he got at this or that mail-order house, and last summer came in to tell us about a great bargain in a cemetery lot in a cemetery being laid out in Kansas City; he bought it on the installment plan, a dollar down and twenty-five cents a month to be paid until he died, and he bragged a great deal about his shrewdness in getting the lot on those terms. He chuckled and said he would be dead in five years at the most and would have a seventy-five-dollar lot for a mere song. He made us promise that when the time came we would write up his obsequies under the head "A Mail-Order Funeral." He added, as he stood with his hand on the door screen, that he had no use for the preachers and the hypocrites in the churches in this town, and that he was taking a paper called the *Magazine of Mysteries* that taught him some new ideas on religion and that he expected to wind up in a mail-order Heaven.[6]

And this is the material with which we do our day's work—Mail-Order Petrie, Marshal Furgeson, the pretty girls in the flower parade, wise club women, the cut-glass society crowd, the proud owner of the automobile, the

---

6. *The Magazine of Mysteries* was an occult periodical published from New York City in the early 1900s.

"respectable parties concerned," the proprietor of the Golden Eagle, the clerks in the Bee Hive, the country crook who aspires to be a professional criminal someday, "the leading citizen" who spends much of his time seeing the sights of his country, the college boys who wear funny clothes and ribbons on their hats, and politicians, greedy for free advertising. They are ordinary two-legged men and women, and if there is one thing more than any other that marks our town, it is its charity, and the mercy that is at the bottom of all its real impulses.

Our business seems to outsiders to be a cruel one, because we have to deal as mere business with such sacred things as death and birth, the meeting and parting of friends, and with tragedies as well as with comedies. This is true. Every man—even a piano tuner—thinks his business leads him a dog's life, and that it shows him only the seamy side of the world. But our business, though it shows the seams, shows us more of good than of bad in men. We are not cynics in our office: for we know in a thousand ways that the world is good. We know that at the end of the day we have set down more good deeds than bad deeds, and that the people in our town will keep the telephone bell ringing tomorrow more to praise the recital of a good action than they will to talk to us about some evil thing that we had to print.

Time and again, we have been surprised at the charity of our people. They are always willing to forgive, and be it man or woman who takes a misstep in our town—which is the counterpart of hundreds of American towns—if the offender shows that he wishes to walk straight, a thousand hands are stretched out to help him and guide him. It is not true that a man or woman who makes a mistake is eternally damned by his fellows. If one persists in wrong after the first misdeed it is not because there is not love and kindness thrown around the wrongdoer for shelter. We have in our town women who have done wrong, and have lived down their errors just as men do, and we have men who have sinned and atoned, and have been forgiven. A hundred times in our office we have talked these things over and have been proud of our people and of their humanity. We are all neighbors and friends, and when sorrow comes, no one is alone. The town's greatest tragedies have proved the town's greatest sympathy, and have been worth their cost.

The Coming of the Leisure Class

(*Saturday Evening Post*, October 14, 1905)

We are all workers in our town, as people are in every small town. It is always proper to ask what a man does for a living with us, for none of us has money enough to live without work, and until the advent of Beverly Amidon our leisure class consisted of Red Martin, the gambler, the only man in town with nothing to do in the middle of the day, and the black boys who loafed on the south side of the bank building through the long afternoons, until it was time to deliver the clothes which their wives and mothers had washed. Everyone else in town works, and, excepting an occasional picnic, there is no social activity among the men until after sundown. But five years ago Beverly Amidon came to town, and brought with him a large leisure and a taste for society which made him easily the glass of fashion and the mould of form not only in our little community, but all over that part of the State. Beverly and his mother, who had come to make their home with her sister, in the big house on the hill, had money. How much, we had no idea. In a small town when one has "money" no one knows just how much or how little, but it must be over fifteen thousand dollars, otherwise one is merely "well fixed."

But Beverly was a blessing to our office. We never could have filled our society column Saturday without him, for he was a continuous social performance. He was the first man in town who dared to wear a flannel tennis suit on the streets, and he was a whole year ahead of the other boys with his Panama hat. It was one of those broad-brimmed Panamas, full of heart-interest, that made him look like a romantic barytone, and when he came tripping into the office under that gala facade in his white duck clothes, with a wide Windsor tie, Miss Larrabee, the society editor, who was the only one of us with whom he ever had any business, would pull the string that unhooked the lock of the gate to her section of the room and say, without looking up: "Come into the garden, Maud." To which he made invariable reply: "Oh, Miss Larrabee, don't be so sarcastic! I have a little item for you."

The little item was always an account of one of his social triumphs. And there was a long list of them to his credit. He introduced ping-pong; he gave us our first "pit party." He held the first barn dance given in the county. His was our first "tacky party," and he gave the first progressive buggy ride the young people had ever enjoyed, and seven girls afterward confessed that on the evening of that affair he hadn't been in the buggy with them five minutes before he began driving with one hand—and his right hand at that. Still, when the crowd assembled for supper at Flat Rock, the girls didn't hold his left handiwork against him, and they admitted that he was just killing when he put on one of their hats and gave an imitation of a girl from Bethany College who had been visiting town the week before. Beverly was always the life of the company.[1] Also he could make three kinds of salad dressing, two kinds of lobster Newburg and four Welsh rarebits, and was often the sole guest of honor at the afternoon meetings of the T. T. T. girls, before whom he was always willing to show his prowess.[2] Sometimes he gave chafing-dish parties whereat he served ginger ale and was real devilish.

He used to ride around the country bareheaded with two or three girls when honest men were at work, and he acquired a fine leather-colored tan. He tried organizing a polo club, but the ponies from the delivery wagons that were available after six o'clock did not take training well, and he gave up polo. But in making horseback riding a social diversion he taught a lot of fine old family buggy horses a number of mincing steps, so that thereafter they were impossible in the family phaeton.[3] He thereby became unpopular with a number of the heads of families, and he had to introduce bridge whist in the old married set to regain their favor. This cost him the good will of the Epworth League to restore himself in the church where he passed the plate on Sundays.[4] Miss Larrabee used to call him the first aid to the ennuied.[5] But the Young Prince who chased runaway teams and wrote personal items never referred to him except as "Queen of the Handholders." For fun we once printed Beverly Amidon's name among those present at a Mothers' League meeting, and it

1. Bethany College: a private Lutheran college established in Lindsborg, Kansas, in 1881.
2. T. T. T. girls: a philanthropic organization started in the late nineteenth century (Time Talent Treasure).
3. A light, horse-drawn carriage popular in the nineteenth century.
4. Epworth league: A Methodist youth organization, founded in 1889.
5. Ennui: French word for boredom.

was almost as much of a hit in the town as the time we put the words, "light refreshments were served and the evening was spent in cards and dancing," at the close of an account of a social meeting of the Ministerial Alliance.[6] The next time Beverly brought in his little item, he stopped long enough to tell us that he thought that the people who laughed at our obvious mistake in the list of guests of the Mothers' League were rather coarse. One word brought on two, and as it was late in the afternoon, the paper was out, we bade Beverly sit down and tell us the story of his life, and his real name; for Miss Larrabee had declared a dozen times that Beverly Amidon sounded so much like a stage name that she was willing to bet that his real name was Jabez Skaggs.

Beverly's greatest joy was in talking about his social conquests in Tiffin, Ohio: therefore he soon was telling us that there was so much culture in Tiffin, such a jolly lot of girls, so many pleasant homes, and a most extraordinary atmosphere of refinement. He rattled along, telling us what great sport they used to have running down to Cleveland for theatre-parties, and how easy it was to 'phone over to Toledo and get the nicest crowd of boys one could ever wish to come over to the parties, and how Tiffin was famous all over that part of Ohio for its exclusive families and its week-end house-parties.

The Young Prince sat by listening for a time and then got up and leaned over the railing around Miss Larrabee's desk. Beverly was confiding to us how he got up the sweetest living pictures you ever saw and took them down to Cleveland, where they made all kinds of money for the King's Daughters. He told what gorgeous costumes the girls wore and what stunning backgrounds he rigged up. The Young Prince winked at Miss Larrabee as he straightened up and started for the door. Then he let fly: "Were you Psyche at the Pool in that show, or a Breakfast Food baby?"[7]

But Beverly deigned no reply and a little later in the conversation remarked that the young men in this town were very bad form. He thought that he had seen some who were certainly no gentlemen. He really didn't see how the young ladies could endure to have such persons in their set. He confided

6. Mothers' League: A nationwide organization of mothers who supported religious education for children and engaged in charity work. Ministerial Alliance: An alliance of Emporia Protestant pastors.

7. This is one of many quips throughout this editorial implying that Amidon has a feminine affect. While not explicitly homophobic, White here connotes a connection between wealth, pretense, effeminate men and "otherness" in regards to his idealized Emporia.

to Miss Larrabee that at a recent lawn-party he had come upon a young man, who should be nameless, with his arm about a young woman's waist.

"And Miss Larrabee," continued Beverly in his solemnest tones, "a young man who will put his arm around a girl will go further—yes, Miss Larrabee— much further. He will kiss her!" Whereat he nodded his head and shook it at the awful thought.

Miss Larrabee drew in a shocked breath and gasped: "Do you really think so, Mr. Amidon? I couldn't imagine such a thing!"

He had a most bedizened college fraternity pin, which he was forever lending to the girls. During his first year in town, Miss Larrabee told us, at least a dozen girls had worn the thing. Wherefore she used to call it the Amidon Loan Exhibit.

He introduced golf into our town, and he was able to find six men to join his fifteen young ladies in the ancient sport. Two preachers, a young dentist and three college professors were the only male creatures who dared walk across our town in plaid stockings and knickerbockers, and certainly it hurt their standing at the banks. For the town frowned on golf, and confined its sport to football in the autumn, baseball in the summer and checkers in the winter.

That was a year ago. In the autumn something happened to Beverly, and he had to go to work. There was nothing in our little town for him, so he went to Kansas City. He did not seem to "make it" socially there, for he wrote to the girls that Kansas City was cold and distant and that everything was ruled by money. He explained that there were some nice people, but they did not belong to the fast set. He was positively shocked, he wrote, at what he heard of the doings at the Country Club—so different from the way things went in Tiffin, Ohio.

For a long time we did not hear his name mentioned in the office. Finally there came a letter addressed to Miss Larrabee. In it Beverly said that he had found his affinity. She was not rich, he admitted, "but," he added, "she belongs to an old, aristocratic, Southern family, through reduced circumstances living in retirement; very exclusive, very haughty. I have counted it a privilege to be constantly associated with people of such rare distinction. Her mother is a grand dame of the old school who has opened her home to a few choice paid guests who feel, as I do, that it is far more refreshing socially to partake of the gracious hospitality of her secluded home than to live in the noisy, vulgar hotels of the city. It was in this relation at her mother's home that I met the woman who is to join her lot with mine." Thereafter followed the date and place of the wedding, a description of the bride's dress, an account of her lineage back to the "Revolutionary Georgia Governor of that name," and fifty cents in stamps for extra papers containing an account of the wedding.

In time we hope to teach our young men to roll down their shirt-sleeves in the summer, our girls to wear their hats, our horses to quit prancing in the shafts of the family buggy. In time bridge whist will wear itself out; in time our social life will resume its old estate, and the owners of the five dress-suits in town will return to their former distinction. In time caste lines set by the advent of leisure class will be obliterated, and it will be no longer bad form for the dry-goods clerk to dance with the grocery clerk's wife at the Charity Ball. But, come what may, we shall always know that there was a time in the social history of our town when we danced the two-step as they dance it in Tiffin, Ohio, and wore knee-breeches and plaid stockings, and quit work at four o'clock. Those were great days—"the glory that was Greece, the grandeur that was Rome."[8]

8. Quoted from Edgar Allan Poe's "To Helen" (1831).

Emporia and New York

(*American Magazine*, January 1907)

Americus, with a population of five hundred souls, lies ten miles northwest of Emporia. It is a town that bit off more than it ever could chew; for it started to go around its public square and only got on one side of it. And to understand well the relations between New York and Emporia, it is necessary to know the relations between Emporia and Americus. For instance, if you get the confidence of an Americus man you will learn that Americus people regard Emporia as an awful place, where the men stay out until all hours of the night, and many of the women are really no better than they should be. Americus people come to Emporia to have a good time, because they believe they are lost in the great city where no one knows them from Adam, though we have a scant ten thousand people in Emporia; and when we see an Americus young man cutting up on Commercial Street we know him as well as his mother knows him. And there are those who say that when an Emporia man or a man from a town like Emporia goes to New York, he is marked as surely as the Americus man in Emporia. And probably the opinion of Emporia people about the doings of New York men and the ways of New York women is just as inaccurate as is the Americus theory of Emporians.

Three years ago we sent Charley Vernon, the best reporter on the *Gazette* force, to New York for a holiday, and he came back with a poor opinion of the town. The first thing that shocked him was to see a funeral clattering down the street at a fast trot and, as we are rather accurate about such matters in Emporia, Charley instinctively counted the carriages and found that there were less than twenty, though he learned afterward that it was the funeral of a man worth a million. We have had only one funeral in our town of a man worth a million, and the procession was three miles long. Charley says also that there were no buggies in that millionaire's funeral procession—the mourners all rode in closed carriages. This is odd to us, for in a funeral procession here in Emporia the hearse is escorted by the wagonette—a long, low, rakish-looking craft, with a seat on each side; the pall-bearers ride in the wagonette and have a moderately good time, and if it is a funeral of prominence the pall-bearers are generally leading lawyers or doctors or business men. Following the hearse come the hacks—never less than three and sometimes as many as a dozen. After the hacks in the funeral procession come the double-seated surreys—and under-cut surreys taking precedence over the others—and after the surreys come the top buggies, and after them come the runabouts, and if the funeral is an unusually long one, the spring wagons of the farmers bring up the rear. It means something to die in Emporia; it is not the every-day event in a man's life that it seems to be in New York.

Indeed, when a prominent man dies, or one whom we love, the mayor in our town issues a proclamation calling on the merchants to close their stores, and the banks close their doors, at the hour of his funeral. And when Mr. Soden, who had run the mill for fifty years, died last summer, though his funeral was on Saturday, when the streets of the town were crowded with farmers who had come in to trade, the stores and banks were closed at the very busiest part of the afternoon, and we slipped on our Sunday clothes and left Commercial Street and sat for an hour on the lawn about his house under the broad trees that he planted half a century ago. And while the preacher preached from the front steps of the porch of the house of mourning, and while the choir moaned inside the house, up town the stores were closed and business stopped. Yet Mr. Soden never held an office in all his life and would be counted a poor man in New York. But unless one contends that the death of a friend is a mere incident of the day like the loss of an old hat, we here in Emporia see some things more sanely and more humanly than they do in New York, where death in a house only interests the servants next door.

Also, here is another thing that we cannot understand in Emporia and that is the attitude New Yorkers take toward weddings in what is known as society. Charley Vernon says that when he was in New York he saw a big crowd gawking in front of a church; policemen had to fight the women back to keep them off the side-lines; and he found that these women—well-dressed women, perfectly proper women, so far as he could see—and he has done "society" on the *Gazette* for three years, and ought to know—women he says who looked to him as though they might be coming home from the meeting of the bridge whist club at Mrs. Cleaver's or Mrs. Larkin's—were jamming and pushing and shoving to get sight of the bride and groom and the wedding party as they came out of the church. Would they do that in Emporia? Well, hardly. The Emporia way for those who are not invited to an important social affair—we call such gatherings "functions" in the *Gazette*—is either to stay at home and sniff at it, and call each other up over the telephone—which always leaks— and laugh at the proud ones, or to give another party the same night. Never would Emporia women riot around a wedding to which they were not invited. They would die first.

But the fact that a number of Americus people, who drove down to hear the Emporia band concert in the park, reined up and watched Mrs. Steele's lawn party eight years ago, leaves an uneasy suspicion bobbing over the sur- face of one's consciousness. Perhaps these handsomely gowned who riot at New York weddings are not New York women at all, but Emporia women, and women from towns like Emporia who chance to be in New York and wish to be able to say when they get home, "You know I just happened to be passing Trinity Church the day of the Vanderbilt wedding," and then launch in and tell the Research Club what the bride wore, and how the bride's maids were dressed, and all about the affair! If being away from home and lost in the whirl of the great city makes Americus women stare at Mrs. Steele's party in Emporia, New York may have the same effect on Emporia women. For women probably are not entirely different from men, and there is this no- ticeable similarity in the attitude of the men in Americus to Emporia, and of Emporia men to the larger cities. When an Emporia man goes to Americus for a day he does not put on his good clothes. He has seen Americus men dressed up in Emporia, shopping and attending the county conventions, and he is astonished to find these men whom he has known dressed up for years stubbing around in their old clothes. But when the Emporia man goes to Kansas City, he puts on what he calls his trotting harness, and there he meets Kansas City men in their every-day clothes. Kansas City men dress up to go to Chicago, and Chicago men put on their fine raiment to go to New York, but on the streets of New York the men who naturally are wearing their every-day clothes seem so faultlessly dressed to us Westerners, who appear to have slept in our every-day clothes, that we gasp as we wonder how the New Yorkers must look when they go to London!

But here the hateful suspicion bobs up again: Perhaps these well-dressed people in New York are not New Yorkers at all, but Emporians and their brethren from the country in their Sunday best, hurrying up town or down town to go to lunch with some one! For New York surely is the eatingest place on this continent. In no other American town do people spend so much time fussing around their food as they spend in New York. Here in Emporia the stores open at seven o'clock, and by eight o'clock all the merchants and professional people are at work. For although the banks do not open until nine, the bankers are down and at work by half-past eight, and Major Hood, who for years ran our leading bank, used to come down town at half-past seven and stay in his office until six o'clock in the evening. There are no nine o'clock jobs in Emporia, and everyone, rich or poor, works nine hours, and many of us ten hours. Most of the clerks get an hour at noon, but the boss—as we call the head of a store or an office or a shop—rarely takes over half an hour. Most men go home for their noon meal, but a few hurry over to the lunch counter and spend fifteen or twenty cents, or at most a quarter, for roast beef and mashed potatoes, or stewed chicken and dumplings, or fried cat-fish and coffee and a piece of pie. The meal has no social significance as it has in New York. An Emporia man would as soon think of inviting his friends to take a bath with him as to take lunch with him; for groceries have not got so far along in Emporia as drygoods!

But it must not be inferred from this that our women are not good cooks; we have passed the point in the gastromic [sic] evolution of the town where the leading citizen goes into the shop and asks for twenty cents' worth of "meat." Our butchers are learning how to put up crown roasts and to save a lot of the interior arrangements of the calves that used to go to the scrap heap. And while, of course, groceries have not gone far in our society, there is the inner temple, our cut-class circles where they have a fish course and a game course with their formal dinners, and wherein the women long since have given up trying to find out how Mrs. Warren makes either of her three kinds of plum pudding.

But our cut-class circle is not a wide circle, not is its circumference wall impassable. At the annual dinners of the Christian Union, given at the Campellite Church—which, of course, no one joins to get into society, as sometimes people are suspected of joining the Episcopal Church or the Congregational Church or the Presbyterian Church—about two hundred people from all the churches, and the Big Church, to which many of the men belong, sit down for an evening's social communion and good fellowship. At this table are the bankers and grocery clerks and lawyers and railroad men and farmers and mechanics, two-percent money lenders and all classes and conditions of men. But the important consideration is that their wives and sisters and mothers are there also. It is no trouble to get men to fraternize. Indeed, it is hard to keep them from it. There isn't a man in Emporia who could refrain from talking politics and business with his footman if he had one. But, on the other hand, there are few women in town who wouldn't be grand ladies in ten minutes if they had maids. But no woman in town has a maid. The prospect of a bride coming to town with a maid once set the town to wondering what the standing of this prospective maid would be with other girls in town who do general housework, and when it turned out that the bride really had no maid, and was a good cook herself, the town was greatly relieved. Thus, for Mrs. Butcher to sit down beside Mrs. Banker, and Mrs. Baker and Mrs. Lawyer to be *vis-à-vis*, and for the haughty Merchant girls and the pretty Mrs. Barber to sit amicably at the same table, indicates that the town is essentially democratic, in spite of the social formaldehyde that the Whist Club uses in preserving its exclusiveness. Excepting the score of children whose parents send them to the Catholic school, through a sense of religious duty, every child in town goes to the public schools. And in the public schools money does not make for leadership. So the boys and girls of one generation, whose high school amalgamations often form the lines of social cleavage in the next, break up any disposition to a hereditary nobility in the town.

Thus, broadly speaking, one may say that in Emporia there is that equality of opportunity for the youth—equality of education, of financial backing, of social standing—which guarantees a democratic community. Not long ago there was a gathering of women from all over Kansas in Emporia, and the leading hotel was a-flutter with silk petticoats. Emporia clubwomen gathered up all the solid silver in town and borrowed both of the cut-class punch-bowls and gave a reception that easily discounted any previous social celebration that we ever held. The hotel glowed with splendor that night. And one of the most prominent guests on that occasion had once been head waitress at that hotel. The town knew it, and respected her for it as much as they would respect a man whose proud boast was that he had once been a bell-boy and had risen in the world. Stronger proof of our real democratic spirit may not be found.

Yet this same degree of democratic enthusiasm is found in nearly every country town of the east and north and west. Emporia is rather typical than exceptional. Country-dwelling American men and most of the women are instinctively democratic. And being democratic, the cities sadden us country people. For the city—and New York is typical of urban America—fosters too much of the sham relation between men that one finds where class lines are set. The eternal presence of a serving class, whose manners may someday petrify into servility, the continual discovery that the man who brings the food, or sweeps the street, or drives the cab, considers wholesome conversation with him from his patrons as a sign of low breeding, the presence of the man who fawns for a quarter, all these make the countryman in New York desire to rush home and organize a Sitting Bull Lodge of Ancient and Amiable Anarchists![1] It is not the extravagances of the rich, but the limber knees of too many of the poor, that disgust the countryman in New York. The saddest thing in that great city, to one who comes from the frank, wholesome, clean, happy faces of the country, is not the painted lady's face, with its glassy eyes, not the overfed, puffy-necked figures of the lazy, respectable hotel-dwelling women, who get no more exercise than stuffed geese, not the besotted faces of the man about the barrel houses—though a merciful God knows they are sad enough; but sadder than they are the loathsome, wooden faces of the men who stand decked out like human manikins in purples and greens and what-not of modish silliness and, for a price, surrender themselves to be made part of the landscape. For years Mickle the painter was the lowest form of humanity we had in Emporia. He was the town drunkard, and once they fined him for beating his wife; drink made him a loafer and a brute. But some way one felt that down in Mickle there was the soul of a man; some way one knew that he would not do certain things for money; some way one always understood that Mickle could still look into the depths of personal degradation below him, and tell whoever tempted him there to go to hell! But, on the other hand, some way the flunkey is just a flunkey, and he seems to have given up the right to resent personal insult when he assumes the miserable part. And for a man to commercialize his American birthright seems a heart-breaking tragedy.

Probably the man in purple and the woman in scarlet are necessary parts of our social order, but they are not necessary parts of our social order in Emporia, and we country people cannot get used to them. So perhaps it is all in

1. While this club is fictional, White here is lightly mocking the American penchant for forming fraternal societies in the nineteenth and early twentieth centuries. These organizations sometimes took their names from American Indians.

the point of view. There are, of course, drawbacks and compensations in every form of human existence, it will be wiser to balance the difference between the town and country, rather than contrast them. Therefore, before we go onward as Christian soldiers from Emporia, marching, as to war on New York, it might be well for us to consider whether New York may not have a just cause against us for some of our shortcomings.

For, after all, the differences between Emporia and New York—differences which antedate those between ancient Rome and the Sabine farm, where Horace sipped his old Falernian—are merely differences of provincialism.[2] Little old New York is provincial; and even though New York is populated with people from Emporia and neighboring towns, these adopted New Yorkers forget, or pretend to forget, all about the old home town. And Emporia is provincial, in that even though we go to New York once or twice a year, we ignore the fact that the very presence of three million people living there argues that they live in some degree of comfort and satisfaction. What New York can't see is how we can live in Emporia with so little going on at the opera house; and what we can't see is how a man who can have one hundred feet of lawn and a kitchen garden to sprinkle with the hose every evening after work, can permit himself to be locked up in a long row of five and six story cell houses, with nothing to distinguish one cell-house from the other but the number on the front door. New York forgets that we have the family horse and buggy and can go jogging over town every summer evening at twilight, looking at our neighbors' porch-boxes and admiring their trees and flowers, and in the spring and autumn take long rides into the country, where the panorama is as good as Belasco ever attempted, and the great comedy of life moves on without waits for the shifting scene.[3] And we in Emporia forget that New York has the ocean and the great playgrounds for the grown-ups, to which they go when they escape from the cell-houses and are happy. And we both forget that the youth who talks books—like the poor—is with us in Emporia, just as persistently as he is in New York. Also, that young Mr. Windeigh, who regales

2. Sabines: The Sabines were rivals of the nearby ancient Roman republic and eventually were conquered. Later, wealthy Romans often had estates in the territories formerly controlled by the Sabines. Horace: Horace (65 BCE–8 BCE) was a Roman poet and contemporary of Emperor Augustus. Falernian: a type of ancient Roman wine.

3. Belasco: likely David Belasco (1853–1931), playwright, producer, and director.

the company with what I said to the boss and what he said and then what I told him and what Miss Stevens said and then what the head buyer said, and what the boss said to me, and what I told the head buyer and what Miss Stevens told me after they both left, is as distinctively a product of Emporia as of New York.

We are of one blood—city and country—in America; our differences are superficial; it is our likeness that is fundamental. We even have the same folk tales. In New York, for instance, they will tell you, with bated breath, that a man named Straus finances the big department stores and controls the policies of the newspapers, and that they do not dare to breathe without consulting him. In Emporia, they say the same thing of George Newman, our leading dry goods merchant. When the *Gazette* takes a stand in local matters people think that the stand is taken because George Newman and Major Hood have some scheme on hand. Though, of course, this is absurd, for often they are just as angry at things that appear in the *Gazette* as the oldest and most valued subscriber, who comes to the office with the previous day's paper folded tightly into a wad, and begins unfolding it and hunting for "that piece." Doubtless this man Straus often sees things in the New York papers that annoy him; but he can't help it. And when people come to him and ask him to stop it, he probably does what George Newman and Major Hood do—makes a note of the grievance and forgets all about it. Major Hood and Mr. Newman and Mr. Straus know that by day after tomorrow something else on the first page of the papers will be so much more terrible than day before yesterday's story that it will be forgotten. For a great deal of the pomp and power in this world are delusions. And no one knows this more than Major Hood and Mr. Straus and George Newman.

But it would be interesting to inquire who gets the most out of life for the money invested—Mr. Straus, the pillar of finance in New York, or George Newman and Major Hood, pillars of finance in Emporia. We who know Emporia well and love her best are inclined to think that a dollar will buy about as much of the comforts that make for happiness here as it will any place in the world. To begin with, the Newman home and the Hood home in Emporia stand on great, wide lawns, and around them are beautiful gardens. Civilization has brought to Emporia every comfort that electricity and gas can afford a man in New York, and after a hard day at the store—a day just as hard as Mr. Straus has at his office—Mr. Newman gets into his automobile and goes to his farm, two miles from town, where he kicks around until dinner time. It is a great, broad, beautiful field, lying in a rich valley; on the farm are blooded

cattle and hogs and pottering with them is a lot of fun—and the fun is en-
hanced by the fact that they pay well. But an hour or two a day on that farm is
making George Newman hale and hearty, and the sweep of the fields and the
close, first-hand relations with men who have not learned the primary lessons
in servility will make him a better, braver, kinder man than life in the store or
shop can make any man. Every year the Newmans can go to New York and see
all that Mr. Straus sees. They have the best of Emporia and New York. But has
New York anything to offer to Mr. Straus every day in the year as compensation for not living in Emporia? New York can offer more money. Yet the house
of Newman in Emporia will endure to the second or the third generation. It
will be a respectable house. It will have peace and plenty, in so much as it really cares for peace and plenty. The house of Straus cannot ask more—and if
it does ask it, probably that's all it will get. We shall all lie down beside George
Newman out in Maplewood on the hill when our time comes, and others will
come after us who will forget this generation and how it strived. Perhaps it is
provincial, perhaps it is merely a countryman's view, but one is constrained
to think that he who lives his life honorably and kindly among real neighbors
will take more with him on his long journey, after leaving all his money here,
than he who lives perhaps just as honorably in an environment full of men
who must needs be strangers, and whose hearts he can never hope to know.

For there is something in touching elbows with men at work—men who
are your equals and make you acknowledge it a thousand times a day—that
gives a man a philosophy worth more than millions. And we are philosophers
here in Emporia—if nothing else. None of us is too busy, none of us is too
poor, nor of too low an estate to have his opinion about things. There was
Zimri Doyle, who went around from church to church year after year and got
religion and joined them all, so as not to burden one church too long with
the keep of his large and growing family; Zimri had a theory of life. When
he finally settled down upon the Congregational Church as having, upon the
whole, more good cooks in it than any other church in town, the women of
the Aid Society claimed that Zimri's theory of life was that women loved babies—vicariously—and that if he could manage to keep one nursling in the
house, the neighbors would never let the family go hungry. So he managed it.

It is a curious thing about human nature that when men live close together, a score or two in a building on a twenty-five-foot lot, they are impelled
to hold one another at arm's length; but when they live as we live here in

Emporia, every family on its fifty-foot lot, with many families living on much larger lots, they feel the need of drawing one another together. And so no one ever starves to death in Emporia, even though we have no more food to give than New Yorkers; but we have what is more essential than food in the human partnership—we have a strong social sympathy.

And that social sympathy is the basis of whatever real difference there is between New York and Emporia, between the city and the country. Not that there is more in one town than in the other—for New Yorkers are more sympathetic when they see suffering. But we in Emporia see the suffering. Our neighbors' lives are a part of our lives. We are so close to one another that we almost anticipate the need of our friends. Therefore in computing what the man at the bottom of the industrial ladder gets out of life, in our town, and in comparing it with wages in New York, the element of social sympathy existing in the country should be considered as a real factor in the calculation. If this social sympathy affects Mr. Straus of New York and Mr. Newman of Emporia, and it does, it surely must affect David Owen, a plasterer who lives up in the Bronx, around 166th street, and Frank McCain, the Emporia plasterer. Mr. Owen makes five dollars a day, and has all the work he can do. Frank McCain is glad if he can get a contract which nets him four dollars a day, and much of the winter he has little work. At the end of a day or a week or a year probably David Owen would have the best of it, in money earned or money saved. In the matter of food and clothing, for themselves and their families, the two men would fare about the same. There would be a balance in their housing. For while Mr. McCain has his home among the trees, where he can have a garden and Mrs. McCain can have flowers, which are denied to the Owens, they have a snug little apartment of four rooms, clean and fresh, well ventilated, and most respectable, and the housekeeping would seem to yield Mrs. Owen more results from the same amount of labor than it yields Mrs. McCain.

And there is this vital advantage that Emporia has for the McCains that New York cannot offer to the Owens: Mr. and Mrs. McCain, in their house of seven rooms, need not move into a larger house if their family grows. Six or seven children may grow up comfortably in that house, and all go through the public schools on Frank McCain's wages. The children of hundreds of families in Emporia have grown up and have got high school and college educations, with the head of the house earning less than a thousand dollars a year. But the four-room apartment which houses the Owens is just enough for Mr. and

Mrs. Owen and the baby; if another baby comes, they will have to move for a twenty-five-dollar apartment to a thirty-dollar apartment and if six or seven babies come, if the Owens live as comfortably as they and the McCains are living now, the Owens will have to rent a fifty-dollar apartment. And, more than that, the kitchen garden, which the McCains depend upon to furnish the family with potatoes all winter and garden truck all summer—the kitchen garden, which keeps the children busy out of school hours, is not to be had by the Owens to piece out the hole in the year's wages made by the increasing rent. Surely this is important. For a community that puts a tax upon children is not organized as it should be.

But eliminating the baby question and considering only the wages, the housing, and the creature comforts, probably at the end of ten or twenty years the McCains will be further along in life than the Owens, assuming that each remains a plasterer and brings up a family in his environment. It is now more than twenty years since Frank McCain left Cincinnati to get along practically without a first-class plasterer, and in that time his family has grown up in Emporia and has been educated in the public schools. His son is a lawyer, graduated from the high school and the law department of the state university, and the only thing that will keep him from being governor of his state is his politics. Frank McCain's opinion on things in his town is more valued than is the opinion of many a store keeper or professional man. His lime-covered working clothes are not the insignia of any status in Emporia lower than that of the banker or the preacher. Indeed, he is not a plasterer at all, but a man among men. And recognizing this, one feels that Frank McCain counts for more in this nation than ever a New York plasterer who sticks to his trowel will count. For Frank McCain can bring considerable influence—personal and political and social—to bear on Major Hood, as every other man in our town can who keeps a bank account—and Major Hood has lent money, to United States Senators, for thirty years. Can David Owen, up in the Bronx, get so close to Mr. Harriman or Mr. Morgan, who have relations with Depew and Platt?

We are all fairly close to the throne in Kansas—and in the West generally. The high priests of politics do not impress us. Two United States Senators were in Emporia last fall, and both went wagging across the town to the depot, carrying their own valises. We refuse to get out the Second Regiment Band for anything less than a Cabinet officer. We are "gentleman unafraid" and a few years ago, when a vice president came through town, making speeches at the end of a railroad train, he pumped in vain for applause by mentioning two of the town's dignitaries. He couldn't fool us; we knew them both. The town gave one a beautiful funeral, and would be happy to do the same service for the other at any time reasonably soon. For, although we live among elm trees, on wide, velvet lawns, in paved streets, and although we have three free public libraries in town, and although we have one four-story sky-scraper, the gentlemen who fifty years ago debated the slavery question through the brush of eastern Kansas, with Colt's Ready Reckoner as their parliamentary guide, are still able to bring in a considerable minority report. And while murder is regarded as such bad form that there has been no crime of violence in the town for over half a decade, a hotly contested primary in the Fourth Ward furnishes all the sportive excitement required by any full-blooded able-bodied man whose appetite for fun has not been surfeited by a plethora of actual homicide. For the first primary or two a president of the United States living in Emporia might have his way in a Fourth Ward primary, but at the third, if he got behind the wrong candidate for sheriff, the president would have to take his chances, and nothing would afford Way and Cagney and Clark and Peach and McCoy and the Haynes boys more joy than to bounce a president in a political blanket at some primary, when his heart was set on handling the delegation to the convention—if they suspected he was merely playing the game.

But probably this is only the spirit of '76; it is the American spirit. That spirit of independence—that intense individualism—is the bond that binds this American nation together; it runs through the townships, the counties, the states, and is dominant in the nation. It is in New York, just as it is in Emporia. And it is tempered in all men through all the nation by that kindness that comes to men who have known the world in the rough at first hand, the real gentility that is bred in those who by the sweat of their brows eat their bread, and know how hard a thing life is when one faces it alone. Hence our institutions for mutual help in the cities—our great benevolent societies, distributing God's mercy upon the poor; here in the country, in Emporia, the social sympathy, the touch of nature always found among neighbors of every class and clique that "makes us a wondrous kind."[4]

---

4. "A veteran see! Whose last act on the stage / Entreats your smiles for sickness and for age; / Their cause I plead,—plead it in heart and mind; / A fellow-feeling makes one wondrous kind," from David Garrick (1717–1779), "Prologue on Quitting the Stage in 1776."

A Slow Process

(*Emporia Gazette*, February 27, 1907)

Governor Hughes's address at Detroit yesterday made at least one point clear—the square deal has got to work from below upwards, as well as to be passed down condescendingly from superior beings on the heights.[1] No government intervention can really serve if individuals are not disposed to be honest in their dealings with their fellows. And from the governor's point of view, that is the hopeful element in the situation. The average business man is averse to lying and cheating. He wants all business, private and public, to be made clean and straight. That is in his own interest, as well as that of the whole community; and hence, as Governor Hughes said, it is absurd to suppose that the run of business men can be opposed to impartial laws equitably enforced. But the impulse must come from the mass of the citizenship. A democratic government will not rise above its source. We cannot get away from that—*New York Evening Post*.[2]

The Lord is in no hurry. We whose active useful life at best is rarely over thirty years, desire to see results, to get work stored away and over with before we go, fearing that others who follow will not see the truth, hasten and splutter. What egoists we are—as if the truth we see was through our own eyes,

1. Charles Evans Hughes (1862–1948) was a progressive Republican who served as Governor of New York from 1907 to 1909. After losing the 1916 presidential election to Woodrow Wilson (1856–1924), Hughes went on to serve as secretary of state from 1921 to 1925 and chief justice of the United States from 1930 to 1941. Here White refers to Hughes's speech at a meeting of the Detroit Board of Trade addressing the role of government in regulating big business.

   The square deal: President Theodore Roosevelt's (1858–1919) progressive reform program for the United States, focusing on corporate regulation, consumer protection, and the conservation of natural resources.

2. White could be referring to the February 23, 1907, edition of *The New York Evening Post*, which covered Hughes's speech at the Detroit Board of Trade.

and not from the Soul of Things in which we move, and the very fact that it is truth proves it must be seen of all men. We wink out, but the truth goes on converting men.

So reformers running ahead of the battle line and beckoning, grow irritable and worry because the line does not advance. It cannot advance until as a line it has made the truth part of its practical creed. It is the creed that moves a man's life that counts—not the creed he professes in church. And so long as the world is full of small dealers in oil who cheat and spy on their competitors, and give short weights—we cannot regulate the large dealer in oil who does the same thing. So long as there are many men who cheat and trade and dicker in politics, we cannot adopt a political system which must be operated fairly. So long as the only demand for an anti-pass law comes from the men who have no passes and would like to have them, an anti-pass law is foolish.[3] Public sentiment that does not carry self-sacrifice with it is merely public clamor. So long as the sentiment against slavery was mushy enough to let men own slaves unmolested, it was moonshine. But when men were willing to give their lives for it, the sentiment was real.

So long as the sentiment against the crookedness of Harriman is mere envy of Harriman, it is ineffective.[4] But when men enough in the country are found who would not be Harriman if they could, then Harriman should tremble.

There is but one way for the world to grow—by every man unselfishly paring off his own faults, and trusting to time to take care of his neighbor. Legislation that tries to pull men ahead of their own instincts is often ineffective.

Unless a state or a nation is composed of a majority of honest men, laws commanding honesty will be of little effect. Honesty is not a set thing. It grows.

3. Distributing passes for free railroad travel to influential local elites was a favorite method used by railroads to buy influence during the Gilded Age. Although the use of free railroad passes was restricted under the 1906 Hepburn Act, many lobbyists were not satisfied with the implementation of the act and pushed for further limitations, arguing that the use of passes gave unfair advantage to holders.

4. Edward Henry Harriman (1848–1909) was an investor and railroad magnate who served as president of the Union Pacific Railroad, Southern Pacific Railroad, and several other major railways. In 1906 and 1907 the Interstate Commerce Commission investigated Harriman's railroad investments, finding that his business practices violated the Interstate Commerce Act of 1887. These findings, combined with a history of questionable business tactics, cemented Harriman's reputation as a robber baron.

What was honest one hundred years ago, is condemned today, and Harriman and Captain Kidd will wander down the fables of the next century together. The hero of yesterday walks stumblingly among the moral restraints of today.

And so runs the world away. Reformers are good for us. But they are sorely trying sometimes. They give us what we need, but it is often bitter medicine. We prod them and sneer at them and revile them, and shorten their lives, so that no Moses ever lives long enough to enter the promised land, and the very thing he nags at the line about, beckoning it impatiently forward, is the thing that keeps him out of the realization of his dream. But it all is evened up someway.

A Look Ahead

(From *The Old Order Changeth: A View of
American Democracy*, May 1910)

It is difficult to imagine what a tremendous splash in the tide of humanity was made by the invention of fire-making, or of the lever, or of the wheel. How the current of affairs was changed by each of these devices. How many ten thousands of years man consumed socializing fire, for instance, slowly and with great labor and many wars taking away the special privileges of priest-craft, or social distinction that went with fire-making to the fire-makers. When fire-making lost its mystery and became common to all the people, what a change had come over mankind—what advancement had been reached. Man had ceased to migrate with the birds, and had separated himself from the herd into families, had learned to cook, and had lost his hairy coat. With the invention of the wheel came the overthrow of the rule of the strong. And as the mystery of the wheels became common to the people—through the centuries—as the wheel became socialized, so that every man might make and have and use a wheel without paying tribute or obeisance, the leash of the strong upon the weak slackened just a little. The history of man has been a story of the socializing of human inventions, taking them from the few who received homage and taxes for them, and distributing the inventions and the blessings they brought among all the people.

The invention of writing gave us commerce and kings; its socialization gave us the invention of printing. Printing took away the special privileges of the priests, but it gave the power of the priests to the traders; gunpowder armed the common man, and the socialization of gunpowder destroyed feudalism, and made our modern democracy possible. Great inventions create classes of men with more or less power over their fellows. Then slowly the people take over the inventions, make them common to the race, and the special privileges attached to a particular invention pass; and with the passing of these privileges the economic, social, and spiritual life of the people changes.

Today the world is trying to socialize the invention of steam. The nineteenth century was one of "many inventions." But all of them, that are of first importance in the world, are subsidiary to the discovery of the power of steam, or are interrelated to it. We have shown that the economic manifestation of the invention of steam is the invention of the corporation. Not that the corporation is new in the world, neither is steam; the vapors of boiling water and the legal partnerships of men have been known for thousands of years. But with the harnessing of steam came the consolidation of capital. The vast physical power of the steam engine produced the vast economic power of capital. The steam engine is too big for the common man to own. It requires two or twenty or two thousand, or two million, or more, to own it, and to furnish material for the engine to work upon. And, moreover, it put out the individual fires in a million little forges; it took from the homes and shops of the people millions of little wheels, and gathered to itself all the levers in the world. It was as though, by some strange reversion to old days, a great pre-Adamite giant had come stalking into the earth gathering unto himself all the fires and their privileges that men had wrested from him in the morning of time, all the wheels and their privileges and all the levers and their special powers that had passed among men in the childhood of the race. The world stood afraid before the steam engine. And to those who controlled it we gave privileges and rights and immunities that we gave of old to the priestly fire-makers, the kingly wheel owners, the royal purveyors of the secrets of the levers. Steam harnessed by capital made a new mystery that demanded our worship. And how we have bowed to it! Kings, potentates, priests, "principalities and powers"—all have paid deference to the captain of industry. He who can control capital has stood before kings. Capital has broken caste, the last vestige of feudalism; and where caste exists today, it is a hollow shell that will crumble before the new century is much older. Our problem in this century must be the socialization of steam; and incidental to that will be the control of capital.

For today, under the present order of things, capital rules the world. Churches are built and creeds formulated to please capital. Wars are begun and ended and nations established and laws enacted for the profit of capital. Politics is the struggle of capital to hold its legal advantage. The priests of capital in the skyscraping temples in the great cities of the world hold dominion over the minds and bodies of the civilized people on this planet as the fire-making priests of primeval days ruled their little worlds from altars and caves. For our high priests today, holding dominion over the fires and wheels and levers of the world, have assumed to make the morals of the world to fit their convenience, and for their services have exacted such tribute as seemed equitable, to wit, all the traffic will bear. But the reaction is inevitable today as it was of old. The difference between the reactions will be only a difference of time. We live in a rapid age. The nineteenth century saw the greatest revolution in the world—that from feudalism to industrialism, from the control of kings to the control of capital. The twentieth century will see even a greater revolution—that from the control of capital to the control of men. Capitalism is republican; the next evolutionary step will be toward democracy. For capital, controlling the fires and wheels and levers of the world, after all has been only the world's servant. Steam has been turning power presses, spreading knowledge among men, making electricity to spread intelligence abroad in the earth, to transform distance into a physical fiction, to draw men together in acquaintanceship that in the nature of things must end in brotherhood. Capital, with all its diabolical self-interest, has been engaged in schooling men well, in housing them warmly, in clothing them decently, in providing them wholesome food, and making them physically and mentally stronger men than ever the world has seen before this generation. It must have been thus that the ancient inventions were socialized. As they made man stronger, he captured them. It is a world-old history of human progress. Moreover, the same human nature is working on this our latest problem that worked upon problems that faced man as a child. We face a new fact in the world; fear it; let it establish our moral relation to it, as a thing apart from our common daily run of life; the new fact becomes a fetish, capturing us with its new creed; we struggle and battle and fret ourselves to little avail; and lo! we see some fine morning that the new fact is to be handled according to no new creed, but according to the old law of kindness that common sense of simple justice between man and man known as righteousness. Thus men have captured and made part of society fires and wheels and levers and printing presses and gunpowder and Christ's creed; and thus we shall capture steam, control capital, and establish democracy, not by intricate laws and elaborate government machinery, but by the fundamental kindness of men to men, the basic unselfishness of man widened and applied to men, in their new relations. Only as man's range of unselfishness has extended from the family to humanity has he grown useful and happy in his usefulness upon this globe. So in the conquest of steam will he win by no new set of morals, but by awakening to the widening life that steam has brought, and applying to that greater life his divinely given kindness.

Now in the contest for the control of capital by society through governments, those who would control capital are divided into differing, if not opposing, schisms or factions or schools: those who would distribute the profits of capital according to the needs of men; and those who would distribute profits according to the achievements of men. "From each according to his ability; to each according to his needs," say the socialists. "From each and to each according to his achievement," say the individualists. "We claim for each man equal rights with all other men," say the socialists. "We claim for each man equal rights to display his inherent inequality to all other men," reply the individualists. "We demand that every man's needs be satisfied," say the socialists. "We concede that certain fundamental needs, such as food and warmth and shelter, be guaranteed by society to every man willing to work— not so much perhaps to help the needy man as to prevent the brutalization of those in plenty," say the individualists, and add, "but after that, all that society should do is to guarantee that every man's actual inequalities of achievement shall be reflected with reasonable accuracy in his social rewards."

And that brings us to the problem of the century: Shall we control capital as socialists or as individualists, distributing the profits of capital according to our needs or according to our achievements, fostering the equality of men or developing their essential inequalities? That we are to control capital and make some much more equitable distribution of the profits of capital than now is made seems indisputable. The vast restlessness of the common people of the world, and particularly of America, proves that. It will be idle for capital to resist control; it will be dangerous to civilization for capital to arrogate to itself the divine right of kings and plead a different and a higher morality to govern its activities. The more capital resists control, the more of it will be destroyed by the struggle to control. The more selfishness capital puts into the struggle of the people to control it, the more selfishness capital will engender. "As ye sow, so also shall ye reap."[1] But on the other hand, the more fundamental faith in the justice and fairness of men organized in government those who control capital exhibit in the arbitrament of the problem of the century, the more capital will there be in the world when the question is settled.

1. Galatians 6:7.

But the folly of capital seems to be like the folly of kings. Capital is making the same struggle against control and distribution according to needs of men, as witnessed by the contest with the socialists of Europe, that capital is making against the control and distribution of capital according to the honest achievements of men, as witnessed in the contest in America. It is, however, the American contest that interests us chiefly. Here the socialists have perhaps the smallest following they find in any civilized country. Here is an earnest attempt to control capital and distribute its profits solely upon the achievements of men, allowing, of course, for that narrow margin of need which must be provided for if those in comfort shall not grow selfish and brutalized by the constant appearance of cruel want.

The American struggle to socialize steam by controlling capital, this vast new economic growth from the physical fact of steam, may be epitomized by the word "democracy." Democracy, the child of steam, is seeking to control capital, its economic brother. The struggle proves that a real force has come into the world—a social element with its two forms of motion—inward and outward, centripetal and centrifugal, egoistic and altruistic, capital and democracy. Now, it may be fairly asked what is democracy trying to do with capital. It may be easily seen that as the control of the government, whether of the city or the state or the nation, passes more directly into the hands of the people, profits shrink. In the earlier chapters of this book, we saw that as money gets out of politics profits decrease in public service corporations. Here are the three concrete typical instances: The referendum in the cities makes it impossible to grant franchises carrying large profits for promoters, and this forces municipal ownership, which, being translated, means bonds issued at a low rate of interest. In the states men nominated by direct primaries are demanding that railroads issue stocks and bonds only upon the valuation of the property; and that means only legitimate profits in flotation. In the nation, as the people are awakening to their power, presidents, legislatures, and courts are curtailing the powers and profits of capital invested in combinations restraining trade. Everywhere that democracy touches capital interest shrinks, profits decrease, dishonest deals and speculations cease. What is democracy trying to do?

Now, as a working hypothesis, let us suppose that our American democracy is trying to distribute the profits of capital according to the achievement, and not—expect secondarily—according to the needs of men. It becomes necessary to define achievement. It may mean one thing yesterday, a certain thing today, and something entirely different tomorrow. Indeed, the world's progress may be read in the changing definition it makes for achievement. One may say achievement is social service. That sounds definite and certain, as the lawyers put it. But every age sees a change in what it regards as social service. In imperial Rome the soldier was the chief social servant. He had the "power and the glory," because the state was so organized that the soldier deserved much credit for the stability of society.[2] In the Middle Ages the priest was the chief social servant; his achievement was best rewarded, because he held the state together. But with the invention of printing and gunpowder the soldier and the priest were no longer needed, and their achievements were unimportant, and they fell back to secondary places in the organization of civilization and took inferior rewards. In the transition state between the days of the power of the soldier and the priest on the one hand, and on the other hand our modern days of republicanism, there was a time when the king and the baron and the feudal servants held the social organism together. Then the achievements of the lord and overlord were important, and they had their rewards according to their talents. But the social organism changed. The time came in the last century when the man who could handle wisely the surplus earnings of the people, invested against a rainy day, was the most important man in the state. So the capitalist's social service was deemed the greatest achievement, and he took the place in public esteem and favor, and consequently in power, of the soldier who gave way to the priest, and of the priest who stepped aside for the overlord.

Now democracy in America is catechizing the capitalist. We are asking him to define his use. We are demanding that he show cause why he should not follow the soldier, the priest, and the baron. That is what all this commotion in our politics is about. Over and over we hear this dialogue: "Where did you get it?" asks old Demos, rubbing his eyes.[3] "I earned it," replies Croesus.[4] "How?" "I built a railroad." "But," insists Demos, "the railroad cost you

---

2. "Power and the glory": a reference to a short hymn at the end of the Lord's Prayer.

3. Demos: a Greek word meaning "the people."

4. Croesus is a term used to refer a wealthy individual. It is derived from the name of the Greek king of Lydia in the sixth century BCE, who was known for his extravagant riches until his defeat by the Persian Empire c. 547 BCE.

only twenty million and you took sixty million." "Promoter's profits," replies Croesus, beginning to move on. "Stop thief," cries old Demos, and hales his friend into court. Or sometimes the dispute occurs over the rate charged for a given service. "This is my business, I have a right to its profits," declares Croesus. "I am your partner," retorts Demos; "but for me you would have no patronage. Let's see the books." And they look at the books, and down come the rates, and old Demos chuckles. Or if there is further hitch in the matter, he says, "Come now—down with the rate, or I'll go into business myself." "Who are you that you should do this un-American thing—invade the domain of a private ownership?" "I," replies old Demos, "I am a man." "A mere man," replies Croesus, "and this is a great mystery—this business." "All right," says the catechizer, "but I am the man who found that the mystery of soldiering was common courage; that the imponderable mystery of the Bible which I took from the priest and opened was common sense, and the inscrutable mystery of government that I took from the overlord was common honesty. Behold, I am ready for another mystery! Come now—down with rates, get your profits down to six percent, or I shall borrow money from the same widows and orphans that supply you at three percent, and go into this business myself." "But the widows and orphans whose earnings I have taken?" whines Croesus. "They are my friends; they will take my notes," replies Demos, and advertises for bids for the municipal plant.

But when Demos finds the man who has invented something, whether a business system, a telephone, a combination of effective men, or a religion, there Demos stops. There society is willing to lavish its rewards. That is achievement. All democracy demands is value received. If the capitalist can show that, he may have his millions and welcome to the care they bring him—or the joy, if he is wise. In this new definition of achievement which democracy is making for the capitalist, the first requirement is that achievement shall return to society value for the money he gets; next that the money shall be taken honestly. And now by inheritance tax laws in thirty-seven American states democracy is demanding that rewards for achievement shall not descend unto the third and the fourth generation.

It is difficult to say what democracy's definition of achievement for capital will be ultimately. But it is not difficult to see that the tendency of the definition today is toward limiting the legitimately rewardable achievement of the capitalist to the accumulation and investment of the actual surplus earnings of the people with a small profit for handling these funds. Obviously the funds are his in trust. He has earned no large part of them. He is acting for the men and women whose thrift has produced the capital. If he invents business systems and combinations that have economic value—that save money for the people and earn large returns honestly—his reward shall be the inventor's rather than the capitalist's. But the day of the rule of the captain of industry is rapidly passing in America. In all the world there is not a soldier ruler of any importance. The day of the temporal power of the pope and the cardinal has gone. The king or overlord in civilization today is but a figurehead. And tomorrow the capitalist who now dominates the civilization will take his place beside the soldier, the priest, and the statesman—each needed, none absolute. For democracy will have many servants, but no masters. The democratic mind of all the civilized world seems to be coming to the conclusion—by leaps and bounds in Europe, and slowly in America—that much of the pretended achievement of capital is empirical. In thousands of instances the people have seen promoters and operators taking great rewards from the public, and giving back slight value to society. So little by little the people have lost their faith in the divine right of capital to rule. They have seen the sham of it, and letter upon letter, word upon word, they have read the dishonesty of these shoddy transactions. Clamor is ceasing. But there is a deepening conviction in the American mind that capital shall not be a law unto itself. Thus we find in many of our great cities, in certain of the states, and in the nation definite legal restrictions upon the issue of stocks and bonds, upon the rates of public service corporations, upon the character of the service required from public service corporations; prohibitions of many activities in which great aggregations of capital are invested, and special taxes upon capital for the mere privilege of doing business. These restrictions, prohibitions, and special taxes are new things in our politics. Ten years ago one heard them referred to as un-American, just as the old Tories of England used to denounce any interference with the king's prerogatives as "treason."[5] But kings and capital are no longer sacred. The once un-American limitations of the activities of capital are increasing steadily. As money leaves politics by special invitation of

---

5. Tories: a term frequently used to describe contemporary conservative parties in the Anglosphere. The Tories were originally an English political party in the late seventeenth century known for their support of monarchism, specifically the divine right of kings.

democracy, the rights of property are growing narrower and narrower; the rights of men, broader and broader. Achievements of men with capital are defining themselves more and more closely into the sphere of rigid honesty; not a new-fashioned legal honesty, but an old-fashioned Mosaic honesty.[6] Morals have not changed, but light is turning upon certain shady transactions, and democracy understands them. It is applying to them not so much a quickened, as an enlightened, conscience. It is not so much a moral awakening that we have had, as a moral enlightenment. The schools have taught the people, the people have revived the politicians, and they have remade the law. But so far as the changes in our national life have been political, they do not seem to be manifest so deeply in laws recasting our moral and economic relations, as they are manifest in laws broadening the scope of the individual's participation in the city, the state, and the national governments.

Democracy is arming itself with the full power of the ballot. It is vastly more important that it shall have weapons and equipment for the fight than that it shall have a programme. The laws enacted during the past ten years restricting capital are unimportant. The prohibitions upon capital are unimportant—though they are widespread. And the taxation of capital is of little permanent significance—though the tendency to tax capital is growing. The important thing, the permanent thing, manifest in our growth as a people is the growth of democratic institutions—the broadening and deepening of the power of the people as shown by the adoption of the secret ballot, the purification of the party system, the spread of the direct primary, and the popular acceptance of the initiative and referendum and the recall. The deepening power of the people means that the people are preparing by some subconscious prescience for a great struggle. They do not know definitely what it is. In the nature of things they may have no programme. A cut and dried platform, a formal declaration of principles, and an economic or a social scheme would limit the scope of the movement and curtail its usefulness. Democracy of the twentieth century may have no prophet now—no leader now. It must grow. Coming events must be met, not by a party or a set of principles, but by an attitude of mind. The reaction must be simple, but inevitable. In the socialization of steam which shall equalize the forces of capital and democracy of only this we may be certain: that in its outward form our social, economic, and political organization shall

6. Mosaic: referring to Moses of the Old Testament.

change; but that human nature, which is essentially kind and also essentially selfish, shall remain the same. But we may hope at least that the essential self-ishness of men may be tempered by the coming change into some form of selfishness wherein kindness may extend the selfishness of the man from his family or his clan, or even from his city or his state, to a larger group, so that he may be greedy for the common good.

For it is indisputable that we are acquiring a national public sentiment. Our public men in office and out of office are giving a national expression to our common aspirations. This national public sentiment is not the belief of our rich men, nor of our slums. It is not the trained judgement of the intellectually fittest, neither is it the bias of the uninformed. It is calm crowd judgment amalgamated in the heat of discussion, but cooled and sober on second thought. It holds about so much selfishness as imbues the average man, and it goes only so far toward reform as the average man is willing to go toward self-reform. But the important thing about it, the net result of agitation in America for ten years, is the nationalization of the opinion of the average man. He now finds himself thinking, not merely in cities, not merely in states, but as an American. The great achievement of the past ten years is the exaltation of the individual by putting him in accord, not with the opinion of the leaders of business, of politics, of the college world, but the opinion of his kind, a coordinated, definitely formed characteristic American conviction of the meaning of life.

But the rise of the people is manifest otherwise than in politics. A certain amount of the complaint against the increased cost of living may be satisfied when one considers the increased standard of living. Men are no longer will-ing to eat and wear and read and believe and enjoy and endure what they did twenty or even ten years ago. Eliminating from consideration for a moment the submerged tenth, and taking the average man who lives on $75 a month, and one finds that the average man's taste is for much better things in food and clothes and houses and books and pleasures and comforts than it was twenty years ago.[7] Millions of men are living on a scale now that was possible only to a few thousands before the Civil War. Modern plumbing, telephones, gas for cooking, and electric lights are no longer luxuries for the American

7. Submerged tenth: a late nineteenth-century phrase referring to the 10 percent of society considered to be an underclass living in permanent poverty.

masses—these things are comforts. They are required, not dreamed of. We are paying more for our meat than we ever paid before in a time of peace. Doubtless a few pennies on the pound are being stolen by the packers' trust; but we are paying the farmer more for the meat on the hoof—more in clothes and food and houses and books and creature comforts than any other farmer on earth ever received. We are paying more for our cotton than we have paid for fifty years. But we are paying the cotton spinner—not so well as we should to be sure—more in housing, food, clothing, and education for his children than any other cotton spinner ever received. We are paying more for our gold than ever we paid before; but much of the increased price goes to the gold miner in better food, better cabins, better tools, and shorter hours than we gave to the men in the mines of '49.[8] We are paying more for our houses than we paid for our houses twenty years ago; but they are better houses, and men in the building trades and the workers in the lumber camps and mines and forges receive a share of the increased price for our houses in increased comforts. Steam enters into all this; steam lightens the burdens of workmen. Steam shortens working hours; steam has converted the luxuries of our fathers into the comforts we demand. Steam has broadened our lives, bringing us books and newspapers and music and thousands of beautiful things. Steam has given us electricity and has made the nation a neighborhood. It has organized the public mind, making democracy articulate. In all these matters of better living, of more complete understanding, of higher aspiration, has steam been socialized. Only as steam manifests itself in great aggregations of capital that assume to dwell apart in a unique moral atmosphere, like kings and priests and warrior gods of old, is steam unsocialized. But even capital is passing rapidly under popular control. Another generation will see the worst of the struggle for the control of capital well finished; not that the millennium will come then—not at all. As life widens, it finds new obstacles. Growth is struggle. "God fulfills himself in many ways."[9] It is a dream to believe that greed may be abolished. In all the centuries lust has not been abolished, nor anger, nor hate, nor envy. Yet they are in chains. It is not visionary to assume if we go forward during this century as rapidly toward the socialization of steam as we went during the last century,

8. Mines of '49: a reference to the California Gold Rush.
9. A quote from "The Passing of Arthur" from the poetry cycle *Idylls of the King* (1859–1885) by Alfred, Lord Tennyson (1809–1892).

that we may put the man who issues what the United States Supreme Court has seen fit to call "fictitious capital," or the man who floats bonds not based on actual valuation of property, on footing with the man who violates a home or assaults a woman.[10] We may put the man who manufactures impure food and poisonous drinks in the same category with the fence and the gambler. We may give the trust magnate who refuses to share exorbitant profits with his employes and his customers a social status with the burglar. We may fetter greed, as we have fettered our other human vices. And it will be done, as all our advancement in this life has been made, not by making laws, but by creating broader lives than our fathers knew.

And what a magnificent breeding place we have, here on this continent! The three fates, variation, segregation, and selection, may weave from our social threads such cloth as the world has never seen. The best blood of the earth is here—a variated blood of strong indomitable men and women brought here by visions of wider lives. But this blood will remain a clean Aryan blood, because there are no hordes of inferior races about us to sweep over us and debase our stock.[11] We are segregated by two oceans from the inferior races, and by that instinctive race revulsion to cross-breeding that marks the American wherever he is found. Our social laws permit the best to choose the best; our customs, our traditions, our ideals, all inspire youth to trust their human instincts, to select their mates, the fairest with the fairest, with little thought of caste or class, or of aught but good mating. Our aristocracy is not wealth or

10. Fictitious capital: profits made by capital not tied to anything tangible such as a product or labor, e.g., land ownership or stock market speculation.

11. White's language here is certain to draw connotations with the Nordicism of the German National Socialists. The context in which White uses the term Aryan, however, is of significant difference. In the late nineteenth and early twentieth centuries it was believed that the Aryans, also called Indo-Europeans, were a prehistoric tribe who migrated out of Central Asia and served as the forebears of the cultures and languages of Indians, Persians, and a variety of European groups. White elucidates upon his conceptualization of Aryan when discussing the population of America in a previous chapter of *The Old Order Changeth*: "Some of us are Latin Aryans from the south of Europe; a few of us are Slavic Aryans from the north of Europe; a distinguishable strain of our blood is Norseman Aryan, from the west of Europe, and many of us are Celtic Aryans, cropping out of any of half a dozen other Aryan breeds . . . " (p. 197). Note the inclusion of Slavic peoples in this distinction. While White's views are Eurocentric, it would be erroneous to associate them with the more explicitly racialist ideologies that developed after the First World War.

station; our leaders are the clean-bred children of a natural selection unknown before in human history. Our children grow up with the feeling of community strongly upon them. The "we" feeling is pressed upon them in the common schools, in the common playgrounds and in homes, linked to humanity as no other homes have ever been joined. The electric wire, the iron pipe, the street railroad, the daily newspaper, the telephone, the lines of transcontinental traffic by rail and water, intimate relations with the city, the state, and the federal government have made us all of one body—socially, industrially, politically. Under our quickened democratic institutions the common man has an equal vote with his uncommon neighbor. The democratic environment fairly burns the spirit of human brotherhood upon the growing child. The world is near him. There are no outlanders. It is possible for all men to understand one another; thus hatreds are minimized, and charity stimulated. Thus in a clean home, with wholesome food, in decent clothes, the average well-bred child enters the environment of our democracy. Wars do not mow down the first-born and degrade the breed. Competition gives his sinews all the strain they will stand. This child of the new century may be trusted to see visions—and to follow them. We of this generation have done somewhat to solve the problems that steam has brought to us. And we are by no means done with our day's work. Indeed it is but dawn in the new day of spiritual awakening. Let us touch those who are still sleeping wear the joy of youth upon their faces and say, with the prophet of old:—"Arise, shine; for thy light is come, and the glory of the Lord is risen upon thee."[12]

In the "Massachusetts Railroad and Railway Laws of 1908" we read:

The provisions of this act shall not impair the rights of the commonwealth, as asserted or reserved in the previous statutes; and the commonwealth may at any time during the continuance of the charter of a railroad corporation, after the expiration of twenty years from the opening of its railroad for use, purchase of the corporation, its railroad and all its franchise, property, rights and privileges, by paying therefore such amount as will reimburse to it the amount of capital paid in, with a net profit thereon of ten per cent a year, from the time of the payment thereof by the stockholders, to the time of the purchase.

(Section 7) The commonwealth may at any time after one year's notice, in

12. Isaiah 60:1.

writing to a railroad corporation, take and possess its railroad franchise and other property and shall pay therefor such compensation as may be awarded by three commissioners, who shall be appointed by the supreme judicial court who shall be sworn to appraise the same justly and fairly, and who shall estimate and determine all damages sustained by it by such taking. A corporation which is aggrieved by their determination, may have its damages assessed by a jury in the superior court for the county of Suffolk, in the manner provided in section 90, chapter 48, of the revised laws.

Standing Together

(*Emporia Gazette*, March 24, 1911)

There is not and cannot be any separation of the various interests in a town like Emporia. The interests of Commercial Street are the interests of the whole town. The rich and poor are all in the same boat in this community. What hurts one hurts all. The laborer has no interest different in a community like this from his employer. Drive business away from town, and we all suffer—the property holder suffers by getting low rent, and renter suffers by low wages, the merchant suffers from dull times.

One end of the town cannot grow if the other end falters. One neighborhood is dependent upon every other.

Therefore men and brethren, let us get together. There are certain material things this town needs; but it needs loyalty to the town—the whole town, and not to any part of the town; it needs good will from all parts and sections and conditions of men toward one another, more than anything else. The man who arrays section against section, rich against poor, is making the same mistake that the man makes who says that all the wisdom, all the patriotism, all the self-sacrifice in a community is in the well-to-do. The rich man of today is the poor man of tomorrow, and today's laborer is tomorrow's merchant. We are all alike, all more good than bad, all imperfect, but doing the best we can. The business man who assumes that he is the town is as bad as the loafer who shies brick at the business man for political effect.[1] It is the common average man, the good citizen who lives within his means, cares nothing for social climbing, who pays his debts, treats his neighbors fairly and does his day's work the best he knows how—he is the man who, after all, has made this town and will keep it going. Sometimes he owns a store, sometimes he works in an office, often he has only his hands and his trade, frequently he has a profession; but he is a good neighbor—he is the salt of the earth.

1. Shies brick: to throw an item at something or someone specific.

As a Town Thinketh

(*The Kansas School Magazine*, September 1913)

A town is much like a man. For, after all, a town is but a number of men and women expressing themselves in social terms. So, a town has a bent or tendency, just as a man has. And thus a town acquires a character and gains a reputation among its fellow. In Kansas, Emporia is known chiefly as a school town. The chief concern is the minds of the people of the town schools. The town is the students and the fullness thereof.

Schools and school interests are in the core of the town's heart. Hence we find the soul of Emporia largely devoted to those things that make for spiritual rather than material well-being. To begin with, the town is a clean town. It was a prohibition town before Kansas adopted prohibition, and it has been forty years since a saloon operated on Commercial Street. The gambler and his lady friend never have been allowed in Emporia. Fifteen miles of paving have been laid down without a penny of the paving money coming from the saloon or the gambler or the plain drunk or the woman of the street. Shady lawns, flower gardens, wide-spreading elms, modern homes, public schools that are models for the state—these are the pride of Emporia. The great Kansas State Normal School—one of the world's great colleges for teachers, the College of Emporia, a Presbyterian institution that ranks among the first of the denominational schools in the West, the Emporia Business College, where two hundred boys and girls learn the theory of business practice every year, the excellent parochial school of the Catholics, these are the things that are close to the Emporia heart. These are our treasures, and where the treasure is there the heart is.[1] Emporia thinks in terms of schools. It is one of the few towns in the West where school interests are business interests.

So when students come to Emporia they come with more than a perfunctory welcome. They are welcomed with all the enthusiasm that a community

---

1. Matthew 6:21.

can know. We watch the registration books of our schools as some men watch the stock exchange ticker or as farmers watch the clouds. As a town thinketh in its heart—so is it, and Emporia's heart is set on schools—and lots of them.

The Country Newspaper

(Harpers Monthly, May 1916)

The country town is one of those things we have worked out for ourselves here in America. Our cities are not unlike other cities in the world; the trolley and the omnibus and the subway, the tender hot-house millionaire and the hardy, perennial crook are found in all cities. Class lines extend from city to city well around the globe. And American aversion to caste disappears when the American finds himself cooped in a city with a million of his fellows. But in the country town—the political unit larger than the village and smaller than the city, the town with a population between three and one hundred thousand—we have built up something distinctively American. Physically, it is of its own kind; the people for the most part live in detached wooden houses on lots with fifty feet of street frontage, and from one hundred to one hundred and fifty feet in depth. Grass is the common heritage of all children—grass and flowers. A kitchen-garden smiles in the backyard, and the service of public utilities is so cheap that in most country towns in America electricity for lighting and household power, water for the kitchen sink and the bathroom, gas for cooking, and the telephone with unlimited use may be found in every house. In the town where these lines are written there are more telephones than there are houses, and as many water intakes as there are families, and more electric lights than there are men, women, and children. Civilization brings its labor-saving devices to all the people of an American country town. The uncivilized area is negligible, if one measures civilization by the use of the conveniences and luxuries that civilization has brought.

In the home, the difference between the rich and the poor, in these towns, is denoted largely by the multiplication of rooms; there is no very great difference in the kinds of rooms in the houses of those who have much and those who have little. And, indeed, the economic differences are of no consequence. The average American thinks he is saving for his children, and for nothing else. But if the child of the rich man and the child of the poor man meet in a common school, graduate from a common high school, and meet in the country college or in the state university—and they do associate thus in the days of their youth—there is no reason why parents should strain themselves for the children; and they do not strain themselves. They relax in their automobiles, go to the movies, inhabit the summer boarding house in the mountains or by the sea, and hoot at the vulgarity and stupidity of those strangers who appear to be rich and to be grunting and sweating and saving and intriguing for more money, but who really are only well-to-do middle-class people.

In the American country town the race for great wealth has slackened down. The traveler who sees our half-dozen great cities, who goes into our industrial centers, loafs about our pleasure resorts, sees much that is significantly American. But he misses much also if he fails to realize that there are in America tens of thousands of miles of asphalted streets arched by elms, bordered by green lawns, fringed with flowers marking the procession of the seasons, and that back from these streets stand millions of houses owned by their tenants—houses of from five to ten rooms, that cost from twenty-five hundred to twenty-five thousand dollars, and that in these houses live a people neither rural nor urban, a people who have traditions, and who are getting a rather large return from civilization for the dollars they spend. Besides the civilization that comes to these people in pipes and on wires, they are buying civilization in the phonograph, the moving picture, the automobile, and the fifty-cent reprint of last year's fiction success. The Woman's City Federation of Clubs is bringing what civic beauty it can lug home from Europe and the Eastern cities; the opportune death of the prominent citizen is opening playgrounds and hospitals and parks; and the country college, which has multiplied as the sands of the sea, supplements the state schools of higher learning in the work of bringing to youth opportunities for more than the common-school education.[1]

Now into this peculiar civilization comes that curious institution, the country newspaper. The country newspaper is the incarnation of the town spirit. The newspaper is more than the voice of the country-town spirit; the newspaper is in a measure the will of the town, and the town's character is displayed with sad realism in the town's newspapers. A newspaper is as honest as its town, is as intelligent as its town, as kind as its town, as brave as

1. Woman's City Federation of Clubs: a national federation of women's clubs that supported social progress, community improvement, and education.

its town. And those curious phases of abnormal psychology often found in men and women, wherein a dual or multiple personality speaks, are found often in communities where many newspapers babble the many voices arising from the disorganized spirits of the place. For ten years and more the tendency seems to show that the spirit of these communities is unifying. The disassociated personalities of the community—the wrangling bankers, the competing public utilities, the wets and the drys, the guises that make for discord in towns—are slowly knitting into the spirit of the place. So one newspaper in the smaller communities—in communities under fifteen thousand, let us say—is becoming the town genus! And in most of the larger towns—so long as they are towns and not cities—one newspaper is rising dominant and authoritative because it interprets and directs the community. The others are merely expressions of vagrant moods; they are unhushed voices that are still uncorrelated, still unbridled in the community's heart.

It is therefore the country newspaper, the one that speaks for the town, that guides and cherishes the town, that embodies the distinctive spirit of the town, wherein one town differeth from another in glory—it is that country newspaper, which gives color back, that shall engage our attention at present. That newspaper shall be our vision.

Of old in this country the newspaper was a sort of poor relation in the commerce of a place. The newspaper required support, and the support was given somewhat in charity, more or less in return for polite blackmail, and the rest for business reasons. The editor was a tolerated person. He had to be put on the chairmanship of some important committee in every community enterprise to secure his help. In times of social or political emergency, he sold stock in his newspaper company to statesmen. That was in those primeval days before corporations were controlled; so the editor's trusty job-press never let the supply of stock fall behind the demand. Those good old days were the days when the editor with the "trenchant pen" stalked to glory through libel-suits and shooting scrapes, and when most American towns were beset by a newspaper row as by a fiendish mania.

But those fine old homicidal days of the newspaper business are past, or are relegated to the less civilized parts of the land. The Colonel and the Major have gone gallantly to dreams of glory, perhaps carrying more buckshot with them to glory than was needed for ballast on their journey; but still they are gone, and their race has died with them. The newspaper man of today is of another breed. How the Colonel or the Major would snort in derision at the youth who pervades the country newspaper office today. For this young man is first of all a manufacturer! The shirt-tail full of type and the cheese press, which in times past were held as emblems of the loathed contemporary's plant, have now grown even in country villages to little factories. The smallest offices now have their typesetting-machines. The lean, sad-visaged country printer, who had tried and burned his wings in the editorial flight, is no more. Instead we have a keen-eyed, dressy young man who makes eyes at the girls in the front office, and can talk shows with the drummer at the best hotel, or books with the high-school teacher in the boarding-house. This young gentleman operates the typesetting-machine. Generally he is exotic; frequently he is a traveler from far countries, but he rides in the Pullman and the clay of no high-way ever stains his dainty feet.[2] In the country town, in the factory that makes even the humblest of our country dailies, the little six and eight page affairs, all unknown, unhonored, and unsung, three or four and sometimes half a dozen of the smart, well-fed, nattily dressed machine operators are hired, and the foreman—the dear old pipe-smoking, un-shaven foreman who prided himself in a long line of apprentice printers, the foreman who edited copy, who wrote the telegraph heads and ruled the reporters in the front office with an iron rod of terror, the foreman who had the power of life and death over everyone around the building but the advertising man, the foreman who spent his princely salary of fifteen dollars a week buying meals for old friends drifting through with the lazy tide of traffic between the great cities, the foreman who could boast that he once held cases on the *Sun* and knew old Dana—that foreman is gone; in his place we know the superintendent.[3] And, alas! The superintendent is not interested in preserving the romance of a day that is past. He is not bothered by the touch of a vanished hand. When the vanished hand tries to touch the superintendent of the country newspaper office today, a ticket to the Associated Charities' wood-yard is his dull response. The superintendent is interested largely in efficiency. The day of romance is past in the back room of the country newspaper.

2. Pullman: a type of furnished railroad passenger and sleeper car.

3. *The Sun* (1833–1916) was New York City's first penny paper, created by Benjamin Day (1810–1889). Charles A. Dana (1819–1897) was an American journalist who became part-owner and editor of *The Sun* in 1868. He was popular for his journalistic style and political commentary.

But in the front room, in the editorial offices, in the business office even, there abides the spirit of high adventure that is incarnate in these marvelous modern times. Never before were there such grand doings in the world as we are seeing today. Screen the great war from us, and still we have a world full of romance, full of poetry, full of an unfolding progress that is like the gorgeous story of some enchanter's spell. Where in all the tales of those *Arabian Nights' Entertainments* is anything so wonderful as wireless telegraphy, so weird and uncanny as talking over the seas without wires?[4] What is Cinderella and her romance compared with the Cinderella story today—the story that tells us how the world is turning into her prince, shortening her hours of work, guaranteeing her a living wage, keeping her little brothers and sisters away from the factory and in school, and pensioning her widowed mother that she may care for her little flock![5] How tame is the old Cinderella story beside this! And Sindbad is losing his load too—slowly, as the years form into decades, Sindbad is sloughing off the old man of the sea; the twelve-hour day is almost gone, and the eight-hour day is coming quickly; the diseases and accidents of labor are falling from his shoulders, being assumed by his employer; his bank savings are guaranteed by his government; his food is no longer poisoned; his tenement is ceasing to be a pit of infection; his shop is no longer a place of torture.[6] And every day the newspaper brings some fresh and inspiring chapter of these great stories to their readers. Stories of progress are the magnificent tales of sorcery and wizarding that come gleaming in celestial light across the pages of our newspapers every day. And in our country papers we rejoice in them, because we know the heroes. We know Cinderella; she works in our button factory. We know her father, who lived on Upper Mud Creek and was a soldier in the big war of the sixties.[7] We know Sindbad; he is our neighbor and friend. He is not a mere number and a wheel-tender to us. We played with him in the lower grades before he had to leave, when his father died, to support the family. We see Cinderella and Sindbad every day, and when we read of their good

---

4. *One Thousand and One Nights*, known in English as *Arabian Nights' Entertainments*, is a collection of Middle-Eastern folktales.

5. Cinderella: a folktale character who falls in love with a prince.

6. Sinbad: a character from *One Thousand and One Nights* who goes on seven voyages and encounters various supernatural creatures and magical kingdoms.

7. The American Civil War (1861–1865).

fortunes we feel kindly toward the paper that tells us of these fine things. We open the country paper that tells us of these fine things. We open the country paper and say, "How blessed on the mountains are the feet of them that bring glad tidings," and so we read it, every line. It is the daily chronicle of the doings of our friends.

Of course our country papers are provincial. We know that as well as anyone. But then, so far as that goes, we know that all papers are provincial. How we laugh at the provincialisms of the New York and Boston and Chicago papers when we visit the cities! For the high gods of civilization, being jealous of the press, have put upon all newspapers this spell: that every one must be limited in interest to its own town and territory. There can be no national daily newspaper, for before it reaches the nation its news is old and dull and as clammy as a cold pancake. News does not keep. Twelve hours from the press it is stale, flat, and highly unprofitable. However the trains may speed, however the organization of the subscription department and the press-room may perfect itself, the news spoils before the ink dries, and there never may be in our land a cosmopolitan press. So the cities' papers find that they must fill up those spaces, which in a nation-wide paper should be filled with the news from the far acorns of our land, with city news. Thus in every country paper we have the local gossip of its little world. And our country papers are duplicated on a rather grander scale in the cities. What we do in six or eight or ten or twelve pages in the country, the city papers do in twenty of forty pages. What they do with certain prominent citizens in the social and criminal and financial world, we do also with our prominent citizens in their little worlds.

And in the matter of mere circulation, our American country newspapers are a feeble folk, yet they do as a matter of fact build their homes upon the rock. The circulation of daily newspapers in our cities—towns of over four hundred thousand—aggregates something over eleven millions. The other daily newspapers in the country circulate more than twelve millions, and the weeklies circulate twenty millions more, and most of these weeklies are printed in our small country towns. We have, therefore, a newspaper circulation of nearly thirty-four millions outside of our great cities, and only eleven millions in the great cities. At least so says our latest census bulletin. And the money we country editors have invested is proportionately larger than that our city brethren have invested.

But the beauty and the joy of our papers and their little worlds is that we who live in the country towns know our own heroes. Who knows Murphy in New York? Only a few. Yet in Emporia we all know Tom O'Connor—and love him. Who knows Morgan in New York? One man in a hundred thousand. Yet in Emporia who does not know George Newman, our banker and merchant prince? Boston people pick up their morning papers and read with shuddering horror of the crimes of their daily villain, yet read without that fine thrill that we all have when we hear that Al Ludorph is in jail again in Emporia. For we all know Al; we've ridden in his hack a score of times. And we take up our paper with the story of his frailties as readers who begin the narrative of an old friend's adventures.

The society columns of our city papers set down the goings and comings, the marriages and the deaths of people who are known only by name; there are gowns realized only in dreams; there are social functions that seem staged upon distant stars. Yet you city people read of these things with avidity. But our social activities, chronicled in our country papers, tell of real people, whose hired girls are sisters to our hired girls, and so we know the secrets of their hearts. We know a gown when it appears three seasons in our society columns, disguised by its trimming and its covering, and it becomes a familiar friend. To read of it recalls other and happier days. And when we read of a funeral in our country newspapers, we do not visualize it as a mere church fight to see the grand persons in their solemn array on dress parade. A funeral notice to us county readers means something human and sad. Between the formal lines that tell of the mournful affair we read many a tragedy; we know the heartache; we realize the destitution that must come when the flowers are taken to the hospital; we know what insurance the dead man carried, and how it must be stretched to meet the needs. We can see the quiet lines on each side of the walk leading from the house of sorrow after the services—the men on one side, the women on the other—waiting to see the mourning families, and to be seen by them; we may smile through our tears at the uncongenial pall-bearers and wonder what common ground of mirth they will find to till on the way back from the cemetery. In lists of wedding-guests in our papers we know just what poor kin was remembered, and what was snubbed. We know when we read of a bankruptcy just which member of the firm or family brought it on, by extravagance or sloth. We read that the wife of the hardware merchant is in Kansas City, and we know the feelings of the dry-goods merchant who reads it and sees his own silks ignored. So when we see a new kind of lawn-mower on the dry-goods merchant's lawn, we don't blame him much for sending to the city for it.

Our papers, our little country papers, seem drab and miserably provincial to strangers; yet we who read them read in their lines the sweet, intimate story of life. And all these touches of nature make us wondrous kind. It is the country newspaper, bringing together daily the threads of the town's life, weaving them into something rich and strange, and setting the pattern as it weaves, directing the loom, and giving the cloth its color by mixing the lives of all the people in its color-pot–it is this country newspaper that reveals us to ourselves, that keeps our country hearts quick and our country minds open and our country faith strong.

When the girl at the glove-counter marries the boy in the wholesale house, the news of their wedding is good for a forty-line wedding-notice, and the forty lines in the country paper give them self-respect. When in due course we know that their baby is a twelve-pounder, named Grover or Theodore or Woodrow, we have that neighborly feeling that breeds the real democracy. When we read of death in that home we can mourn with them that mourn. When we see them moving upward in the world, into a firm, and out toward the country club neighborhood, we rejoice with them that rejoice. Therefore, men and brethren, when you are riding through this vale of tears upon the California Limited, and by chance pick up the little country newspaper with its meager telegraph service of three or four thousand words—or, at best, fifteen or twenty thousand; when you see its array of countryside items; its interminable local stories; its tiresome editorials on the waterworks, the schools, the street railroad, the crops, and the city printing, don't throw down the contemptible little rag with the verdict that there is nothing in it.[8] But know this, and know it well: if you could take the clay from your ears and read the little paper as it is written, you would find all of God's beautiful sorrowing, struggling, aspiring world in it, and what you saw would make you touch the little paper with reverent hands.

8. California Limited: a train that traveled between Chicago and Los Angeles, running from 1892 to 1954.

The League and Things

(Emporia Weekly Gazette, July 14, 1919)

The League of Nations is in its pioneer stage. It is a kind of board sidewalk, dirt street, wooden awning concern with hitching posts and rough characters more or less in evidence. The Italians are running a dance hall; the French are running a faro outfit, the Russians are laying out a rival county seat, the Germans are cattle rustling and the British are buying up all the "soldier rights" and grabbing all the bottom land adjoining themselves.[1] The United States is about to go out and pull the badger and then go snipe hunting.[2]

It's a rough outfit; but from such beginnings springs civilization. Moreover, the League is on a good site, and is here to stay. Times will be better in the spring; one more rain will save the corn crop and town lots never will be cheaper than they are today. Pious people who object to the rough element, in ten years will be glad to brag that they were in on the ground floor and shot deer where the court house now stands. Don't ever forget that in every community the "rude forefathers of the village" were mostly wanted for something before they came West.[3] The same thing is true of the League: but that doesn't make it undesirable. In the slow grind of close association men and nations lose their sharp corners and settle into a solid foundation upon which civilization rests and grows powerfully into human service.

---

1. Faro: a card game where players bet on the order specific cards will appear as they are drawn from the deck.

2. Pull the badger: a reference to a blood sport known as "badger-baiting," where a badger is coerced into fighting a dog, often resulting in the severe injury or death of one or both of the animals. Snipe hunting: a nineteenth-century practical joke where members of a community trick a newcomer into hunting a fictitious animal.

3. "Rude forefathers of the village": possibly a variation of a verse from the poem *Elegy Written in a Country Churchyard* (1751) by Thomas Gray (1716–1771), "rude forefathers of the hamlet."

PART II

MID-VICTORIAN MODERN

We Who Are About to Die

(*The New Republic*, March 9, 1921)

Here is the mainspring of the world's oldest tragedy: To fight for change, to establish it firmly, and then to see it fall before inevitable change. "The fear of youth," writes Mr. H. G. Wells, "is the beginning of wisdom."[1] So much for a text.

How American youngsters in their teens and twenties rallied around Mr. Howells when he came out of Ohio by way of New England in the eighties.[2] Walking abreast of him came Mary E. Wilkins, Charles Egbert Craddock, Hamlin Garland, George W. Cable, Thomas Nelson Page, Richard Harding Davis, Margaret Deland, Hopkinson Smith, and soon they gathered about them a group of realists who established a new order of writers in this country—an eager body of literary explorers of waste places. With the fiction writers came Riley and the dialect rhymers, all—story tellers and rhymers—looking joyously for new things to write about;[3] unexplored corners of the heart, unstaked literary lands; New England's flinty emotions, the rough ways of "our great Middle West," the soft and luxurious South, denuded by the war of its exterior beauty, the rugged ways of the mountain folk, and California with which Frank Norris came wagging in.

In the middle nineties Chicago assumed a little brief authority as a publishing centre. Stone & Kimball, Way & Williams, the Chapbook, a blithe band of revolutionists, assembled to watch the sunrise in the Little Room. And Henry Fuller, Harry Webster, George Ade, Peter Dunne, Octave Thanet, Harriet Monroe and the World's Fair, which was as much of a personage as any

1. An ironic revision of Proverbs 9:10, "The fear of the Lord is the beginning of wisdom." No source written by H. G. Wells (1866–1946) could be found to match this quote.

2. William Dean Howells (1837–1920) was a novelist and critic known for pioneering literary realism in the United States.

3. James Whitcomb Riley (1849–1916) was an American poet known for writing in rural Midwestern dialects.

of the others, became fixed stars in the dawn. The Bowen Merrill Company at Indianapolis began to branch out into fiction and poetry—a group of writers clustering around Riley; reviving Maurice Thompson, developing Meredith Nicholson, Mary Hartwell Catherwood, and then with the effulgence of the dawn that "comes up like thunder" appeared Sam McClure![4] He streaked zigzag across the country, peddling Mr. Howell's *The Quality of Mercy* for his syndicate; McClure gave Howells the unheard of price of ten thousand dollars, count them—ten, for the syndicate rights of the story. Probably no other American ever gave the writing craft of this country such a quick cosmic kick, which amounted to impulse, as Sam McClure, aided, controlled, and transformed by John S. Phillips. McClure's magazine gathered about it Booth Tarkington, Ray Stannard Baker, Miss Tarbell, Stewart Edward White, Steffens, Willa Cather and a husky lot of young adventurers, the Pilgrim Fathers of the muckrakers of ten years later—mostly from the West and all of the West in their divine impudence. San Francisco developed its lively crowd—a sort of renaissance of the Bret Harte–Mark Twain days, and the whole order around Mr. Howells, around Chicago, around Indianapolis, around McClure's, became one rather definite school of American writers. It was not great; but it had a certain sure quality, and it was recording the story of the times.

The writers of this school let themselves go; they believed in emotions. Things were fairly black-and-white, with gray areas conspicuously restricted. As children and youths they had come through the sixties, seventies, and eighties, and they had seen the physical miracle which populated the Mississippi valley, the mountain states, and the Pacific coast. They marveled at it; they frankly admired it, even if they almost invariably made villains of the community captains who did the job; the railway builders, the timber thieves, the bankers, the public utility magnates, the mine operators, the land speculators. Christopher Columbus did not disembark upon his new America with a more awed and joyous soul than these explorers of the New America took into their wilderness. These joyous souls revolted at the materialism of the times and the leaders who embodied that materialism in each community;

4. "comes up like thunder": From the song "On the Road to Mandalay" (1907) by Oley Speaks (1874–1948) with lyrics by Rudyard Kipling (1865–1936). Samuel McClure (1857–1949) was an American publisher and cofounder of *McClure's Magazine*, known for popularizing muckraking journalism.

so the leaders became the villains, but the heroes written in the books of that hour were the people, or the embodied courage and faith and devotion of the people to the American spirit of progress. Of course this spirit was puritanism in a new dress—puritanism which is the consecration of the economic main chance as a moral issue. And so these joyous souls of the nineties and of the first decade of this century, wandering about their new wilderness, typewriter in hand, saw beauty in the landscape, heroism in the people, and the promise of a greater American life in all the significances that arrested their attention.

"It is great," read the sign across the carnival entrance, "to be bug house!" And literary life in those good old days was a carnival of optimism. A modern critic of Booth Tarkington accuses him of "swallowing Midland city whole." Of course he did; for he loved it. Booth Tarkington subscribes to support the art gallery, probably heads the list of sponsors and guarantors for the week of grand opera, is a subscriber to the fund to sustain the symphony concerts, is a member of the country club, lives in a suburban place with wide verandahs, velvet lawns, and one hired girl—why shouldn't he swallow it whole? We all swallow it whole. And we buy Main Street in car load lots out here as the digestoid tablet to relieve us after the meal.

Which brings us to the meat of the matter. Main Street is of the new order. And the new order is here. The story teller under the old order may as well "learn of her ways and be wise."[5] Ten years ago it was fashionable to write stories which dramatized the wisdom of the ages, as it is reflected in the Ten Commandments, the beatitudes, and the Golden Rule. Ten years ago virtue was rewarded—in one way or another, either by raw material bon-bons or frothy spiritual satisfactions. Ten years ago vice was punished either by death or remorse or spiritual atrophy. Today "Doc" Kennicott takes his night off, bats his eyes at the domestic environment next morning for an uneasy moment, and that's all.[6] We have moved, during the war, "somewhere east of Suez!"[7] We are no longer interested in "nice people."[8] It is no longer popular to hang their dirty linen upon the line and let its embroideries and filmy grace make amends for its exposure. We must write of the men who fresco the

---

5. Proverbs 6:10.
6. A character from *Main Street* (1920) by Sinclair Lewis (1885–1951).
7. From "Mandalay" (1890) by Rudyard Kipling (1865–1936).
8. Possibly referencing the 1921 play *Nice People* by Rachel Crothers (1878–1958).

railing around the area-way leading down to the "Bon-ton barber shop," and our sordid literary laundry exposes the "short and simple" flannels "of the poor"—mostly red![9] But above all we must not be sorry for the poor. We must not be sorry for anyone. Pride under the new dispensation is bad enough; pride in the town, pride in the state, pride in the country, pride in the heroic patience of humanity; pride in the slow groping of mankind through the dark toward justice, toward that bungling institutionalized kindness called democracy—bah, that's the delusion of the cheerful idiot! But bad as pride is, wicked and weak as it may be, it is infinitely preferable to pity.

So we have witnessed the coming of a new school of fiction, in which enthusiasm, humor, and pathos are as old fashioned as the bustle and the hired mourner! We psycho-analyze our subjects in fiction under an anaesthetic; they don't writhe; blood indicates bad technique! And as for tears—

The Silent Tear which once glittered upon the pages of American fiction is going dry along with the rest of the country under some sort of literary Volstead act.[10] Probably the Mencken group was the dry league that closed our literary tear ducts.[11] But whoever did it, the new books and plays of the new men who write of our national life are absolutely waterproof. Edgar Lee Masters harrows our hearts, but without even the use of the knife. It's dry surgery. Sherwood Anderson in *Winesburg, Ohio*, and in *Poor White* gets away with every sort of cruelty and oppression to his heroes and performs every sort of literary malpractice upon his heroines. We observe the flinching of his cursed creatures with merely scientific interest. We even pin up, in the laboratory, the suppressed sex emanations of Scott Fitzgerald's kids without releasing a temperature. It is all impersonal—this grief and pain and passion of the fiction writers in our new dry era. Yet, somehow, a middle-aged mid-Victorian with natural emotions, who likes a good periodical souse, longs for the splash of the vanished tear, the cramp of the throat that is limp.

9. Referring to Thomas Gray's (1716–1771) frequently parodied "Elegy Written in a Country Churchyard." The original line is "the short and simple annals of the Poor."

10. The National Prohibition Act of 1919, which enforced the Eighteenth Amendment's ban on the manufacture and sale of alcohol.

11. Henry Louis Mencken (1880–1956) was an American writer and cultural critic. Known for his cynicism, Mencken was closely associated with many prominent figures in the literary scene of the 1920s, including Sinclair Lewis (1885–1951) and F. Scott Fitzgerald (1896–1940). White's metaphor here is ironic as Menken was vehemently anti-prohibition.

And here is a curious natural reaction: We are developing a group of literary bootleggers; obliging artists who slip the emotional hootch to us in queer packages. Take Zona Gale. Of course Miss Gale once distilled tears along with the rest of her elders. Her *Friendship Village*, of the first decade of the century, was as wet as Milwaukee. But in *Birth*, her book of two years ago, the dry movement was clearly in evidence; not a sparkling tear in four hundred beautiful crystalline pages. Then came Miss Gale's *Miss Lulu Bett*, which on the face of it would fool any Volstead agent. Even Mencken could smell nothing on Miss Lulu's virgin breath in the book. But it's there; glory be—it's surely there! The good old stuff is concealed in Miss Lulu Bett's calico skirt and the hussy is in New York, and in a theatre on Forty-Eighth Street amidst the smartest set of the Avenue smarties, peddling contraband, lachrymal fluid shamelessly in the play—even more shamelessly than it is dispensed in the Lulu Bett book. In the play the tears are all in the humor—a curious but convenient place to carry them. A comedy will break your heart as surely as the pathos in *The Old Homestead* or *East Lynne*.[12] But Miss Gale goes blandly around in literary dry circles looking as innocent as a cat full of canary. And while Miss Gale has left the old tear mixers, she peddles a secret sorrow in Miss Lulu Bett and winks the other eye to Edna Ferber and her former leaky pals with commendable joy. She is fooling the dry agents.

Possibly the younger crowd in our fiction will discover this violation of the new dry literary law and will get after Miss Gale and her kind; and then again possibly Miss Gale is finding a legitimate way around the law. Miss Willa Cather sneaked around the dry fiction law last year in *My Antonia*, which contained gallons of fine tasty tears in its pages, though the tears were dehydrated and not immediately discernible as tears. She concealed her tears, not in her humor as Miss Gale conceals pathos in Lulu Bett's keenest comedy; but *My Antonia* carried her tear jug in her sex repressions, where no one would look for it.

Floyd Dell's *Moon-Calf*, which is bone dry, evidently is to be followed by a sequence story. Possibly *The Bull*, if that is to be its logical title, may find how to get around the law and we may have an American school of bootlegging fiction. In that day the dear old emotional booze fighters of the time when a

12. *The Old Homestead* (1855), by Ann Sophia Stephens (1810–1886); *East Lynne* (1861), by Ellen Wood (1814–1887).

silent social tear was no crime in our literature and our drama, may slip back into respectable company. In the meantime the old crowd will watch with mourning hopeful interest the shy adventure out of puritanical literalism and dry naturalism which Miss Lulu Bett is making into poignant comedy. If she runs the blockade—the law won't hold us. In another year we'll all go out on one big pathetic toot—and we'll drown Mencken and Van Wyck Brooks, Waldo Frank, and Nathan at the town pump.[13]

These are probably vain hopes. We must not fool ourselves. The old order is passing; the new is well under way. The star of empire which once rested over Indianapolis and all points west, has been put back half a thousand miles and now illumines a shining area bounded on the east by the Brevoort, on the north by the Civic Club, on the west by Greenwich village and on the south by Anthony Comstock![14] Here the new Ebenezer has been raised! It will do no good to rail at the new dispensation, to hoot at "Nietzsche and Mencken and god" with a small "g."[15] We only show our green eyes when we lift them in supplication to a providence that has been junked by our youngers and betters asking for the Restoration. So "gone are the days when our hearts were young and gay—"[16]

"We who are about to die salute you!"[17]

13. Van Wyck Brooks (1886–1963), literary critic; Waldo Frank (1889–1967), literary critic and labor activist; George Jean Nathan (1882–1958), an editor, drama critic, and close associate of H. L. Mencken.

14. Anthony Comstock (1844–1915) was an American reformer and anti-vice lobbyist.

15. Mencken was a supporter of German philosopher Friedrich Nietzsche (1844–1900) and was known for his opposition to organized religion.

16. Referring to the song "Old Black Joe" (1860) by Stephen Foster (1826–1864).

17. A phrase well-known in the twentieth century as the traditional salute of gladiators to the emperor. Despite its pervasiveness in pop culture, there is no historical evidence that this salute was used by gladiators.

The Other Side of Main Street

(*Collier's*, July 30, 1921)

American fiction is developing a new triangle—the man, the woman, and the country town. Sometimes the country town is the hero of a tale, sometimes the villain. Typically, as in "Main Street," the country town is the villain.[1] The lady turns from the country town to drop into Lewis's Gopher Prairie, Minnesota, to be a long-haired Swede. But in "The Brimming Cup" Dorothy Canfield takes the heroine and snatches her from the clutches of the villain, who in her story is a tired business man, and turns her over for better or for worse to Ashley, Vermont, and its rural delights.[2]

The husband of the lady in each novel—and these are good novels—incarnates and somewhat impersonates the country town. The heroine in each novel is more than a woman; she is the spirit of challenge. And the difference between "Main Street" and "The Brimming Cup" are the profound oppositions between the old and the new in American life and letters. "Main Street" presents admirably and with scientific consistency the case for the new; "The Brimming Cup" defends the old. The American country town stands in each book only as a symbol in two contending philosophies.

So for a moment it may be profitable to consider these two novels, for therein American civilization is undergoing rather a serious discussion.

Such pedantic talk may scare many gentle readers from two most interesting books. But if the gentle reader deserts "Main Street" and "The Brimming Cup" and goes to nearly any other American novel of recent years he will find it concealing the same discussion. Indeed, the whole controversy raging between the American naturalists and the romanticists is upon the question involved in these two books.

1. *Main Street* (1920), by Sinclair Lewis (1885–1951).
2. *The Brimming Cup* (1921), written by Dorothy Canfield (1879–1958).

Step Across the Street, Please

The plots of "Main Street" and the "The Brimming Cup" are much the same. Stripped to the bone and the bones bleached, the two plots are like this: An intelligent woman, living with a kind American husband who is of the environing soil, meets a man from beyond the horizon. She takes a good look at the third party and goes back to the environing soil. In "Main Street" she is impelled to return to her bed and board because she has not the moral or spiritual courage nor the visible means of support nor the grit to follow her inclinations. She comes back a grouchy pest. She hates the soil, and accepts her husband as a cross. In "The Brimming Cup" she comes back to the soil, and her husband because she feels that they are of all things in her universe most worth while. So the question is this: Is the soil worth while? Mr. Sinclair Lewis says "no" for the naturalists; Dorothy Canfield says "yes" for the idealists.

Mr. Lewis seems to be dealing with facts; but he has only the facts about the east side of "Main Street," the side containing the hardware stores, the grocery stores, the pool hall, and the drug store; he omits the facts about the pleasant west side of the street—the side which contains the dry-goods stores, the millinery and suit shops, the music store, and the book store. So far as his facts go, they are irrefutable arguments for his thesis, that the American country town, and the American city for that matter, are not worth while. But his facts fall short of the truth. Dorothy Canfield in "The Brimming Cup" aims at the truth. She considers both sides of the street.

It is not that "Gopher Prairie," Minnesota, is uglier than "Ahsley," Vermont. Neither town is beautiful. Both have their dreary spots. So has New York; so has Rome; so has Paris. The average city dweller coming into a country town sees the iron foundry, the ice plant, the small storage houses, the miserable little eating places, the garages and what not of the town's sordid and melancholy prospect, and he sighs at the wasted lives of the townsmen that have no joy in them. The countryman going into New York through tunnels, past poverty-stricken tenements or dirty river fronts, across slimy wharfs or among heaps of wreckage where the builder is making dreams come true, might as well make moan and lament at the ugliness of all cities.

So also, going into books and touring these American towns, it is a question whether one sees externals or internals—the facts or the truth. "Winesburg, Ohio," is the picture of a maggoty mind; a snapshot from a wapperjawed camera.[3] An artist would paint another picture of the same town and make us understand it well enough to like it. The American country town is not Utopia; for Utopia is the hay on the end of the stick before the donkey's nose, moving forward as he strains under his load to get his heart's desire. But the American country town is much like the Utopia of the mid-Victorian dream.

Did This Happen in Your Town?

Here great wealth is as unusual as bitter poverty. Water, light, communication, heat, books, grass plots, sanitation, clean streets, transportation are distributed equitably, almost equally. The telephone, the library, electric lights, running water in houses, schools, colleges, sewers, automobiles are either owned in common or used in common. What a sinful spectacle such socialism would be in the eyes of "Josiah Bounderby" and how "Sissy Jupe" would rejoice in it.[4] And that is not all nor a hint of all. For behold the uplift.

In the beginning there was the Chamber of Commerce. Of old the Chamber of Commerce rented a room, subscribed for half a dozen daily papers, a dozen magazines, hired a steward to take care of the lockers when prohibition came to the States twenty years ago, and used the place as a resort of more or less guilty joy where a little poker, some chess and occasional checkers were played, a few bad cocktails were consumed and much idle time. But that tarnished palace of sin has gone. In the place of the steward to look after the liquor lockers, we have the full-time paid secretary, who belongs to the secretaries' union and attends national conventions of his kind, where he is developing the rudiments of a new-learned profession—one which promotes the gentle and applied art of "boosting."

The Chamber of Commerce today in the American small town and in the American city is the leading exponent of altruism in the community. It is not a wide interurban altruism that the Chamber of Commerce fosters; it is Higginsville first. But it is for Higginsville all the time. The Chamber of Commerce

3. Wapperjawed: crooked.

4. Characters from *Hard Times* (1854), written by Charles Dickens (1812–1870). Josiah Bounderby is a wealthy factory owner who symbolizes the upper-class elites. Sissy Jupe is the poor daughter of a circus performer who symbolizes the lower class.

modifies the innate cussedness of the average selfish, hard-boiled, picayunish, penny-pinching, narrow-gauged human porker, and lifts up his snout; makes him see further than his home, his business, and his personal interest, and sets him rooting for his community.

The New Order of Fellowship

It is a shorter step from the city to the State, from the State to the nation, and from the nation to humanity than the tremendous jump which a man must take to consider his city before his own interest. And the town Chamber of Commerce is giving the first lesson in practical Christianity to millions of savages in America. It is not a full baptism, but it helps.

A man, no matter how greedy and squint-eyed he may be, cannot work a year upon any moderately important committee of his town's Chamber of Commerce without being a better father, a better husband, a better citizen, a better brother.

After this apprenticeship he falls an easy victim to the Rotarians, or the Lions or the Kiwanis Club. These groups interest men in a somewhat broader fellowship than the one which the Chamber of Commerce promotes. They are interested in the neighboring underdog; in man as a suffering or as an aspiring creature. The Rotarians typify the others. "He who serves best thrives most," they declare.[5] They are interested in friendship, in boys, in jollying up the country people around the towns, in "the pore and needy ones that clusters all about," in parks and playgrounds, and they nationalize a number of highly altruistic activities.[6]

Men in these gay groups of rough-necked, low-browed Samaritans are making the Jericho Road a fairly safe and recently comfortable highway wherever they roll their chariots along.[7] And they interlock with the Chamber of Commerce. It is bad form of a Rotarian or for a member of any of these societies not to be a member of the Chamber of Commerce. Thus a stream of rather intelligent altruism keeps flowing into the Chamber of Commerce.

5. "He who serves best": a motto of the Rotary Club.
6. "The pore and needy": quoted from "Little Orphant Annie" (1885), written by James Whitcomb Riley (1849–1916).
7. Referencing Luke 10:25–37.

Around these influences, and largely of them and deeply affected by the organized altruism of the country town, are the Masons, the Knights of Columbus, the Red Men, the Elks, and the Moose, whose chief reason for being is fellowship. And he is a rather measly citizen who is not a member of one of these bodies. And being a member, no matter what mean motives may sneak him in, he must be a cast-iron man who resists the infection of neighborliness that saturates them all. He cannot escape the uplift except by going indoors and sealing himself and his family behind air-tight openings. Once he could go to church and get away from Christianity, but now it will get him even there. And he is liable to find a whole congregation in a raging fever of altruistic desire. In which case the church blossoms out with a parish house or a Plymouth Hall, or a basement for gymnastic and social activities for the young–even dances–or a hospital or a recreational center of some kind.

All over America in the small towns—towns of from 1,500 to 250,000, the churches are burning with the new order of fellowship, which the old deacons, elders, or wardens still call socialistic in want of a profaner term of opprobrium.

Something for Nothing

Then, pyramided upon the Chamber of Commerce, the Rotarians and their kith and kin, upon the lodges and the churches, rise in every community of over three thousand American people the real professional uplifters—the flower of community altruism, those provident, or benevolent, or welfare, or charitable associations which in one way or another look after the down and out. The Red Cross, since the war, has continued its work in thousands of country towns.[8] And here is a curious thing: If in the business community there is a network of interlocking directorates which control public utilities, banks, local industries and newspapers, one finds also in the uplift another labyrinth of directorates tightly interlocked with the Chamber of Commerce, the Rotarians, and their associate societies, the lodges and the benevolent institutions. There is no marked line where the altruism of the Chamber of Commerce crowd tops and the professional uplifter begins. Good-fellowship has

8. Since the war: The First World War (1914–1918).

shot its virus through the whole community. It is an American disease—or blessing, whichever way one looks at it.

Collective neighborliness has marked the American small town for its own. The farmer still is an individualist. He is as independent as a hog on ice; he still retains his suspicions, his reservations, his self-sufficiency, and votes them in politics. So does your urbanite. Broadway is hard. It has no neighbors. Death, poverty, grief, tragedy visit the city and no friends hurry in to heal the wounds. But good will in the American country town is institutionalized. In some organized way the town's good will touches every family. Men feel the strength of it, take courage from it, give themselves to it more or less, and thus grow in stature by what they give. This big growth of curious, emotional kindliness in the heart of the American country town dweller has sown the seed of our national belief in fair[ness]. This belief more than any other—this belief that if you are good to somebody, somebody will be good to you; this conviction that you can get something for nothing by giving something for nothing—distinguishes Americans from the rest of mankind. And it is not the product of our great cities, and not primarily is it a farm product. It is made in our country towns.

Of course it is crass sentimentality, this belief in the efficacy of mutual aid. And much of the mutual aid may be misapplied. A lot of it is gorgeously funny. Nothing is funnier than to see the lime-stained brogans of the man who lays cement sidewalks protruding from beneath a five-hundred-dollar silk night-gown, bespangled with mystic symbols, as its wearer parades a long lodge room with a quid of tobacco pumping the juice from his salivary glands and no chance to spit for five minutes while he proclaims that God is good to the assembled crowd of brethren; nothing unless it is the spectacle of the Rotarians in fantastic medieval garb at the district convention, cutting such capers before high heaven as would make the patients of Bedlam seem wooden images; or if that fails to land the funny prize, try the picture of the Chamber of Commerce giving a dinner to the head of the railroad, trying to coax a division point location out of him for some prairie metropolis.

Yet the lodge does carry the cement dealer through sickness and keeps his widow after his death. The Rotarians do look after the boys of the community and see that they are decently clad and in school; and the Chamber of Commerce does land the new ice plant, and under its activities a park system is established and the waterworks are municipalized and rates cut down. Always, in every one of thousands of American towns, these agencies are working for the common good. They are more powerful than governmental institutions; they are as universal as law. They form an essential part of American life. The forms of iron and stone and wood in the modern civilizations of Europe and of America differ but little, it is in the sentimental relations of men that the civilizations of the old and the new worlds vary.

Which contention is the core of the difference between the idealists and the naturalists in American fiction. The "Main Street" of Mr. Sinclair Lewis is a great book; but it is written in ignorance of the tremendous forces that make for the righteousness in every American town. Dorothy Canfield's "The Brimming Cup" is a truer book because it takes account of these righteous currents that are moving–however muddily, however sluggishly–moving with the current of progress which is surely directing humanity away from a barbarous past to a kindlier, broader, better way of living.

The Jack Horner School

Man as a biological specimen, endowed with hunger and its stimulating organs, and equipped with a desire and a capacity to reproduce his kind, and given hands and feet and eyes and ears and his other sensory organs, climbed down from the trees a long time ago—maybe one hundred thousand years ago, maybe ten times that long ago—it is unimportant. But the first biologic specimen of man was as good as the average specimen today, and perhaps he could run faster, smell better, hear more, and see farther than man runs and smells and hears and sees today. The only progress man has made is in things outside himself. Biologically he is what he was. Socially his inheritance has increased a thousand thousand fold. He has added physical things to his equipment, lengthened his arms by clubs, speeded up his legs by wheels, widened his bill of fare and beautified his home and his raiment by the uses of fire. And every time he has discovered some material substance to aid him, he has seen it develop vast institutions which inexorably pull him into more complex relations with his fellows; and incidentally, but inevitably—as soon as his hand clutches a material weapon, club, or fire or lever or gun or lightning or steam— intangible but still more powerful institutions come to establish a wider justice among men.

This social inheritance of man is today so much more important than man as a biological specimen that he is inclined to forget that he is after all a bundle of muscles and bones and nerves, a brother to the beasts of the field. About every other generation along comes a group of bright young men in the writing game and discovers that beneath the clothes of men are the bodies of men. Aha, they declare in joy upon their peaks in Darien: behold, man has intestines and means for reproducing his kind! This Jack Horner school of literature, which pulls out the preadamic plums from the pudding of humanity, and says "What a big boy am I," is no new school. It is just ignorant. It can see nothing in man but his stomach and the caprices of his affections. Upon these things, but always above them, the whole journey of man from the crotch of the palm tree to the crumbling of the Saint-Mihiel sector has been made. One must not forget the man of biology; but to ignore the social man is gross and fantastic ignorance. And in writing of America to observe this ponderous academic blunder would make a laughing hyena weep its eyes out if it could read.

For America may be crazy with sentimentality, America perhaps may have proved that in every historic crisis Americans are governed by sentiment rather than reason. Yet after all America is America, and not France, not Germany, not even England. And being America it is a literary joke to set "Madame Bovary" down in Gopher Prairie and to put "Mlle. de Maupin" in "Winesburg, Ohio," or to whitewash Rousseau and set him on four legs in the Middle West and call him a "Mooncalf."[9]

America is what it is, not what its critics think it should be, and it is no sign of literary acumen to present what should be as what is. To fail to see the sheer power of sentiment in American life merely because you dislike sentimentality is bad art. Damn sentimentality if you will; but don't deny its presence and power in American life.

Find the Villain

And this new triangle that is appearing in American fiction, the two lovers and the country town incarnated as villain or hero, is set up as a literary frame upon

9. *Madame Bovary* (1857), written by Gustave Flaubert (1821–1880), is a novel about a woman who seeks to escape rural life, and embrace high society and fine arts; Mademoiselle

which to work out this discussion of American life. Typically in the discussion "Main Steet" and "The Brimming Cup" are the challengers, the heavyweights, the Dempsey and Carpentier of the combat; big books both of them.[10] The powerful array of country town facts in "Main Street" is notable achievement. And it is a book that all Americans should read—to take the conceit out of them. It should be on the compulsory reading list of every professor who tries to tell his student about American life.

And then "The Brimming Cup" should be read as an antidote. Ashley, Vermont, is as small and mean a town as Mr. Sinclair Lewis's Gopher Prairie, Minnesota. But in Ashley one sees the social inheritance of man and its inexorable force in controlling his destiny. Bigger than sex, stronger than hunger, the urge of Ashley dominates the woman in "The Brimming Cup." It turns her from a perfectly good lover, from a life of luxury and wide intellectual growth to the thing called duty.

And the thing called duty was not stark, hard, incessant work, but chiefly the rewards of that stark, hard, incessant work: the love of a man, the joy of children, the sweet communion with neighbors, the contact with simple life's raw tragedies, and the eager satisfaction that comes to one who is forever wrestling with a neighborhood, a town, a community, a State—any organized group of people—in the effort to arouse their wider, wiser moral and intellectual capacities, and to lead them to enjoy more abundantly. Let us shamelessly call it the uplift.

"Is Not the Life More Than Meat?"

To this life of long marches and hard bivouacs the woman turns from the gratification of a natural desire for a new lover.[11] And she turns not to satisfy a New England conscience, not even because she is afraid of the lady next door,

Maupin (1673–1707) was a French opera singer known for her extravagant lifestyle. Floyd Dell's *Moon-Calf* was published in 1920 and tells a coming-of-age story set in the Midwest. White appears to be calling Dell's novel derivative of Rousseau's *Emile* (1762). "Mooncalf" is also a colloquial term for a still-born calf.

10. Jack Dempsey (1895–1983) and Georges Carpentier (1894–1975) were heavyweight champions who fought in 1921.

11. "Is not the life more than meat": Matthew 6:25.

nor of her husband's wrath. She turns from the physical joy to the spiritual joy because in rather cold blood she finds the social man more worth while than the biological man. In "Main Street" the woman turns from her lover because she is a coward; fearing her husband, fearing Gopher Prairie, fearing for her own comfort, fearing the hardship of the life into which she returns, blind to its rewards, hating the duties which bring its rewards.

In "Main Street" the heroine wants the biological man. The social creature with a big American social inheritance she loathes. She is a gross materialist.

There the problem of American life is squarely stated. Is man a belly plus sex; or is he these two plus his social inheritance which makes him vastly more than hunger and desire? Of course this is the world problem. Yet in America, and in the American country town, the problem has a peculiarly illuminating setting, at least as the American country town is contrasted with Europe. Probably in South Africa and Australia and certainly in Canada, American country town conditions are duplicated. But they are not duplicated in Europe. They are not duplicated in great cities anywhere in the world. And the distinguishing thing which marks the American country town is the distribution of its economic surplus. That is big talk, and more or less prig talk. Translated it means that in the American country town no one is disgustingly rich; no one poor for a long time. There is enough to go around, and it is passed around. Most people have more than they need; more money, more time, more education, more health, more energy.

While the Top Spins

It is because we have set our economic top spinning and don't have to spend all our time watching it that we in American towns have developed this thing called uplift, this organized, standardized, Yankee-patented business of spreading social sunshine. "Brighten the Corner Where You Are" sang the Billy Sundayites.[12] And "Brighten the Corners Where They Are" sang the Red Cross.

---

12. "Brighten the Corner Where You Are": taken from the hymn "Brighten the Corner Where You Are" (1913), written by Ina D. Ogdon (1872–1964). Sundayites: followers of Billy Sunday (1862–1935). Billy Sunday was a popular evangelist during the early twentieth century who gave sermons all around the United States.

And the whole land began brightening up the corners. Every philosophy from, let us say, Nietzsche's icy mountains to Dr. Frank Crane's coral strand, would like to brighten up the corners, but only communities that can afford it, only communities where there is no horrible pinch of need felt in large masses of the population, will spend time and substance brightening up the corners.[13] In American country towns we can afford it. So we follow the natural human impulse to do so.

It is not the American blood, nor the Puritan spirit, nor the melting pot, nor "the voice that breathed o'er Eden," nor manifest destiny that makes us tender-hearted about our weaker neighbors.[14] The American country town uplift, which expresses itself rather frequently in the slogan "Vote the bonds," comes from our economic surplus.[15] Anyone who has plenty and is not afraid of losing it likes to give. For two or three generations the fear of poverty has been bred out of the average American dwellers on farms and in country towns, and though they may be temporarily hard up, their credit is good, so they give and keep giving, trying to make this a better world than the one they found. They function in crowds as social men more and more, and as biological men less and less.

The literary invasion of the country town makes the social geography of the community valuable. It is entirely possible for a writer to move about in one locality and think he is enjoying the whole town. In every town, however small, are various sets and sections. The differing abilities of men and women make different kinds of men and women. A person seeks his kind.

How They Line Up

There is the country club crowd, which can do little more than make money and spend it. The country club members are interested enormously in home

13. Friedrich Nietzsche (1844–1900) was a German philosopher. Frank Crane (1861–1928) was a Presbyterian minister.

14. "The Voice that Breathed Over Eden" (1857) is a hymn written by John Keble (1792–1866).

15. The slogan "Vote the bonds" was often used in late nineteenth and early twentieth-century newspapers to support bond projects for public works and utilities.

brew and home wrecking. They move around like the covers on "Vogue" and, having come up from shirt sleeves in two generations, return in a third or fourth. They are interesting, but they are not the whole town, though they think they are.

Then there is the church crowd—the older generation—filled with bankers, merchants, judges, elderly doctors—dull but essentially kind.

There is the "booster bunch"; busier than a wilderness of bird pups in a rubber shoe store, and sometimes the boosters get things done. They are forever having committee luncheons and putting on drives and sticking visiting convention delegates in other people's houses, and organizing parades and passing subscription papers and whirling around the country on trade tours in high-powered cars, and in summer sending post cards all over the earth to one another declaring "I wish you were here." The booster bunch isn't the town; though it has more justification for this hallucination than has the country club crowd.

Opposite the "booster bunch" is the labor crowd, the Building Trades Council, the City Federation of Labor—the boys who sail out and clean up the booster bunch and the country club crowd and the church crowd every other spring at the city election. The labor crowd also is given to saying it with food; its membership dines, never lunches, together. And at every labor dinner sits some nice fat amiable vulture of a politician blinking blandly at his food.

The labor bunch would like to be class conscious. But it can't be done, with the high school. The children stop that. How can a downtrodden, horny-handed son of toil be class conscious when his earless daughter is tripping the street in tricolette, and his son is sitting on the small of his back in a home-made racing car, or filling a limousine alongside of the sons of the rich and the twanging ukuleles as they spin fifty miles after school over to the next county seat to give the entertainment of the High School Glee Club? If the high school doesn't wring out all his class consciousness from country town labor, the country college does, and every hundred miles in any direction, from the Missouri Valley eastward, one finds the country college; sometimes a State institution, sometimes a denominational school, but always a replica of Harvard or Princeton or Yale or Vassar or Wellesley or Smith or all of them, differing only in size and prestige. The labor crowd sends its children to the country college and the children come home more intelligent about labor's wrongs. But less inclined to enjoy them.

And around the country college, which is as typical of the country town as the railroad division roundhouse, clusters the academic crowd. The academies manage to make a better social showing on less money than the labor crowd because their womenkind know more about domestic science. The average country college professor is making somewhat less than $2,500 a year. Yet the professors make their homes around the bankers and lawyers and owners of public utilities and wholesale grocers. Some of their womenkind mingle among the airy-fairy Lillians who take tea on the wide verandas of the country club. And generally the president of the college and one or two of the deans and the bachelor professors play golf on the country club links. How they do it is the wonder of the town.

Filling in the Picture

The most democratic group in the community is the woman's group—the city federation of women's clubs, by whatever name it is known. Here all castes and classes meet. Here the country club woman stands upon her own qualities, and battles with the women from the Mothers' Club below the tracks. Here the banker's wife is just as good as the railroader's wife if she can make good. These women's organizations are rather fashionable, for the women who count socially in the community lead them, not because these women count socially, but because they generally have the qualities of leadership which make them count socially. Generally they are part of a State and a national organization, and are doing much the same things that women are doing all over America. But they are doing the job well. And they are making the American town more livable by their activities.

Beneath them all is the submerged tenth, the unskilled laborers, the draymen, the odd-job people, the day laborers, some white, some black, some living in homes huddled around the town factory, some living in the few mean tenements that infest the community. They are the poor. They are always on the move; occasionally upward in the economic scale, often sideways, from one quarter of the town to another, from one kind of profitless job to another. Into their homes go the "good fellows" on Christmas Eve. These sad people are the "cases" of the Welfare Association and the Red Cross. For them mothers' pensions are distributed by the county, and to them free clinical aid is given at the hospital. They are the job that is never finished on the work table of the world.

If it is an industrial town, the shop workers form another social group, with their own aristocracy, their own middle class, their own poor. The farmers around about these American country towns sometimes wax rich and move to town. They make a small, lonely group—generally gravitating to the church crowd. But their sons and daughters get into high school and college and the next generation sees them in the country club.

Speaking broadly and allowing for certain Southern and New England exceptions where color or caste or both blur the picture, there is your American town; it may be two thousand or a quarter of a million. The differences between towns large and small are not so great as they seem, if the town spirit is there to bind people together. The country town, of course, is not God's final message to the world about human organization. The American town has the American faults with its American virtues. Chiefly these faults gather about mass production. We are doing things in carload lots—the town halls, for example; great barnlike steel and cement structures seating from a thousand to ten thousand people. Before the war we called them convention halls, now we call them memorial halls. Every town has one or is getting one. They house the innumerable conventions to which American town dwellers are conspicuously addicted. In these halls banquets are served where people sit down by the thousands to eat bad lukewarm food and to watch the gestures of the worst after-dinner orators in the world, men who have nothing to say and can't say it and can't quit trying to say it. They are all enlisted in good causes, but why talk about them?

Together with a zeal to build memorial halls just because other towns have them comes a desire for parks and playgrounds, an entirely laudable desire; parks and playgrounds are needed adjuncts to every civilized community. But some way the vastness of the movement indicates momentum rather than conviction in its spread, and these parks and playgrounds are all alike. So are the good works of the Elks, the Rotarians, the Masons, the Y.M.C.A., the Knights of Columbus, the Moose—the list becomes interminable, but the purpose limited. All American towns are releasing tremendous currents of energy upon certain small areas of ugliness or selfishness or stupidity; leaving vaster but different areas of the same vices untouched. The basic fault of the American town is its lack of distinction. A few towns have distinction. Rochester,

Minn., has one of the world's great medical clinics. It copies no other town's achievement in that. Lindsborg, Kas., has the greatest choral society in America and has given "The Messiah" every year for thirty years.[16] Minneapolis has an orchestra of note. Riverside, Cal., has its famous hotel. East Aurora, N.Y., has its artful and crafty shops; Battle Creek and Grand Rapids, Mich., stand out in the public consciousness for genuine contributions to American civilization. Northfield, Mass., has St. Olaf's choir. But the towns that have attained distinction are so few! Municipally we are a menagerie of copy cats!

Wanted, a Daniel

In the florid seventies and eighties someone down in Connecticut built a big house with towers on it, and jigsaw filigree and round bulging tumors and fiercely bedizened verandas. Then we all built that house in miniature or enlarged upon it for twenty years. Every four-room cottage had to ooze jigsaw effluvia, and to squirt out of its top an ornate iron fence protecting the chimney. And every larger house had to squeeze up a peaked Normandy gable somewhere, or erupt a tower. Then we began to build square houses, and for twenty years plain square houses blossomed all over the continent. Now we are mad with bungalows. The minareted house of the seventies reflected a grandeur that was much pretense and half aspiration and some actual achievement in conquering a continent. The square house reflected our candor, our simplicity, our blunt bald desire for efficiency and scorn of tradition, and the bungalow marks us for a nest-building nation, softened by time and house broken to a degree. But why do these things descend upon us like pestilences? Why this terrific mass production of everything? Will no one be himself–no town in America dare to be a Daniel?

We have a great spirit in these American towns—a spirit of mutual help, a spirit of militant altruism. We are plastic to a fault. Like Athens of Paul's day, we have all the gods in heaven or earth set up for worship and we are "altogether superstitious." But no town, with a few notable exceptions like those named above, sets up the gods of its own household. Citizens are not trying to make their towns great on their own account. No one is saying in

16. *Messiah* (1741) is an oratorio composed by George Handel (1685–1759).

these American towns; "Let's harness this resistless surplus of social energy which makes for righteousness to something that will make this town stand out from all the other towns, make this town a shining example of what a town may do that no other town ever has done before." Then when the writer folks come to a town to set it up in their literacy triangles they will find in that new type of town, not the obvious thing that characterizes all American towns, and therefore seems hardly worth while, however splendid it may be in contrast to towns in other lands; but the writer will find in the new town something vivid, something consecrated, something heroic that separates that town from the firmament of towns and makes it worthy of sacrifice.

As it is, we have "Gopher Prairie," Minnesota, and "Ashley," Vermont, deeply and essentially "one and inseparable, now and forever"; yet we observe the author of "Main Street" setting down the facts about Gopher Prairie and hating it, and Dorothy Canfield telling something of the truth about Ashley and loving it. And a not too discerning public wonders why.

Will They Fool Us Twice?

(*Collier's*, October 15, 1921)

"Fool me once," says the proverb, "and it's shame on you; fool me twice and it's shame on me!" The United States of America should blazon that proverb upon the public buildings of the land for the next few weeks and while the Disarmament Conference is in session.[1] For in that conference the problems of the Peace Conference in Paris will arise again. Those problems are to nearer sentiment than they were the day after the armistice, nearly three years ago.[2] Indeed, the Paris conference and the Versailles Treaty added to the problems of the war the grievous burdens of secret diplomacy.[3] And in the three years that have followed the war the world—that portion of it which we are pleased to call civilized—has stagnated until decay threatens seriously.

Something awful has happened to Christendom. It is more than the paralysis of commerce, though that is a part of it. It is more than industrial debility, which surely is a part of the cataclysm. It is more than political reaction and apathy that chokes and poisons the springs of progress. It is something deeper than the social decadence which is seen in every caste and class and country— the loosening of moral stays and the wilting of ancient standards. The things that are so hopelessly apparent in the realms of business, of industry, of politics, of the social order, are mere symptoms of a spiritual disease. Christendom is sick for lack of Christianity. Faith is dying—faith in men largely. For it is faith that bellies the sails of commerce when the ship goes out; faith that honest men will man her, that honest men will take her cargo, that honest men

1. The Washington Naval Conference took place between November 1921 and February 1922. The conference set tonnage limits on navies in an attempt to prevent an arms race between major powers in the aftermath of the First World War.
2. November 11, 1918, the end of hostilities during the First World War.
3. The treaty that ended the First World War, signed on June 28, 1919. The US Senate did not ratify the treaty, though President Woodrow Wilson took an active part in negotiations.

will send back a decent gain to the owners. It is faith that makes men sweat in industry; faith that their day's work will bring them a decent living, that their day's planning will yield them a good profit. Faith that the centripetal force that holds men together in states, in nations, in associated power; faith that the word of rulers is dependable, faith that the common sense of the people may be trusted to respond to humanity's decent needs under government. Faith holds home inviolate and makes the social compact strong and wholesome.

And the Golden Rule, which is the essence of the Christian philosophy, is the basis of faith. But the Golden Rule is badly tarnished today. It has fallen into desuetude. The pessimist, the grouch, the greedy-gut, even the cynic, are expounding the world's current philosophy, and everywhere men are dwelling in fear. The terror of a vast unbelief is gripping mankind in some sort of spiritual glacial epoch, which threatens chaos. And what is in the hearts of men reflects itself in their counsel. "As a man thinketh in his heart, so is he," and so will he make the events that are conceived in his head.[4]

What has happened? Surely it was not entirely the war. In November 1918, men had high hopes. "The day of glory has arrived." The happiest day the world ever saw was November 11, three years ago. The vanquished believed in the chivalry of the victors, and the victors believed in themselves. Disillusion came at Paris, slowly in an excruciating anticlimax, but inexorably and without extenuation or relief.

We are all in one boat on this planet. Civilization cannot rot in spots. Like "the little dog whose name was Rover," when civilization is dead it is dead all over. If it rots, we rot with it, and the blight of war has touched us all. And the dry rot of civilization comes from the aphis of hate that the war released. The world must have faith before it can resume the business of civilization—faith of men in men, faith of nations in nations, faith of all of us in the general decency of mankind and the changeless goodness of God. But faith never grows behind closed doors and in secret conclaves. Men make their noblest professions and square them with their greatest deeds while they are being watched. Open diplomacy is the safest diplomacy.

"Fool me once, and it's shame on you; fool me twice, and it's shame on me."

---

4. "As a man thinketh": Proverbs 23:7.

What's the Matter with America

(*Collier's*, July 1, 1922)

Go east, west, north, or south and enter the regional metropolis; pick up the local newspaper and you will read accounts of banditry, thuggery, burglary, car stealing, murder and violence, a long train of dastardly and abominable crimes.

Look on the inside pages of the same papers and you will notice, under small headings, certain accounts of other crimes—similar crimes—for which offenders are grinding slowly through the courts, or for which offenders have been released through mistrial or want of evidence, or have been paroled or pardoned, or saved by bail sharks.

Any place you look in the paper you will find festive items recounting the tax waste and inefficiency of the city government; paving-contract robbery, stuffed pay rolls, grafting public servants, department heads selling special privileges to cheat, poison and swindle and blackmail the citizens of the town.

Generally in the newspapers you also will find some account of the activities of various small bands of intrepid protesters struggling rather futilely for their rights. For the most part these protesters are upheld by the editorial columns of the paper. These columns are bitter in their complaints or may be merely cynical and hopeless in their jibes at the crime, inefficiency, and corruption all about them in municipal government.

Occasionally, as in Pennsylvania or in Illinois or Massachusetts, where the urban population outvotes the rural population, where cities overcome the farmers and the towns under 50,000, the conditions of the regional metropolis are reflected in the State government. Then you will find a great political cancer slowly overcoming the institutions which the founders of the commonwealth established.

Quarreling with the Majority

No form of democracy seems able to cope with the situation. For a bad major-ity may be assembled, and usually is assembled at any election, State or mu-nicipal. And the State house is a replica of the city halls, with the little band of protesters recruited from the small towns and rural districts. The political cancer in States usually attacks the treasury first, then captures a senator and as many congressmen as can be assimilated, and forms a State legislative combine which is sustained by the same thugs who rob, bludgeon, and terrorize honest men in the cities.

The only difference between the States which have developed this cancer and the States which have not developed it is a matter of time. For when the cities of a State grow sufficiently large, they will capture the State and impose upon it the evils which beset them. The evils are only symptoms.

What is the matter with America?[1]

One man's guess is a good as another's in a free country, so let us venture a diagnosis and call the trouble a moron majority.

The typical political situation in any American city is about this: The forces in the community that stand for what is obviously good government in the old-fashioned sense line up behind a candidate, conspicuously honest and cold-nosed, often high-browed, and sometimes even a "Christian gentleman."

Those Who Don't Care

All the newspapers support him. All the organizations devoted to orderly pro-cesses of government get behind him. It becomes evident as the campaign grows warm that around his opponent are gathered the evil influences of the town: the grafters, the underworld, the racial blocks, the devotees of special privilege in political grafting—the market-house graft, the paving graft, the

---

1. The repetition of the titular question draws upon the themes of White's 1896 piece "What's the Matter with Kansas?" The two articles share a similarity in that White is iden-tifying problems within the polity as being caused by a particular group that does not align with his conception of American values, Populists in the former article and immigrants from outside northwestern Europe in this article.

printing graft, the public-works graft—and a score of smaller activities where men may pick up a few hundreds or a few thousands, and, if persistent and diligent, a few millions of dollars.

During the campaign disclosures of the activities of these grafters and blackmailers and representatives of petty larceny in city politics come thick and fast.

They are convincing to the mind and heart of the old-fashioned American, who is pained and surprised to discover that thousands of his fellow citizens are not even cynical about it. These care-free fellow citizens accept the situation, desiring for their soul's salvation only to feel that the stories of graft are true; accepting the principle of special privilege with a sincerity which makes the overwhelming proof of a graft only a further reason to stand by their maligned and long-suffering friend, the candidate opposed by the truly good.

And this candidate always runs true to certain definite types. He seems destined to be our future ruler, so we may pause to consider him. If he is recruited from politics, he generally exploits himself as a sort of he-Cinderella, who has come up from the ash can.

He is a smiler and a handshaker; sometimes an orator, and occasionally a lawyer who has graduated from the criminal courts into a decent practice among the more shady of the public-service corporations. He has the confidence of those in high finance in the city who know exactly what they want.

If he is not of that type, he is a partisan business man of the genus dub. He knows nothing of politics; can be depended upon to accept the dictum of the party leaders who control the machine that protects the underworld, and the boodlers, and he has illicit relations with the men who pay big money for franchises and the frills and fripperies of special privilege in public corporations.[2]

These two types, the political confidence man or the political straw man, attract the voters of immature minds. Their candidate does not try to make them think. He makes them hate, makes them laugh, and shows them their own advantage in his candidacy. And when he gets into office he gives them the kind of government they desire.

The child mind is satisfied with childish things: parks, playgrounds, parades, gambling, bootlegging, and plug-hatted politicians in shiny motor cars,

---

2. Boodlers: a late nineteenth-century term referring to individuals who engage in bribery and the misuse of public funds.

who are conspicuous he-Cinderellas exemplifying America as the land of opportunity. The child's conception of the land of opportunity is satisfied with the opportunity to rise by graft, or by boodling, or by cunning blackmail. And as for the crime wave, well, boys will be boys, and it's only the goo-goos who are complaining, and who are they to kick? If they didn't get their share, it's their fault. So the children citizens hoot at the "Christian gentleman" on the independent ticket and stand by the man who brags that he supported his poor old mother when he was five years old by selling papers and always gave a penny to the orphans' home.

They are a simple people who make up this moron majority. "Sure, there's graft," they say. "What did you suppose we were going into politics for if not for special privilege? What's the use of getting ahead in this country if a man can't have a friend in the courts? If the poor man has the same chance of getting justice that the rich man has, why all this talk of thrift? If I can't sell a stall in the market house to my friends, what's the use of having friends? You guys at the City Club get us poor devils all excited about saving money, and getting on in the world; but why?"

"What's the use of rising in the world if we are no better than anyone else, and have to submit to the same laws as anyone else? What's the good of getting money, if it won't buy you anything?"

Voters with Children's Minds

So speak the masses in our cities, and all the newspapers, all the preachers, all the chambers of commerce, and all the traditional Americans unite against the mass majority to make a brave but negligible minority. When the majority has rolled over the unimportant but eloquent minority, its voices, chiefly through the newspapers and in pulpits, sound a lot of different kinds of clarion notes and warning tocsins about boss rule. Then, after a few weeks, or at the most a few months, the minority calms down and becomes confident that the next time conditions will be different.

But they will not be different. For something permanent and fundamental is happening in our cites, and sooner or later it will get us all. We may well pause in this glorious Fourth of July season to consider these morons.

They are the political bacilli that are tearing down the tissue of our institutions. Here, according to the enlistment figures in our late draft, are 45 million people with intelligences which stopped developing at the green age of fourteen. Of the 45 millions probably 20 millions stopped growing up mentally at eleven, and of the 55 millions left of our 100 millions probably 20 millions stopped growing before they reached sixteen. So we have a working majority of voters who have children's minds.

Add to the political children a considerable minority of the mentally adult who have a blind spot of party prejudice, who will follow any party in any record of crime, and you have furnished the morons in any community a political crystal around which to cluster.

In New York it is the Democratic party. In Pennsylvania and Illinois it is the Republican party; in each State the crystalline form of hidebound partisanship is different. But the result of the crystallization is always the same. The crooks and boodlers and thugs of Philadelphia are no better than those of New York or Boston or Kansas City.

We Assume All Men Are Equal

But, granted the presence of the morons in our country, what makes them worse than their fellow half-wits of Europe? What is our distinction? What is the matter with America?

Well, for one thing it is our peculiar institutions. A nose counts too heavily under the American system, whether it is a dirty nose, or a clean one, a pug, a Roman, or a Greek. We fashioned this blooming land for men who are mental adults. The European statesmen took account of the weak-witted in making their institutions. We Americans assume all men are created equal. It was a good enough assumption in Jefferson's day. But our blood is changing.

We are filling up our cities with men and women who lack the mental grasp of the colonists who fought our Revolution, who established our land, who wrote our Constitution and so made America. The moron cannot take in all this tall talk about the Constitution.

Yet, in spite of the evidence that considerable masses of our population do not comprehend our institutions, a puzzled minority in every community still acts as though American institutions were functioning perfectly. This puzzled minority still believes that the "land of the free" will become eventually "the home of the brave," forgetting that the moron majority sees nothing in our institutions to excite its enthusiasm.

Land of the Pilgrim's Pride

This puzzled minority that reads the editorials in the newspapers form good-government clubs, "deplores" "views with alarm," and "demands that something be done," considers that America is a melting pot where the lower racial plasms may by some alchemy be purified and exalted. But the plasm of the lame brain keeps right on producing lame brains, and the plasm of the American stock of fifty years ago keeps producing unhappy minorities. And these unhappy people keep on talking of the Constitution as a sacred document. They cling to the belief that there is virtue in law and order. They contend passionately that the courts must be impartial and beyond corrupting influences—the stern and implacable dispensers of equal and exact justice.

Ideals something like that made this the "land of the Pilgrim's pride," and for some such shibboleths "our fathers died."[3] The political notion that government should be free from special privilege seems to be commonly held among English-speaking people everywhere; it is held even among the Teutonic nations, and by the Scandinavian races generally.[4]

But government without special privilege is by no means an axiomatic principle of civilized men. Government without special privilege is a heritage of what must be loosely grouped as the Anglo-Saxon people, the northern races. They settled Colonial America. They largely dominated its political

---

3. Quoted from "My Country, 'tis of Thee," also called "America," by Francis Samuel Smith (1808–1895).

4. The Northwestern European chauvinism White displays here was a growing sentiment in the late nineteenth and early twentieth centuries, increasing in the wake of the First World War (1914–1918) and the First Red Scare (1919–1921). These anxieties surrounding immigrants reached their culmination with the passage of the Immigration Act of 1924, barring immigration from Asia entirely and placing heavily restrictive quotas on immigration from southern and eastern Europe. This law would form the foundation of US immigration policy until 1965. For further information, see Kristofer Allerfeldt, "'And We Got Here First': Albert Johnson, National Origins and Self-Interest in the Immigration Debate of the 1920s," *Journal of Contemporary History* 45, no. 1 (2010): 7–26.

thought, and their institutions when transplanted in a pioneer environment became the America of the last century. And the whole trouble with the little group of hangover Americans that make the minority in our great cities is that they think, when they have stated the principle of government without special privilege, and have proved the facts of its violation, that their case is made.

But it isn't. Far from it. Another civilization has invaded these shores, one not reared to hold ardent opinions about the Anglo-Saxon political taboos.

So the more these descendants of an austere past uncover graft and special privilege, the more they disclose loose and unvirtuous conditions in the courts, the stronger the gay and festive sons of the world's sunny climes gathered in our midst rally around the standards of the grafters and the boodlers and the amiable judiciary. They want what we abhor. We show them where it is, and then we marvel that they go to it.

Shadowy Ghosts of Our Past

What's the matter with America? Well, it's not a simple question nor an easy one to answer. Either we who believe in the old order must teach these care-free children of sunnier skies and gayer lives than ours that our ideals are better than theirs or their ideals will overcome ours. For our darker-skinned neighbors breed faster than we.

In another hundred years we shall have an America for which our fathers didn't die, by a long shot. We may come back to the USA and find, not the land of the Pilgrim's pride, but Italy, Greece, or the Balkans, or all three gorgeously blended.

In that day we may find that Washington, Lincoln, John Hancock, Miles Standish, and Andy Jackson—the decent and circumspect Rover boys of our earlier politics—are shadowy ghosts without conjuring power in our country.[5]

They may be regarded somewhat as the Huns and Vandals are esteemed in modern Rome, while the ruling statesmen of the next century cavort about

---

5. Miles Standish (c.1584–1656) was an English officer hired by the Pilgrims to serve as the military advisor to their journey to North America and was instrumental in the foundation of the Plymouth Colony in 1620. The Rover boys refers to *The Rover Boys*, a book series for adolescent boys published from 1899 to 1926.

from revolution to revolution, distributing largess to the electorate in bread and circuses and complicate our politics with assassination. It is quite possible. Hyland and Thompson are forecasting shadows.[6] And every American city has men of the same type.

The type is no accident. It is here to stay, unless the Puritan ideal can overcome the ideals of the darker skinned peoples who have come by express invitation to our shores. They are here. They have the same right to make this their kind of country that we have to maintain our kind of country. And, instead of bewailing the machinery of democracy which gives these lively and impulsive people the right to change America into "something rich and strange," we should take stock and see where we are failing.[7]

Breeding the Bonehead

For a hundred years we have pinned our faith to two improving agents in this country: education and a rising economic status.

We have said you can take the low-grade stock of Europe and teach it three years of Latin, spherical trigonometry, a year of physics, a modern language, some United States history and Longfellow's epics and make it fit for a self-governing democracy, if only you give it modern plumbing, fresh air, motor cars, a living wage, and a helping hand.[8]

But these things are not working. The motor-car bandits, grafters, thugs, city-hall bosses, and municipal tyrants of various sorts all live in the pink cotton and tinfoil environment to which we have pinned our faith. Indeed, most of these rascals have been so educated through our taxes, and so taught to undo us.

Education and environment will help, but they will not cure, for we are missing something somewhere. We are wasting something.

We must still ask what is the matter with America. Wherein has it failed?

6. Likely referring to James R. Hyland (c.1877–1959), a state senator for Kansas, and William H. Thompson (1871–1928), a US senator of the same state.

7. "Something rich and strange": a quote from "Ariel's Song" in the play *The Tempest* (1611) by William Shakespeare (1564–1616).

8. Henry Wadsworth Longfellow (1807–1882) was a New England poet who wrote popular epics about mythology and American history.

Why do not the dreams our fathers dreamed about the blessings of a free country come true? Why do the morons keep breeding morons? If the glass eye does not beget its kind, why does the bonehead? Why are the second and third generations from the low breeds of Europe, living under our economic conditions and educational advantages, still producing a breed so little improved that the ballot box is almost as dangerous as dynamite in their hands?

Teach Them the Truth

Somewhat, if not entirely, it is our own fault. We spend billions to educate these children of the immigrant, but we neglect to teach them the important things that good citizens should know. We teach them facts, but too often neglect the truth. The truth which every American should know is what is good conduct; what acts are social, and what is antisocial.

Why is a grafter and enemy of society? Why is it wrong to consider a public office a private snap? Why is a tip a misdemeanor and a bribe a felony? Why is the public-service corporation a traitor when it resorts to legal technicalities to evade a contract?

These are simple things, not hard for a child of ten to understand. They are as easy of comprehension as the arithmetic lesson of the fifth grade. They are much simpler than many things taught in the seventh and eighth grades, and vastly more important than much that is taught the child in high school.

Social education is one of the things that will clear the clouded mind of the moron about public affairs.

Education will not quicken his intelligence. But it will clarify certain conceptions of right and wrong, and put the child upon another moral plane. He can then help to contribute to an American public opinion, and reasonably may be expected to contribute to a majority which will respond to the call of American ideals.

We are taxing ourselves by the billion to teach the children absolutely nothing that will help them in their relation to the state. It is not the public schools alone that are to blame. Our private schools for the rich and for the poor have the same faults. A lot of people bemoan the fact that children in our private schools learn too much of the catechism. But what better than the catechism do our public schools teach them?

Does the average high-school graduate know more than an idiot about practical civic mortality as we of the last century like to imagine we knew civic morality? We keep feeding our beloved progeny educational folderol and fudge and wonder why our children have no stamina, why they are morally undernourished.

We stand astounded before the menace to our ancient ideals and the best we can offer is to curb free speech and curtail a free press. We are timid, stupid, and lazy, and if the civilization of the languorous south overwhelms us, no one but our bigoted selves will be to blame.

And even when we consider the faults of our education the failure of our environment to make Americans out of the job lots from southern and eastern Europe, we have not found out all that is the matter with America.

The Puritan Ideal

America is an attempt to institutionalize the Puritan ideal. Now, the Puritan ideal is basically an economic aspiration. It hopes for the greatest good for the greatest number, and is crass enough at heart to mean goods where it reads good. The thought that all men are created equal is true only in the sense that they should be equal before the law and should have about the same economic start in the race.

The equality idea implies a certain feeling of equality in another direction, a brotherhood more or less limited, but a brotherhood which makes the strong responsible for the weak. It is dangerous biologically; but socially, economically, and politically it may be made to work.

In rural America the thing is working fairly well. No one is offensively rich, and few are unjustly exploited. But in rural America, at least in rural America of the Middle West and of the Pacific Coast, the substance of the Puritan ideal is taught to childhood in tradition, in example, and in the precepts of his religion.

This teaching produces a public opinion that is dependable in time of stress. The preponderance of the stock is of English or Teutonic or Scandinavian blood.

There the moron does not breed with his kind. The life plasm changes. The melting pot actually melts and fuses the strains.

But in the cities which slowly are growing larger, a new biological condition faces us. That biological condition has its political reflex. And that reflex is the moron majority which piles up in every great American city.

The Fundamental Clash

It creates the spawning ground of the thug, of the assassin, of the boodler, of the greedy corporation manager who exploits the people by buying privilege from the pliant bosses. We have written our Constitution, created our laws, established our government for one kind of people—and the ships from across the sea have brought us another kind of people. And the government that we have builded here is nuts for them.

All our grand national policies, all our pompous parties, all our crucial issues—all the flubdubbery of politics, are subsidiary to this fundamental clash of ideals: the Puritan ideal and its festive foe, that shrugs a gay shoulder, denies our brotherhood, rejects our cold justice, and giggles out of our homely duties.[9]

9. Flubdubbery: bombastic language.

Emporia and the Strike

(Emporia Gazette, July 3, 1922)

Emporia has two conflicting interests in this strike.[1] This is a railroad town, and the men who work here are our friends and neighbors; good citizens, all of them, mostly taxpayers and property owners, and each a reasonable human being who deserves the confidence and friendship of his fellow townsmen. That is interest number one, the big primary interest, and we should not violate it by expressing hostility-formed opinions about the rights and wrongs of the strike. These neighbors and friends of ours have not risked all that is at stake in this strike today without reasoning it all out from their own standpoint. But it is theirs and they have a right to it.

Interest number two is the Santa Fe railroad.[2] It has always been a friend to Emporia. Generally speaking it is the fairest of all American roads in its treatment of its workers, and of the public. This road has done the town many a good turn and is about to do others. Therefore we cannot take a position of bitter antagonism to the Santa Fe without hurting the town.

The Santa Fe has its side of the contention. It is associated with the other railroads of the country in making a fight for lower wages. These lower wages presumably will be reflected in lower freight rates. And so prosperity will become general.

The men have their side, and it is this: They were promised by the rail board over a year ago that in all questions of wage adjustments, wages should be adjusted upon the basis of a living wage for the unskilled workers. When the recent cut was made and the workers tried to show that the cut was below

1. The Railroad Strike of 1922 last from July to September, and involved four hundred thousand workers. The strike began with a reduction in wages.

2. The Santa Fe line started in Kansas in 1859 and was instrumental in settling the state in the late nineteenth century. The western branch of the line ultimately bypassed Santa Fe and reached its western terminus in Los Angeles. A line also ran from Atchison, Kansas, through Emporia, to Oklahoma City and, finally, to Galveston, Texas.

a living wage for the unskilled, the board declared that it could not consider that phase of the matter. Thus the workers feel that they are striking against a gross violation of contract. Again: about a year ago the rail board, which is today outlawing the strikers for disobeying its orders, issued an order demanding that the railroad owners cease farming out shop work to non-union shops. The railroads flatly disobeyed this order. They disobeyed this order of the same board that the strikers are now disobeying. But the railroads did more; they went to the courts and got an order restraining the rail board from making public protest against the disobedience of the railroads. So the railroads were not outlawed as the strikers are.

The strikers in Emporia are peaceful men. They are just as much interested in peace as the Santa Fe, or as we other citizens are. If this is a prolonged strike, it will bring disorder.[3] If it was a strike of bankers and lawyers and doctors when the strike was prolonged and looked bad some ignorant bankers and some stupid lawyers and a few rattle-brained doctors would go to making trouble. But the lawyers, doctors, and bankers as such should not be blamed. So we must keep our heads, as neighbors and friends of these men and of this railroad, and realize that a strike is a war, and in war, rough things are done and said that are not justified in peace.

The property of the Santa Fe should be protected. Any good citizen should be willing to help protect it. But these men who are striking are normal, decent, intelligent human beings, our neighbors and friends, and we should also see that it is as [friends] that we meet them in [any] emergency that may arise. Their friendship, their good will to the town, their self-respect as American citizens striving for what they believe is right—all these are vital things to maintain.

And as for the rest of us, we who merely look upon the conflict from the outside, it is of greatest importance that we keep our heads cool and our hearts always kind.

3. On July 12, 1922, the *Gazette* reported President Harding's proclamation that obstructing interstate trade was a federal crime and that the rail lines would be defended by federal troops.

Blood of the Conquerors

(*Collier's*, March 10, 1923)

In America most of us are Emporians in one way or another. Some of us live in towns ranging from five thousand to a quarter of a million, others were born in or around these towns, and still others of us cherish golden dreams of going back to some Emporia, there to see life in the sunset. People say to us Emporia dwellers: "Why do you live in Emporia?" and the answer seems simple: "Everyone does—more or less." But is than an answer? Isn't it a mere reply, an evasion? Does it explain why everyone in reality or in dreams lives in some old town?

To find the answer to that question—to know why America is country-minded at the bottom of its consciousness—there is a proposition worth considering. We Americans are so conspicuously neighborly in all out aspirations—political, economic, social. We insist upon voting only for our neighbors and will have none of the European system which would elect men from afar who are merely distinguished and competent. We demand that our neighbor's daughter shall have a living wage, that his children be kept out of the factories and in good schools, that the factory owner shall pay our neighbor for accidents in the factory, that our neighbor shall have fair rates for everything he buys and sells. Moreover, we have a long economic creed which considers our neighbors' welfare, and socially we are convinced that it is bad for our neighbor to waste his substance upon the corner saloon. We just naturally soak the fabric of our consciousness in what may be called the milk of neighborly kindness. And cold-nozzled and cold-hearted urban dwellers observing our neighbor-mindedness hoot raucously and call to us to look after number one first, to let the devil take the hindmost, and generally to keep our long noses out of other people's business.

*This is the first part of a two-part series. Part Two, "The Dawn of a Great Tomorrow," follows.

But for a generation—indeed, for more than thirty years—America had been passing through a revolutionary period, and the spirit of the revolution had been the application of a neighborly, village-minded aspiration to our national life. So we who have lived in Emporia, in the flesh or in the spirit, have had a box seat at the revolution, and that is the reason why so many of us live here. We admire the show; we like to be a part of it. We dislike deeply to be unimportant figures moved about on the checkerboard of events. And we must be unimportant figures in a country-ruled nation if we live and dream in cities. It is the love of power in our blood, the blood of the conquerors, that keeps us all in Emporia. We are Emporians all, because we desire to belong to the governing classes.

Emporia Was America Then as Now

To know about our uprising, which is only America's expression on the world revolution, the revolution that has come with the amazing increase in the production of manufactured goods—to know how that gentle insurrection has changed us all—it may be interesting to look back at the Emporia that was before the change; back in to the mid-eighties. And, looking back, let us set down things as they were then. For the social and economic and political status of the mid-eighties was substantially what it had been in America from the beginning of our nation. Emporia was in Kansas. But it was only New England and the Middle States fused and transplanted upon the plains. Emporia was America in little in those days, even as it is today.

It was in the middle eighties that Major Calvin Hood built his big house—two full stories with a ballroom and servants' bedrooms in the attic.[1] Hardwood floors adorned the first story, and the town newspaper of the period spoke in some awe of the magnificence of the mansion, because of its "woodwork all in quarter-sawed oak." The elaborately carved banisters and newel posts of its grand staircase excited the reporter who wrote up the house at the opening party; also he had a passionate moment before the colored glass

---

1. Major Calvin Hood (1832–1910) was the president of the Emporia National Bank in Emporia Kansas. He was also active in local and state politics and had earned his title of major from his service in the Eleventh Michigan Infantry during the American Civil War.

windows in the hallway where the stairway with a regal sweep descended to the long hall dividing the house. The reporter noted a reception room, a front parlor, a back parlor, and a dining room. That was before the coming of the cubbyhole which the rich and the great now call their breakfast room.

The Hood house sat far back among large transplanted elm trees upon a velvet lawn. And in the rear of the house was a big barn, and there the Major kept his spanking sorrell team that pulled his glittering carriage about town. The place was baronial. Nothing in the town equaled it.

A few years later Colonel Cross, the rival banker, built another house, bulging with Oriental towers and minarets, indicating a degree of pomp and magnificence in its precincts that impressed the people of the prairie town with the power and grandeur or the potentate who came out of its heavy carved doors.[2] He was a great, hulking man with a moon-shaped vest and iron-gray side whiskers. He strutted with a stringhalted gait and waved a wicked cane to clear the way around him.

Naturally the Colonel had to own a newspaper to combat the Major's newspaper. And the agony of the reporter on the Colonel's newspaper over the magnificence of the Colonel's new house was heart-rending. Even the reporter on the paper which the Major owned was respectful about the Cross house.

The two newspapers were, of course, organs of the rival banks. The editors were forever barking at each other and snapping at the rival bankers as viciously as they dared, considering the libel laws. And whenever in the town one bank backed a project—as, for instance, a new hotel or a street railway or a water franchise or a new railroad for the county—the other bank and its editor opposed the project. And there was a terrible time. The people did not vote for franchises then: promoters controlled public servants and got the franchises late at night. The next night the losing faction appeared with ropes at the courthouse or city hall, but no one was ever hanged. The franchises were held, and if riot became too general the banks divided the spoils.

2. Harrison C. Cross (1835–1894) was a businessman and banker in Emporia, Kansas, and president of the rival bank to Major Hood. He earned his title of colonel from his service in the 153rd Ohio Volunteer Infantry during the American Civil War.

Pet Lawyers and Private Editors

For the splendor of the bankers' homes was typical of the bankers' lives. They were our temporal rulers. The politics of the town and county they held in the hollow of their hand. Often they fought to hold suzerainty from one another, but never to give it to the people. The people in the little houses, and even in the common run of houses, lived in another political world from the bankers' world.

Just under the bankers were the lawyers. Each bank had its pet lawyers, just as it maintained its private editors. The lawyers were more important in ruling the people than the editors. For through the lawyers the courts and the legislatures were manned and controlled. Politics was managed through the county convention, and a good lawyer talking to two hundred delegates in a county convention was more effective than an editor addressing twenty thousand people outside the convention. For the people outside were powerless when the convention was in session and in those days minorities had no rights.

The great struggle in our politics was for the nomination of members of the State Legislature. They were nominated in county conventions. The importance of members of the Legislature lay in the fact that when they got to Topeka they chose our United States senators. So every banker in the State had to have at least one privately owned member of the Legislature if the banker had a say in the election of a United States senator. Through United States senators, politics in the State was controlled, and through politics business favors were distributed.

An Endless Chain of Favors

United States senators appointed Federal judges, and Federal judges appointed receiverships, and receivers cut all the fine melons that flourished on the vines. Therefore a banker in Emporia just had to control his home member of the Legislature. And, incidentally, through the Legislature the banker had a voice in making the laws of his state—such, for instance, as the banking laws and the railroad laws and the mortgage laws. And, by controlling several members of the Legislature through smaller banks in smaller towns and counties, often a banker had standing with the powerful State railroad attorneys who had passes to give, system passes for "self and family," trip passes for henchmen.

From Emporia Major Hood controlled half a dozen members of the Legislature, and often a dozen or twenty, because many smaller bankers owed money to the Major's bank. So the Major was a person of consequence in the State. Once he ran for United States senator himself, and lacked but a few votes of winning; he did control the nominee, and through that control was a great figure in the State and in the West generally. Railroad presidents invited the Major to ride in their private cars. Famous railroad attorneys were chummy with him. He was an overlord, a knight of the inner chamber. He had a pass once which read, not merely for "self and family," but for "Major Calvin Hood and party." He had a telegraph frank and an express frank.

His great house represented the real difference in the government of the United States that existed between the Major and the rest of us. Around him grew up a group of powerful lawyers—all good fellows and true, who later became distinguished attorneys for the railroads. Tom Sedgewick became general counsel for the Katy, Clinton Sterry became general counsel for the Santa Fe in its western system.[3] C. B. Graves became a justice of the Supreme Court.[4] I. E. Lambert became United States district attorney and a district railroad attorney of influence.[5]

There was no question of the honesty and integrity of these men. But they played politics under the government that was, and no one in those days cared to change it. It was representative government, with the representatives interested largely in those whom they chiefly represented, which was the people in the big house who controlled politics for business reasons and so naturally were able to build big houses.

3. Thomas Noble Sedgewick (1848–1905) was a railroad attorney in Emporia and the general attorney of the Missouri, Kansas & Texas Railroad until his death from stomach cancer. The Katy: a nickname for the Missouri, Kansas & Texas railroad. Clinton Norman Sterry (1840–1903) worked for the Santa Fe railroad in their law department in Topeka before moving to California.

4. Charles B. Graves (1841–1912) was a Kansas Supreme Court justice who lived in Emporia.

5. Isaac E. Lambert Sr. (1854–1909) was a prominent Kansas lawyer, who had a law practice in Emporia, served as postmaster of Emporia, and served as the district attorney of Kansas.

To the banks in those days we went for our water and light and power, for our city ordinances, for our State laws, for our county government, for our congressmen. The bank *was* representative government. But the class that governed governed honestly in the main, and, considering the advantages they had for loot, the free hand they had in the business of government, the bankers and their lawyer satellites and kept editors took little except their maintenance. None of the great fortunes of Emporia, of the State today, are founded upon the graft of yesterday.

Moreover, it was a most interesting civilization. Strong men came out of it, and the nobility of the day had its distinction. In the Attic ballrooms of the time gathered the sons and daughters of the lawyers, doctors, and merchant princes of the countryside. From nearby towns on private cars came young hopefuls of special privilege, quite innocent of wrongdoing and most happy in their elevation above the common herd. The carriage, flashing with silver plating, which held the Major and his family as they drove about town summer evenings, rumbled with the rich luxuriant murmur of a circus wagon. Some of us had horses and buggies, mostly we had phaetons and surreys, only a few could afford two horses, and none such a team as the Major's.[6] We kept our cows and chickens in our back lots and the more shameless souls kept a pig. The thrifty had a vegetable pit near the kitchen door, but we commonly ate dried fruit and vegetables and the best of us took our fruit from the can. But the Major and the Colonel brought exotic food from afar—pineapples from Chicago, lake fish from Kansas City, sea food "from the coast," meaning the Gulf of Mexico, and early strawberries from Arkansas. There was no question that the meat upon which Cæsar fed was a different meat from that which the rest of us ate. Our representative rulers lived in another world.

We, the common people, endured no hardships. We lived about as our grandfathers had lived. Sewers in the town traversed but few streets; water was installed in only a few houses. Electricity was for the stores and only the gentry enjoyed the telephone. As for the poor—the Major saw to it that a dozen Christmas baskets went out, and he carried five-dollar gold pieces with him during the holiday—a pocketful—and distributed largess superbly as befitting one who in government had the power and the glory of a grand vizier. The

6. Phaetons and surreys: types of light drawn carriages popular at the time.

comforts, the luxuries, the magnificences, which he had assembled in his big house for our awe and admiration, represented political privileges and powers which established him and his court as our master.

True, we could change masters at will. Colonel Cross always stood waiting for the call to the throne and was not above blowing up the throne when he could, but never for the purpose of handing it over to the folks. He wanted to rule as the Major ruled and, once in a while, had his day.

Of course the situation was not static. The man in the big house always had to fight to keep his control, and in fighting often lost his money and died poor. Colonel Cross went that way. His son inherited the failing bank. As a boy he owned the only Shetland pony in the town, went away to boarding school, was the town beau, married the prettiest girl in the State, built a house nearly as large as his father's, and bought a royal blooded stock farm. Then, when the elder Cross died, his son inherited a criminal shortage, carried it himself until exposure was upon him, and then went out to his farm and put a bullet in his brain—a tragic victim, if ever there was one, of the ruthless system of government by special privilege.

In the bank records they found all sorts of worthless public-utility stock from various parts of the State that represented the politics of the father; also sheaves of notes and checks signed in blank by minor politicians to make up shortages in the bank's accounts and all sorts of crooked banking paraphernalia, much like burglars' kits. That was the seamy side of the grand government of the time.

And that is the order that was. Thirty years ago America was ruled like that. Our nation was a feudal republic. Each State was a baronial holding; each county a shire governed by the squire and the nobility; each large town a citadel of privilege. But we were prosperous and happy. Possibly we were as well governed as we are today. Certainly it was as easy for an able man to rise to power as it is today. Strong men were rising out of the mass all the time. It was the day of the strong individual. But masses were stationary. They had no consciousness, no aspiration. They accepted the government which was bestowed upon them. Restless minorities had small success.

Goods were unevenly distributed. But they were few. Crimes of violence and cunning were generally punished, and graft was conventionalized. Life and property were safe and taxes low, but exceedingly hard to pay. It was a government as honest as the people who lived under it, and about as good as their courage and enterprise deserved. They were proud of it, made songs and poems and orations to it and about it, and were correct in considering it the best government on earth.

Then the Feud Was Forgotten

Only, those who thought it was the best possible government on earth were wrong. And they were most sadly wrong, as people are who are self-satisfied, when they grew bitter and angry at those who thought we might have a better order of things and went to work to get it. And those who were striving to make it a better order made the mistake of vilifying those who upheld the old: as it was in the beginning, is now and ever shall be. Which is all just a bit beside the point. The point is that it was a different government thirty years ago from what we have today. The revolution has been coming slowly, but it is here.

With what consternation did Emporia behold the first signs of change! They came in the early nineties. And they dropped out of a clear sky. A political party called the Farmers' Alliance appeared.[7] First it found its strength in the country, where 10-cent corn and 60-cent wheat had bred discontent. The alliance leaders got an organization fee, and that fee was made the issue by the pillars of society in town. Someway, that issue did not interest the farmers greatly. But the alliance leaders did interest the farmers tremendously with talk of a direct primary, talk of the initiative and the referendum, talk of national farm loan banks, talk of credit on the products of the farm, talk of lower railroad rates, and talk of a longer time in which to pay defaulted mortgages before a foreclosure. These things were vital to the farmer's existence. So by the thousands all over the West, the farmers followed the alliance leaders. Then certain town dwellers joined the revolt. Like a great wind, the spirit of rebellion against the existing system moved the country people.

When it became obvious that the alliance was gathering a majority of the farmers, the Major and the Colonel forgot their ancient feud and stood together for the salvation of organized society. Their satellites even began to

7. In the late nineteenth century farmers formed local political alliances to achieve economic security. For a history of Populism, see Charles Postel, *The Populist Vision* (Oxford University Press, 2007).

make up. The Major's lawyers rode over the county campaigning with the Colonel's lawyers, and their editors turned their artillery upon the "socialists" and "anarchists" who were threatening to overturn the world. Long processions of singing farmers and their wives and children riding in farm wagons, bearing here and there some banner with a strange device, moved down Commercial Street. The banners declared for "Equal rights for all, special privileges for none," and demanded a currency that could reach $50 per capita, which was considerably above the current issue.[8] The banners also were flashy with Lincoln's phrase about "government of the people, for the people, and by the people."[9] These farmers puzzled the good Major, who stood in the front door of the bank and saw many an old friend ride by glaring at the gilded bank sign above the Major's head.

"What is this special privilege they are complaining about, Ike?" quoth the Major to his youngest and dearest lawyer, the apple of his eye, as a particularly long and noisy procession went roaring down the street, miles and miles of it.

"That's what I can't make out, Major," answered Lambert. "But one thing's dead sure. They are hot after us, whatever it is."

It never occurred to the Major and Ike and the rest of us that special privilege was our railroad passes, our inside rates for cattle shipments, our easy access to credit without security or the unquestioned right to usury upon the borrower who was hard up. We had free water and free light and we had a thousand little favors that come with politics to insiders, but those favors seemed to us who enjoyed them our royal American right. We did not dream that we were enjoying "special privileges." Probably the farmer did not know exactly what our special privileges were, nor could he have listed all the privileges we had.

The farmers did not realize how tightly we held the reins of government in the hands of the few who were using our representative powers as means of getting what we did not earn from those who earned what they did not get. We worked for the party. It was our party. We had a right to the governors we nominated and elected, to the senators we made with the sweat of our brow,

8. "Equal rights for all": a popular quote credited to Thomas Jefferson (1743–1826). Other Democrats, such as Williams Jennings Bryan (1860–1925), have used this quote in various political capacities.

9. From President Lincoln's (1809–1865) Gettysburg Address.

and to the incidental railroad passes that we held. Well—if we used our governor for our own ends, whose business was it? If one would complain, let him go and get a governor and a senator of his own. And that is what the alliance did. They got the Legislature and elected a United States senator.

Populism Comes and Goes

But their isolated officials did not bring much relief to the farmers in the early nineties. They scared the Republicans in the North and the Democrats in the South. And the fear the farmers bred helped a little, but only a little. Then in the mid-nineties came the Populists and the free-silver Republicans, and we saw the wave of reform beat even higher than it washed in its first inundation. More processions passed the bank, where the Major stood and reviewed the ranks of his enemies with a mild and implacable face. The Colonel had died. His son was president of the bank then, but the procession meant little to the younger man. He was born to the purple. He was interested in his bulls and calves at the stock farm.

But the Major sensed the revolution in the air—and hardened his heart against it. Also he tightened his grip on the party machinery and conferred with the directors of the rival bank about everything. Party harmony was capitalized, emphasized, deified. It was an intrepid band of zealots that faced the mob in those days, and in the end defeated the mob. The Populists disappeared; and by giving good jobs to their leaders, and by thanking Heaven for good crops, the Major and Ike and the organization won. The Populist party faded into the mist of the day. The dawn of the revolution seemed to have passed.

The Dawn of a Great Tomorrow

(*Collier's*, March 17, 1923)

Then came the new century to town. A fine, hopeful young thing was that new century, that seemed especially endowed with the task of brightening up and perpetuating forever the established order. It was a grand and lofty time. God had given us the Philippines, and we were going to play Providence to the brown men there.[1] The obsession of Manifest Destiny was becoming a national vice.[2] But more important things than that were happening in Emporia. Major Hood's house and Colonel Cross's house were becoming old-fashioned. Moreover, scores of new houses were going up in the town—fairly good houses, not so grand as those that the Major or Colonel built, but better houses, on the whole. Lawyers, merchants, doctors, teachers, and retired cattlemen were building these houses. They filled in the gap between the little house and the big house that had spelled out the story of the economic feudalism of the earlier times.

The waterworks had become publicly owned; also the light plant. Telephones were coming into general use, one to every house in town, and the rural phone was common. Sewers went everywhere. Gas was used for fuel in hundreds of homes, and bank deposits began to rise. Prosperity was passing around. The world's unheard-of flood of manufactured goods was inundating Emporia, and so the houses of the Major and the Colonel were becoming old-fashioned, and we became conscious of our jigsaws and their devilish work.

The revolution which the Populists had threatened ten years before was upon us, and we did not realize what is was—a more equitable distribution of

*This essay is the second in a two-part series that began with "Blood of the Conquerors."

1. The United States acquired the Philippines from Spain in 1898 after the Spanish-American war, shortly after a Philippine-American war ensued (1899–1902), wherein Filipinos sought independence from the United States.

2. The thought that Americans had the divine right to settle North America, which drove westward expansion and the removal of Native populations.

the products of agriculture and industry. And, with the rise of the common man in the possession of worldly goods, by some strange alchemy the political power of the Major seemed to be decaying. Ike Lambert, his political arm, became stronger than the Major himself. The pair were named in parlance "Ike and the Major," instead of the other way round. The Banker was losing his power. His power was based upon his influence over his debtors. But only a few people in the new world were borrowers. Thousands of others living in substantial houses and with rising economic status had to be considered, for the first time. It took a lawyer. So the bankers first divided and then surrendered their power. In Emporia Ike Lambert's rise typified the change. Ike branched out in business, invested in an ice plant and a blooded trotting stallion. He was no longer a satellite, but a star in his own right. He had passes. He delt with the farmers. He had power of his very own.

The Last of the Barons

And we were all Eminently Respectable. We lived well. We were proud of ourselves—just a mite middleclass-conscious. And—because our houses were good square, well-furnished homes, with water and electric lights and gas and telephones in them; because we ate head lettuce all winter and enjoyed tropic fruits in season; because we were all well clad, and well traveled, by way of excursion to the four corners of the world, and because our sons and daughters were in colleges and high school, and we were all better educated than the Major—we felt a certain condescension toward even his nominal suzerainty. Emporia was Major Hood's town, of course, but we also felt rather definitely that the line would end with him. He was to be the last of the barons.

And what Emporia was feeling, thousands of other mid-Western towns were feeling. The Revolution was indeed world-wide. But it was visible more clearly in the country than in the great cities. We were closer than the urbanite to the ringside where the battle was going on.

We joined the Roosevelt mutiny with a hurrah against what he called "the aggrandizement of great wealth."[3] Even the Major joined. Ike was skeptical. Being a railroad attorney, having a district as large as a New England State, Ike

---

3. President Theodore Roosevelt (1858–1919).

was inclined to sniff. He knew what it meant, this Rooseveltian middle-class uprising. At the meeting of the State Bar Association, Ike and the other lawyers had a great powwow about [the] Constitution and all that threatened it.

But the Bankers' Association was not greatly excited. The bankers knew what the lawyers were doing to them. Therefore the country bankers—who owned no railroad stock to speak of, who had no great amount of "aggrandized wealth" compared with their suddenly prosperous neighbors, and who felt the power of the great financial forces centering in New York—were rather with Roosevelt in those early days of the century than against him. The Rooseveltian revolution was successful, not because the downtrodden and oppressed rallied to it; the banner of Roosevelt was surrounded and carried by the Eminently Respectable, who felt piqued at the arrogance of those above them in the financial world and also honestly feared the power of the industrial captains and masters of finance.

The Eminently Respectable, all over America, but more definitely west of the Alleghenies, saw with angry astonishment that the seat of real power in government had passed from the country banker to that intangible force or place or principality called, for short, "Wall Street." So as the Populists of the nineties had risen against the Major and Colonel, now the Major and all Emporia rose with Roosevelt. Ike and the Major went out to Colorado to ride into Emporia on Roosevelt's train, and the town gathered to cheer them when they got off and Roosevelt made a speech. But Ike still had reservations. The local leaders of the Roosevelt revolt were Ike's friends. But he festively referred to them as "you damned reformers." Fancy that to the Major!

As the first decade of the new century grew older, prosperity came in an overwhelming flood to Emporia—but only because Emporia was what and where and when it was. And as more and more people cooked with gas and got their names in the society columns, so more and more people joined the Roosevelt insurgency. It was more than a mutiny. It was an overturning of the old order.

The man in the brown derby had overthrown the man in the plug hat. And the wearer of the derby did a number of deeply revolutionary things. He put the railroads out of politics with the primary law. Then he took away the railroad pass and brought the whole operation of the railroads under the control of the government. He regulated every activity of the man in the plug hat—the insurance companies, the packing houses, the brewers, the banks and trust companies, the big industrial combinations selling oil, gas, coal, lumber, flour, power, and all the public utilities that deal with the average man.

Emporia for ten years sent to the Legislature her leading citizens who were not to be bought or bulldozed and could not be fooled. They, and literally thousands of others of their kind in various legislatures and in Congress, changed the seat of power in America from a central, invisible government, ruled from the great cities of the Atlantic seaboard, to the Eminently Respectable who live west of Buffalo.

Why the Major Joined

Transportation, currency, industry, and finance are today under the control of the Republic. Twenty years ago the Republic was under the control of our dominant commercial leaders. The thing that made the Major pause and then join the rebels was the news that his candidate for the United States Senate in 1902 had to stand hat in hand before the door of the financial powers in New York before getting permission to run for the Senate.

Senators used to stand in the Major's outer office and pull a respectful forelock when they came in. Ike might work for Wall Street if he would; but the Major fought in the Civil War, rode the old cattle trail when a man was as good as his gun, and the Major was a free man! Also Roosevelt wrote letters to the Major from the White House. He understood the phrase: "Men of our type!"

Liberty Wrestling with Equality

So the Major joined, rather dubiously but yet definitely, the movement to Restore the Republic to the people—a man-sized job for any nation at any time. It was a big job twenty years ago; to get control of business we had to rewrite many of our State constitutions, change most of them fundamentally, and amend the Federal Constitution four times. Each amendment was a leveler. We taxed incomes to equalize and redistribute our national wealth. We elected our United States senators directly, to take away the political power of great wealth centered in New England and New York. We adopted prohibition to prevent economic waste and to break the political power of the saloon. And, finally, we gave women the ballot to lift the home into politics; thus again clinching and cleating underneath the revolution of the Eminently Respectful by doubling its voting power and increasing its leadership.

And, as if these changes in our economic and political life were not enough, we are even now seeking four other constitutional amendments, each along the lines of the last four. First, we are seeking to exalt the middle-class home by prohibiting child labor. Second, we are going to check the rich tax dodger and make him pay more for government by abolishing tax-free securities. Third, we are trying to get a new strangle hold upon government by making our congressmen and president go to work immediately after election. Fourth, we are seriously considering limiting the veto powers of the courts upon legislation. All amendments a part of the middle-class revolution, all parts of a greater Emporia platform, all devices to equalize the opportunities of the common man! It is as though the constitution of the fathers had been struggling for thirty years with the Declaration of Independence; liberty in a losing match wrestling with equality! . . .

The Colonel died a generation ago, but he died an enfettered spirit who swung his cane freely in the throughfare and let the people take care of their own shins. The Major and Ike have been dead these dozen years now, but they saw the pink dawn of the revolution. Ike detested it to the last, and the Major was always bewildered. It was not his world. His world came to an end when we began to blush for shame of our jigsaw's deadly work. The Major lived to see many houses as fine as his in town. And, in the end, Mrs. Hood had in her kitchen nothing that was not in two thousand homes in the town—water, heat, light, power, communication—all at hand when she turned a tap or pressed a button!

When the Major went he had nothing on his table, in his barn, over his head that was not common to the average run of his neighbors. He had a fine car, but a flivver was nearer its equal than any rig in town ever was to his big spanking sorrel team and his costly carriage.[4] The primary left the Major one vote. Suffrage made him split that with his womenfolk. He paid his way on the railroads and scarcely knew the man who managed the roads that ran through Emporia. He had been leveled by the age. Steam had done for him. So many,

4. Flivver: term used to describe an automobile of lower quality and smaller size.

many things had been made by all the factories in the world that the Major and his heirs and assigns could not even pretend to control them.

When the tide of material things made by a million machines—food, clothing, building materials, and a hundred luxuries of which the Major in his youth never dreamed—came sweeping over the town, everyone got a lot of them, and most people got their share. Was it strange that they had to readjust their politics to their economics? Is it not easy to understand why the Major's son, or someone in his place, did not inherit the Major's power?

Those who still hoped to continue the old order made their last stand at the two great party conventions of 1912. They represented a sad and hopeless minority—the old order that was good in its day. It had prevailed here in America for more than a century. But its passing left the new order, raw and green and unstable. The leveling process had been from above—a leveling down. The leveling up was only incidental.

Then came the war, when a new process was manifest in the social order—a leveling up.[5] This process had little political expression. It made itself manifest in Emporia curiously. For ten years before the war the sign of a flock of motor cars before a house meant two things: a party inside or someone sick there. After 1919 it meant workmen on some adjacent job—plumbers, carpenters, plasterers, bricklayers, or electricians. The rise of wages we knew about. But the mere story of the rise meant little. When it began expressing itself in motor cars and bungalows and dry goods and clothing; when the attendance at high school began to show a definite increase; when the two colleges in the town began to fill up to the crowding point; when the market for fresh vegetables began to double, we knew the thing had happened.

The skilled laborer was taking his social and economic place beside the professor, the doctor, the merchant, the lawyer. The middle class, which had been for twenty years leveling down, began to be leveled up. The Adamson Law was the only legal expression this revolution had.[6] But its aspiration was written in a group of proposed legislation—the Plumb plan, the nationalization of the coal industry, the resolution of impeachment against the attorney

---

5. Referring to the First World War (1914–1918); the United States entered the war in 1917.

6. Called the Adamson Act, it established work rights for railroad workers such as an eight-hour work day and extra pay for overtime. It was passed in 1916.

general, the repeal of the Esch-Cummins Law, and the La Follette legislative program.[7]

An Uprising a Generation Old

In the election of 1922 a coterie of so-called radicals appeared in Congress, and a number of ultraliberal governors were chosen in the West who represented with startling accuracy what is in the mind of these new acquisitions to the governing class. The revolution is merely trying to put into law what the rise of wages and the consequent rise in living standards have put into the social order. But it is the same uprising that began a generation ago when the Major asked Ike: "What is special privilege?"

And here in Emporia during the thirty passing years we have seen it all—a revolution none the less complete because it has been bloodless. We have seen the Major and the Colonel looking surly and amazed at the upstarts who tried to crowd the established overlords out of their appointed places. And now, with high prices pinching those who ten years ago thought God was in his heaven, we see them also looking askance at the newcomers in the places of power whose increased wage is causing the maladjustment of our social order.

The professors in our colleges find it hard to live decently on their salaries. Emporia's academic colony has fewer motor cars than the engineers and conductors who make this division point on the Santa Fe their home. Babies are not coming to the professors and clerks as they came fifteen years ago. The times are out of joint. We are in a period of adjustment. The country club is not what it was when it was built a dozen years ago. It is not so exclusive. The wards down by the roundhouse have controlled the city for the last five years. They vote down there for what they want, because they know exactly what

7. The Plumb plan: a proposed plan by lawyer Glenn Plumb (1866–1922) in 1919 that would have the railroads owned cooperatively. The federal government would use bonds to buy the railroads and half the profits from the railroads would go to the workers and the other half for the bonds. The proposal was never passed. Esch-Cummins Law: Also known as the Transportation Act of 1920, it returned railroad operation to private operations after the railroads had been nationalized during the First World War. Robert La Follette (1855–1925) was a progressive Republican senator from Wisconsin.

they want. The wards near the two colleges are divided and dazed. Once they ruled by a sort of divine right. But not now.

Just One Drive After Another

Major Hood's grandson runs the largest bank in town. But he has his place through no money or influence that the Major left him. Moreover, his politics never enters the bank. He knows the member of the Legislature in his district but slightly. He has hardly met the State senator. Neither is under the slightest obligation to the Major's grandson for nomination or election. He is consulted by those who play the politics of the town no more than the foreman of the roundhouse or the registrar of the college. The Major's grandson had a bank three or four times as large as the bank that his grandfather controlled. But the grandson lives in one of a dozen good houses, and outside of banking hours he works with the town boosters. He is the best man on the town site as a team captain in a drive.

And life in the town is just one drive after another. A dozen activities are motived by community effort that once were the result of individual largess. The Major's grandson carries no gold pieces around for the poor at Christmas. We look after the poor by organizing unemployment, look after the boys through the Y.M.C.A and summer camps, and the girls through the Y.W.C.A. in the same way; after the money for the new hotel and the new college dormitory through the Chamber of Commerce; after milk for underfed children in the schools through the Woman's City Club; after the "broken soldiers" through the Red Cross, which also hires the county nurse and is securing a full-time public-health officer.[8] Every job in town is done in some organized way. No serious need is neglected. The population is thoroughly socialized. This socialization also is part of the revolution. We have come into a more abundant life.

And the list of our common activities indicates the seat of American government. It is in organized minorities. In Emporia the laboring men have their City Trade Council, the farmers have their union, their grange, their bureaus, the women their City Federation of Clubs, the merchants their Chamber of

---

8. Many soldiers returning home after the First World War had "shell shock," what we now recognize as PTSD.

Commerce and their retailers' association. The organized churches federate in the Y.M.C.A and Y.W.C.A. The benevolently inclined crystalize around the Red Cross and the Welfare Association, the politicians rally around their party organizations—all minorities. And each minority has its outside affiliation, in the district, in the State, in the nation. So every citizen has at least two district votes; one rather unimportant—his vote at the polls; the other generally most important in making public sentiment—his vote in his club or his trade union, his professional guild or his craft society. Through that second vote he controls legislatures, congresses, executives. Some citizens have a dozen extralegal votes, for each group maintains a lobby at the State and national capital to see that the private sentiment of the group is made public sentiment by law and through law enforcement.

What the Major and the Colonel did a third of a century ago by controlling politics, these organized minorities do today through their hired representatives in the capitals of the country. We have overcome certain defects of representation by territorial delegates by substituting a practical government by crafts, trades, professions, creeds, leagues, cults, and allied interests. It is not a democracy. But it is nearer representative government—even though the representation is extralegal—than the old order was. The Major and the Colonel were benevolent despots. We now have in Emporia government by altruistic closely organized Boosters. In the change is the essential machinery of the great middle-class revolution that has transformed America. The deluge of manufactured goods produced the revolution. But these social, economic, and political devices for voicing public sentiment gave the revolution its outward form. And we are still "going strong."

The "we" does not mean just Emporia. It means America. A generation has made us over. Even the individualistic farmer is organizing rapidly and effectively. The thing that we dreamed of forty years ago we have in our lives today. And the ideals of today will be realized tomorrow. But in a little country town where men and women live close to one another's lives, it is somewhat easier to observe the growth of our institutions than it is in a city where one scarcely knows the man sheltered under the same roof with him. We in Emporia—seeing whole sections of the community changing their political status, seeing one economic group after another push itself upward and thus change its political relation to the community—can realize what the passing decades are bringing to us.

The revolution may be only a phrase to those who live in crowded places, where changes are impersonal. But we who have seen the vast difference between the life and activities of the Major and his grandson, we who have seen a mayor inaugurated in his overalls making good in the college ward, we who have seen the rise and decline of the railroad attorneys and have seen printers and things going around the golf course at the country club—we know what the revolution has done. We have watched it from box seats. And that's why we live in Emporia—forty millions of us. We like the show.

A Brave Man

(*Emporia Gazette*, April 21, 1923)

It seems to be settled that President Harding will take his issue of the world court to the people.[1] He can do nothing less. For him to retire the issue, for him to surrender to a few malcontents in his own party who have no plan for world peace but American isolation, would brand President Harding as either insincere in his first position or cowardly in a later one. The world court offers a simple, sane, and workable plan by which America can participate with dignity in world affairs, and keep America free from binding covenants which would imperil us and embroil us in foreign wars. Europe and Christian civilization generally is seriously menaced by conditions that have arisen since the world war. If Christian civilization degenerates, America will go down with the rest of the world. We have a duty toward our neighbors. It is not a duty to commit suicide, but it is a duty to help humanity help itself.

The president's vision of America's part in world affairs is not impractical. He is a conservative of conservatives. He has taken a middle position. He should have the support of every American who believes that America in the neighborhood of nations must play a neighbor's part.

The president who for two years has held a steady helm through economic and industrial storms, who has kept America going straight ahead, who has kept us the soundest nation on earth, who has preserved our prosperity at home and maintained our integrity in the world abroad certainly should have the faith and confidence of the American people now. Neither the endorsement of cranks nor the malice of his political foes should shake our faith in this sane, kindly, courageous man's high purpose and his deep common sense.

---

1. Warren G. Harding (1865–1923) was the twenty-ninth president of the United States (1921–1923). The World Court, or Permanent Court of International Justice (1922–1946), was the judicial branch of the League of Nations.

A Holy American Day

(*Emporia Gazette*, September 17, 1924)

Today celebrates the 137th anniversary of the adoption of the constitution of the United States. The American constitution is the wisest human document that has been written since the Sermon on the Mount.[1] It gathered into the fundamental law of the nation a code of living which guarantees to the average man more justice than is guaranteed by any other charter, covenant, or constitution in the world up to this hour. It had its foundation, this American constitution, in the Sermon on the Mount. Our constitution attempted to make a practical, living political instrument which would put into practice the golden rule in so far as it was livable under human conditions in this world. Of course our constitution is not perfect. It is full of flaws. It must be amended and reamended with every decade, as changing conditions bring new responsibilities upon it. But fundamentally it does guarantee to man in his relations with other men under government more justice, more self-respect, and an easier path in living kindly, bravely and wisely than does any other document in the world.

It is more responsible for America as America is today, the land of the free and the home of the brave, than any other document in our institutions. Charity, religious tolerance, neighborly give and take, political compromise, and the high aspirations of far-seeing men all are provided for under that constitution and its amendments. It has instituted in America the rule of reason and law rather than the rule of force. We are today the freest people in the world because of that constitution and our freedom comes from the institutions of neighborly kindness which the constitution fosters. We use less force in our practical government than any other government in the world. We Americans, of course, have a small portion of force back of our laws, but they are chiefly enforced by reason, by the sense of justice, by an intelligent public opinion, all of which our constitution has promoted.

1. Matthew 5:7.

There is and always has been and always will be an impatient minority in this country which believes in force. An ignorant minority, a bigoted minority, a shallow minority that wants to solve all problems by ukase and decree.[2] But alas, problems are not solved so. They are solved by mutual give and take, by reasonableness and kindliness, by institutionalized Christianity; by the golden rule slowly working upon a problem until it solves it. There is nothing so dynamic in life as neighborly affection; but this intolerant minority, this small group of bigots which always has existed and always will in America, attacking various problems whether slavery, or religion, or temperance, or race prejudice, or the menace of low bred humanity, will get nowhere. It never has got anywhere. Only those generous, patient, wise souls who see our problems and apply to them the constitutional methods, the kindly methods, the neighborly methods, the reasonable methods, the legal methods, ever go far in putting America forward in progress.

So let us face the problems made by this poor, blind "breed without the law."[3] Let us go forward as Americans full of hope, full of faith that our country under its constitution will survive, will grow, will work out its problems. Unless we approach our serious problems sanely, kindly, patiently and with a deep faith in the unswerving purpose of God and a corollary faith in the essential goodness of common man, we get nowhere, and the work of the fathers who established our constitution is bound in the end to come to naught. This day celebrating the adoption of our constitution should be one of the great days in our national life, as great as the Fourth of July, a time of common thanksgiving, a time for parades, a time for patriotic observance. For it is a holy day in the history of mankind.

2. Ukase: an edict or decree, typically used to refer to orders by the tsar of imperial Russia.

3. A line adapted from the poem "Recessional" (1897) by Rudyard Kipling (1865–1936).

Klanism vs. Americanism

(*Emporia Gazette*, September 26, 1924)

The candidates for lieutenant governor and governor in Kansas filing independently in a protest against the activities of the Ku Klux Klan in both political parties, have done so in the hope of restoring to our politics a respect for the constitutions of our state and nation.[1] The philosophy of the Ku Klux is a philosophy or terror and force. It institutes boycotts without giving a man his day in court. It ostracizes families merely because of their skin or race or belief. It punishes by taunts and jibes innocent children merely because of what their parents may think, or how they look, or what their grandparents may have been. Now our constitutions, both state and nation, provide that men may have their day in court, that a man may have his property until it is taken by due process of law, that he may have his self-respect, the greatest blessing guaranteed to man, upon good behavior. All these things the Ku Klux takes from a man ruthlessly, lawlessly, and in terror. For 2,000 years our fathers have been striving to institute into government the ideals of the philosophy of Nazareth. Slowly through the centuries, gaining a little age by age, Christian civilization has put into its political institutions more and more of the Nazarene creed— the creed that was proclaimed in the Sermon on the Mount.[2] We have been protecting the weak against the strong, the righteous against the unruly, the kindly against the cruel, making it more and more possible with every century, under law, for man to live with his neighbors decently, kindly and generously. The men who wrote the Constitution of the United States produced the greatest document that has been written on this planet since the Sermon on the Mount. It was a charter of freedom, under which men may live with one

1. Ku Klux Klan: a white supremacist hate group revived in the 1920s. The Ku Klux Klan grew from the southern United States across the Midwest and West and influenced members of both parties.

2. A sermon given by Jesus in chapters 5, 6, and 7 of the Gospel of Matthew focusing on the importance of humility, equality, and caring for one's neighbors.

another under a rule of fraternity and neighborly consideration—a charter of freedom fairer and broader than ever had been conceived in the world before. The soul of the American Constitution is that clause which abolishes caste and title in America. Under it every man knows that he may rise as far as his merits entitle him to rise. He stands on the taw mark at birth equal with every other man in America.[3] He and his children know that whatever they have in them that is of good report may come out, may develop and may lift them in a social scale to their full stature. Not race, not creed, nor ancestry makes a man or hinders him in this land. This freedom, this divine self-respect guaranteed by our constitution and guaranteed to us Americans more than to any other people on earth, is the sacred heritage of our country which the Ku Klux Klan is attacking. It would take self-respect from the Negro. It would take self-respect from the foreign born. It would take self-respect from the Catholic because of his creed and only because of his creed.

And yet Ben Paulen, our Republican candidate for governor took an [e]ndorsement from this un-American, oath-bound crew and has not had the courage to disavow it.[4] He wants the votes of the klan. He would rather have the votes of the klan than to defend the American constitution and the constitution of Kansas. How can he be governor with the knowledge in the back of his head that 40,000 klansmen nominated him and that 50,000 klansmen are voting for him? Why did he go into the state convention and stand by the klan? Why did he use his prestige as a Republican nominee to shut off debate upon the subject of the klan in the state convention? Why does he deny his membership in the klan in exactly the same language that every well-known kleagle, cyclops, or calathumpian uses when he denies his membership in the klan?[5] Why does he send out John S. Dean, the official attorney for the klan, to represent Ben Paulen at governors' days, fairs, and homecomings?[6] This klan issue is not being made by the independent candidates. It was made when

3. "Taw mark" refers to the border behind which players at marbles must shoot into the center.

4. Benjamin Paulen (1869–1961) was the Republican governor of Kansas from 1925 to 1929. He was supported by the Ku Klux Klan in the 1924 Republican primary election.

5. "Kleagle" and "cyclops" refer to titles within the Ku Klux Klan. A calathumpian is a noisy parade of discordant music or someone who participates in such a parade.

6. John Sullivan Dean (1861–1937) was a Kansas lawyer, member of the Republican party, and legal spokesperson for the Ku Klux Klan.

the kleagles came up from Oklahoma and endorsed Ben Paulen and when he took that endorsement, went to the state convention and tied the Republican platform to the Ku Klux Klan. The independent ticket came out for the rank and file of the Republican party who were denied a voice in their convention. The independent candidates believe in the philosophy of the Nazarene, the philosophy of reason, not the philosophy of force and terror. They believe in the constitution that was founded upon reason to give men self-respect and not in the philosophy that would make castes and cults and chasms in our society, based on creed and race and birth. This klan philosophy menaces Kansas. We, of all the states, have fewer of the foreign born. We need no hooded gangs in cow pastures to amend our constitution by rewriting K. K. K. into its preamble. We stand for the old-fashioned, visible government that our fathers founded upon the age-long struggle for tolerance, for self-respect, for the basic philosophy of Christendom. And the independent candidates call upon all good citizens, all believers in Christian civilization, to go with them in this fight.

Forward or Backward

(*Emporia Gazette*, September 27, 1924)

Kansas is a parallelogram of prosperity, 200 miles wide and 400 miles long. Within that parallelogram are gathered something less than 2 million people. These people are the most civilized people in the world. They have more of the material comforts, which make the white man's civilization, than any other 2 million people on this planet. Steam, electricity, the schoolhouse, and the printing press have produced a citizenship here which is better housed, better clad, better educated, than any other 2 million people in the world. Moreover, they worked out, with the heritage of 2,000 years of Christian civilization, the most equitable government in the world.

Our wealth is justly distributed, not divided as the Socialists would divide it, but given to each man in justice. In Kansas every man earns what he gets, and gets what he earns. This is a Utopian dream. For thousands of years, men have dreamed of such a civilization as this is in Kansas.

Here wealth is equitably distributed, and there are no rich and no poor. More than this, we are a people of one heritage, one tradition, one aspiration. We have shown that we can work out a beautiful and just civilization. Now into all this horn of plenty, Providence has poured natural wealth far beyond the dreams of avarice. More than any other parallelogram of equal size on this planet, Kansas has been given material for food and fuel for all this continent. Wheat, oil, meat and coal, a veritable cornucopia of plenty is this Kansas. But it is not finished. The newer world is upon us. We are going forward, to even greater things than we have.

The Kansan has been stationary too long, it is not his natural state. It is the unnatural state of a domain provided with all this natural richness.

We must keep our minds on converting into salable commodities things that are raised more and more. We must take the advantages of our blessings and not give these advantages idly to who would take them. We must wake up and go forward.

How can we do that if every neighbor is at his neighbor's throat, criticizing his religion, scanning his skin, demanding for birth certificates, before beginning the day's work for Kansas?

Will a philosophy of terror and fear and hate make the great Kansas that is to be? Will the Ku Klux Klan, under the leadership of Paulen or Davis, in the next two years develop the Kansas that must be?[1] If we deliver and fritter away our powers, we will be hiding our talents in a napkin. But if Kansas is united with the old Kansas spirit, the spirit of the glorious boom, the spirit of days of free-soilers, the crusading spirit in business, that launches forth to high enterprises, Kansas can keep her high place among the stars.

1. Benjamin S. Paulen (1869–1961) was the Republican candidate in the 1924 gubernatorial election in Kansas; he was supported by the Ku Klux Klan. Jonathan M. Davis (1871–1943) was the Democratic candidate who ran on an anti-Klan platform but refused to publicly denounce the Klan.

At the Crossroads

(*Emporia Gazette*, November 1, 1924)

One hundred thirty-seven years ago our fathers wrote, here in America, the wisest document ever penned by human hands—the American constitution. It is great because for the first time it devised a government under which men could live, based on reason with forces only implied, and that far in the background. We have here a government based on tolerance and religious liberty.

Sighting across 2,000 years we can see now that, when the message of the Sermon on the Mount came to man, the greatest miracle that man has witnessed was performed, the miracle which the infidel cannot question nor the atheist deny, the miracle of putting into the earth where once force ruled, a government based upon reasonableness, upon mutual respect, upon a fellowship of men who have faith in each other.

Yet here comes the new cult, this empire, this invisible empire.[1] Where in its institutions do men meet reason? If one is accused by the invisible empire, to what reasoning place in the empire may he go with his cause? Have the rank and file of any vote in the empire upon the policies of the empire—any reasoning places where they make its policies? No. For the imperial wizard of the empire appoints the grand dragons of the empire and the grand dragons of the empire appoint the imperial wizard.[2] Below that is the scurf of the earth in the empire, no ballot box, no courts, nothing but the will of the few

---

1. The revived Ku Klux Klan of the 1920s promoted "100 percent Americanism," by which it meant white, Protestant, largely rural membership as part of an "invisible empire" against Catholics, descendants of Eastern and Southern Europeans, Jews, and Black Americans. For more information on the Ku Klux Klan in the 1920s, see William Rawlings, *The Second Coming of the Invisible Empire: The Ku Klux Klan of the 1920s* (Mercer University Press, 2016).

2. "Imperial wizards" and "grand dragons" were ranks within the Ku Klux Klan, both in the nineteenth century and during the 1920s. An imperial wizard's purview was national in scope, while grand dragons oversaw particular regions, or "realms."

governing the sections of the many. Yet under the Ku Klux Klan boycott they take away property of citizens outside the realm without due process of law.[3] The cow pasture edicts of this invisible empire wreck our country banks in Kansas with impunity, destroy the business of our merchants, take from our citizens their rights to earn an honest living by boycotting their employers.

Everywhere that the invisible empire of the Ku Klux Klan touches life it touches it with a brutal hand using only force and never with a reasoning head or a kindly heart.

This empire cannot remain in our democracy. Their aims diverge. We must either crush the empire or the empire will change our lives. They represent, this empire and our government, two bitterly antagonist forces, and one must go down. America cannot remain half empire and half democracy.

3. During its iteration in the 1920s, the Ku Klux Klan promoted what it called "Klannishness" by encouraging boycotts of businesses that refused to support the organization, especially in eastern Kansas. For example, the Klan encouraged boycotting merchants who refused to advertise in the Kansas City *Kansan*, a newspaper it claimed was sympathetic to its ideology. See Timothy D. Rives, "The Ku Klux Klan in Kansas City, Kansas 1921–1930" (MA thesis, Emporia State University, 1995), 37.

Annihilate the Klan!

(*The Nation*, January 1925)

The Ku Klux Klan is the flower of reaction. It could not bloom in liberal days.

The heart of man would not travel in the Ku Klux path, if the heart of man were considering humanity from the liberal viewpoint. The whole Ku Klux philosophy is a philosophy of force as opposed to reason, based upon a centripetal rather than a centrifugal movement in life. It is intolerant and egoistic, this Ku Klux philosophy relying upon terror and suspicion and malice to achieve its unholy ends.

Of course it appears to classes that are essentially unintelligent morally and spiritually, but it does grip them with a tremendous force. If the powerful, conscious, egoistic forces that control our government and control governments internationally had employed their wisest publicity men, their shrewdest psychologists, their most fiendish and devilish agencies to corrupt and mislead and cauterize the hearts of humanity for the purpose of making the third- and fourth-raters in life immune to altruistic ideals, these great sinister ruling forces could have hit upon nothing more perfectly fitted for their purposes than the Ku Klux Klan. So long as the Ku Klux Klan is operating in any considerable minority in any American State, that State will be absolutely closed to liberal ideals. The labor movement in America has not had, in a generation, such a staggering blow as it has received from the Ku Klux Klan. The Klan is deeply divisory in every progressive movement but it has diverted labor from its aims and divided the rank and file of organized labor as nothing else has done for a generation.

The leaders of the Klan know well that when other issues than the Pope and the dominance of the Jew and the fear of the Negro enter into the election, their own issue pales and dies. So they are bitter in their denunciation of other politicians and other political movements which have for their object the amelioration of the conditions of the submerged part of our population. Labor got to thinking so bitterly and intensely about the wrongs which the Pope was inflicting this fall that labor forgot all about its own rights.[1]

Of course the thing we call Wall Street for short did not go down into Georgia and finance the high-powered salesmen of the Klan to go out and sell the Klan doctrine to the laboring people; but if Wall Street had done that Wall Street would have exhibited more sense than it has done since capitalism began to dominate humanity.

The Klan is the most amazingly clever capitalization of all recent psychological researches, offering dull and negligible people an escape from the inferiority complex into the realm of the secretly powerful. Wall Street need fear no "dangerous unrest" as long as the Ku Klux Klan is abroad in the land. The discontented are peacefully diverted from the realization of the causes of their condition. And with this diversion their capacity for meeting real injustice is turned in the safer by-paths of hating their neighbor, nosing into their neighbor's religion, or despising their neighbor's race and color. If there were such a thing in a democracy as Machiavellian statecraft it would seem almost childish in comparison with the efficiency of this Invisible Empire in spreading this tremendously effective gospel of reaction among the oppressed.

But if the Klan would only relieve such evils as the Klan itself complains of and states so puerilely one might get some satisfaction in seeing the Klan thrive. But even those evils which are not religious or racial but are largely the result of overcrowding in great cities, of congestion of people of one race or creed or blood in almost segregated sections of our cities and States—those evils are not lessened by the Klan. Hating these segregated peoples because of their race or religion or birth will not Americanize them, will not bring them into any reasonable and righteous relation with our nation, which they may lack. The evils of which the Klan complains must be met with reason, not with force—with indeed "a sweet reasonableness," with a fraternal sympathy, with a centrifugal philosophy.[2] But alas, what we have is bitterness and malice and wicked, unneighborly persecution, unreasoning, unprofitable, futile beyond words except that it promotes the very injustices of which they complain. To

1. This is likely a reference to Cardinal William Henry O'Connell of Boston, who in 1924 lobbied against a proposed amendment to the US Constitution prohibiting child labor.

2. "Sweet reasonableness": Matthew Arnold's translation of Paul from Philippians 4:4–7; Matthew Arnold, *Literature and Dogma: An Essay Towards a Better Apprehension of the Bible* (Macmillan, 1873).

state merely a side issue on these fundamental questions simply, we may say that the net results of the Klan has been to unite Catholicism as it has not been united in America before in our history, and to divide Protestantism hopelessly. Similarly, the Klan has given the power of unison to all of the evil forces of capitalism without giving to the altruistic forces of capitalism anything but discord, diversion, and disunion.

The immediate problem of the liberal statesman is the annihilation of the Ku Klux Klan.

Lyon County

February 15, 1926

If you are a good citizen, if you want to do your full duty to your neighbor, if you realize that you are merely one unit in a community with higher duties to others in many things than to yourself, you should be proud that you live in Lyon County.[1] Here is a socialized county. Here is a county where every man puts his pennies into the county treasury to help his fellows, to pay his own way, to care for the common health of community, and so preserve his own, to provide for transportation, quickly and cheaply, to markets so the Lyon County farmers may receive the most for their produce, to educate the children, to help the poor, to heal the sick, and to prevent poverty. No other county in Kansas, and probably few in the big world, have so organized life that every man is doing his public duty to his neighbors as it is done by the average taxpayer in Lyon County.

We have a splendid home for the indigent poor.

We have a careful tax-saving organization which is looking after the able-bodied poor, keeping them supplied with work, and where families are in need supplying them with necessaries.

We have a splendid county hospital where from 60 to 70 people every day are cared for through illness, and where contagious diseases are segregated and cured.

We are putting down a splendid hard-surfaced road system from the south end county to the north, from the east to the west. And we have one hundred miles of graded, guttered, dragged roads up to the government standard, the best dirt roads in America—good for 300 days in the year.

We have a county health unit and two county nurses fighting against the spread of contagious disease in every part of the county.

We have a high school supported by taxes at large every five miles in any direction from any place on the map.

---

1. The county in Kansas where Emporia is located.

We have law and order and we have always had and always will have competent, faithful, honest corps of public officials from judge down to constable, to guard our property and safeguard our lives without corruption, waste or neglect.

And no human being need lie down to rest at night and feel the pinch of want if he is poor, nor a twinge of conscience if he is rich that he is in serious danger of want if he is poor, or of cauterizing his immortal soul by mean avoidance of his duty if he is rich. A mighty good old county is Lyon, named for Nathaniel Lyon, the only abolitionist graduated from West Point in the American Army at the outbreak of the Civil War.[2] We came from conscientious blood. It is in our practice, our traditions and in our aspirations.

2. Nathaniel Lyon (1818–1861) was the first Union general to be killed in battle during the Civil War (1861–1865). West Point: A prestigious US military academy known for producing famous and exceptional officers located in West Point, New York.

Al Smith, City Feller

(*Collier's*, August 21, 1926)

Observe, a man—stocky but not pudgy—five feet seven, who looks five feet nine or ten sitting down, for he has a long, sturdy body. He is a blond, well kept, with clear, fine, healthy skin (pink and white, in fact), blue eyes and fair hair that may have been red, possibly even tow, in childhood. He is a smooth-shaven, oval-faced, mean-jawed, with a pugnacious set to his head—a head which wags with fine self-assertion.

It is a self-assertion that is never quite vanity. As he talks, one begins to realize that he is merely gesticulating with his long neck above sloping shoulders, over a broad chest, set upon a competent though not distinguished accouterment of intestinal equipment all built upon a scaffolding of nimble legs. He is articulate in every inch of his body.

Now let's dress him, for Alfred Emanuel Smith, governor of New York, is a dresser, which fact brands him a city chap, as do the smart clothes he wears.[1] Behold a pink hair-striped collar on top of a dark, wine-colored bow tie, set above a V of shirt front which shows small brownish-crimson figures in a white background, with a slight pink thread running through.

Protruding from the top pocket of a dark, well-tailored coat are the scarlet tips of a handkerchief. Tan shoes, with appropriate silk socks, set off his properly creased gray trousers. He is a tailored man who gives thought to wherewithal he should be clad; again the habit of a city chap.

His blue eyes, looking casually at a man or a scene, remain curtained, bright, flickering specks under dark lashes. Only when his emotions begin to appear do his eyelids open. Then his eyes glow with some incandescence which reveals a deeply earnest nature. His laughter is casual and incidental, but purpose glows in those wide, scathing eyes.

---

1. Alfred Smith (1873–1944) served as governor of New York from 1919 to 1920 and again from 1923 to 1928. He was the Democratic nominee for president in the 1928 election.

Turn some inner switch in his heart, and affection can burn there as well as purpose, for he is a man of passions, with a capacity for feeling almost as strong as his ability to reason. One gets, therefore, from his spirit, as it is revealed in a well-knit yet nervous body, beautifully controlled, the impression of balance—this kind of balance: a big heart and a clear brain; a balance that makes a man capable of loyalties based upon qualities of both heart and mind.

He can be loyal to a friend, but he can go to the stake for an idea over the body of his friend. Sometimes nice persons, and over-well-bred, come into his office and are shocked at his manner. They who place manner above the inner gifts of heart and mind have revolted at a number of our presidents; indeed, at a number of our great presidents. Alfred Emanuel Smith, beloved of his fellow urbanites as Al Smith, as deeply offends the ultra-mannerly of his generation as any other of our statesmen might offend these nice people. They see on him, these most conventional people, the same horns and hoofs which have frightened men from the beginning of time: horns and hoofs of manners growing out of environmental habits; horns and hoofs which every strong man wears as he comes struggling out of his past into leadership.

The background of Al Smith's childhood was the old Brooklyn Bridge. As a boy he played ball under the arches of the old bridge that run in from the river into the water front—cool, deep, shady arches. Here he heroized the policeman on the beat. Here he hopped proudly on the fire wagon. Here he picked up balls on the streets and in alleys back of the saloons, to sell for spending money. Here he led the bridge gang in his early teens. And the Brooklyn Bridge was to him what the woods must have been to the boy of two generations before him in interior America—the great bridge that was suspended like a steel dream across two worlds. Men said, "Ah, it's a great bridge, and it will hold up under the feet of men, but wait until Jumbo, the elephant, comes across!"[2] And the bridge gang under the arches waited, and Jumbo came, and the bridge stood, and Al Smith learned to hoot at the skeptic.

2. Jumbo the elephant (1860–1885) was an African elephant exported to European zoos from Sudan. In 1882 he was purchased by American businessman P. T. Barnum (1810–1891) and put on exhibition around North America.

Jackson, Lincoln—and Al Smith

He learned from the bridge what backwoods boys learned from the trees and the creatures of the forest, from the Indian and the frontiersman. But now, in a new day, the backwoods boy and the backwoodsman, indeed the backwoods themselves, are passing from American life.

The backwoodsmen of the last century, of whom Andrew Jackson and Andrew Johnson were types and Lincoln not far out of the picture, seem to be threatened now by the city type. For a hundred years the self-made farmer boy has been too busy to smooth off. American politics has produced thousands of local leaders with sixth-grade education—leaders who came out of the backwoods. Now from the back alley under Brooklyn Bridge comes Al Smith, the new type.

There is no reason why the back alley cannot produce as good moral, spiritual, mental and physical timber for politics as the backwoods. This historical equation reads something like this: As Andrew Jackson was to Clay and Webster, so is Al Smith to Coolidge and Lowden.[3] Let us therefore consider the back alley form which Al Smith sprang.

Certainly it was, in the seventies, as clean and wholesome a place as the backwoods from which Andrew Jackson sprang in Revolutionary times. Here was a three-story wooden New York City tenement facing the river front, cobblestones running down past the old fish market to the tide; square riggers coming in with cargoes and drunken sailors running up over the cobbles eager for the river-front saloon and for the fat prostitute sitting in her window barearmed and as alluring as sin in adipose can be.

On the third floor of the tenement where Al Smith was born his father, a dock workman, teamster, day laborer, ready for any job, maintained his little family. The real head of that family was Catherine Mulvehill, his wife, a girl whose father and mother were born in America, but who was, nevertheless,

---

3. Henry Clay (1777–1852) was a politician who represented Kentucky in key positions in Congress. Daniel Webster (1782–1852) was a politician who represented Massachusetts and New Hampshire in Congress. Both men were founding members of the Whig Party, which was created in opposition to the presidency of Andrew Jackson (1767–1845). Calvin Coolidge (1872–1933) was a Republican who served as president of the United States from 1923 to 1929. Frank Lowden (1861–1943) was a Republican who served as governor of Illinois from 1917 to 1921 and ran for the Republican nomination for president in 1920 and 1928.

of the good old Irish stock, energetic, faithful, full of visions and dreams, and never afraid of humble work. She was widowed in her twenties and held her brood together by keeping store and doing such honest work as came to her hands: a strong, vigorous character, Roman Catholic in religion and no bigot.

The Boy, Alfred Emanuel Smith, went sometimes to the public schools and sometimes to the parochial schools, as the circumstances warranted. And when he had learned to read, write, spell and figure a little, somewhere between the seventh and eighth grades, he fell out of school and went to work.

In his teens he was a clerk in the fish market. In his late teens he and the bridge gang went into Tammany.[4] And at twenty-one he was holding office, serving summonses for jurors in the local court of the water-front district. So the streets educated him as the woods and fields and wars educated Lincoln and as the woods and fields and wars educated Andrew Jackson. Their backgrounds are typical even if different.

The psychological effect upon each education was exactly the same upon this pioneer type of mind, the Jackson type, the Lincoln type, the Smith type. And Smith has exactly the faults and virtues that marked Jackson and Lincoln.

Backwoods virtues in education become back-alley excellences. Men of both types learn about evil early, and if it poisons them it poisons them, and they go down. If it does not, it gives them faith and charity, and they go up. Men educated in the back alley and the backwoods learn to think vigorously but without scientific restrictions and limitations. They see life in blacks and whites—not in grays. And so they live with the forces of life—tragically.

Go to the Devil for Light

Nothing sustains the human spirit so firmly as the presence of tragedy if the fiber of the spirit is tough enough to learn its lesson. Al Smith learned. He moved through Tammany in Croker's time, when it was corrupt, when politics

---

4. Tammany Hall, a Democratic political organization founded in New York City in 1789, acted as a patronage network to help the party win elections. While it is frequently associated with corruption and acting as a partisan political machine, it also gave assistance to the working class and immigrant populations of the city through a complex patronage system.

took much of its sinews from vice, form blackmail, and some of it—strength from plutocracy in bribes.[5] The Tammany of his youth sold special privileges alike to the rich and the poor, the corporations, the touts, the harlots, and the saloonkeepers, with equal frankness and cheerful dishonor.

Crokerism waned with the coming of a new century. Croker passed. A new order appeared. All the politics that Al Smith learned of the old order under Tom Foley, the local leader, was a capacity for teamwork, a habit of industry and the precious moral precept that it does not pay to lie.[6]

All of our presidents, except Wilson and Grant, in the past fifty years have gone through a somewhat similar training, and Wilson and Grant were the losers rather than the gainers by entering politics late in life. Grant's administration was in many respects deplorably weak and obviously corrupt. Wilson's ignorance of politics was his chief handicap.

Because Cleveland, McKinley, Roosevelt and Coolidge knew the game— the dirty game, if you will—they avoided many pitfalls and were able to walk with the children of light much farther than they would have walked had they not learned much from the Angel of Darkness.

Up the Escalator to Freedom

Al Smith, a young Tammany leader, who had worked his way up through the precinct into the ward—and so to the district in the moving stairway which takes forward and upward men who are industrious, honest and intelligent— found himself in his early thirties a member of the New York Assembly. The escalator also took him from the river front.

He maintained a decent Christian home. He had married Katherine Dunn. Their children were appearing with proper regularity, and Al Smith was a coming man in the district—something better than a leader. He was going to school in politics, in Albany politics, under Barnes, Platt, Bill Ward and Lou Payn, Republican leaders, and under the tutelage of men who had their

5. Richard Croker (1843–1922), also known as "Boss Croker," was the leader of Tammany Hall from 1886 to 1902.

6. Thomas Foley (1852–1925), also known as "Big Tom," was a saloon owner and Tammany Hall politician notorious for corruption.

political education from Croker, Bill Devery, Tom Foley, Judge Van Wyck, and later Mayor Gaynor, who thrust a certain practical idealism into the situation.[7]

But idealism in politics has never greatly affected Al Smith. It was a part of his political education to learn the routine of the public business: how taxes are levied, collected and disbursed; how political appointments are made; what wires hold what men and what ambitions govern others. Thus his education was not unlike that of the good gambler.

Smith was quick to learn the rules. He became party leader and Speaker of the House. His legislative career was curiously typical of the coming new order that he was to represent. Loyalty is a major virtue in an urban organization.

Smith took orders from Tammany until he was able to give orders. In his first legislative years his record was classed as bad by the nonpartisan organization which was trying to promote the rather rural program of welfare legislation which occupied the hearts of the political altruists of the hour.

Smith voted with the Tammany group against the direct primary, for instance, and certain welfare legislation which reformers were seeking. But Tammany thought Smith's record was good. When he took leadership in the Assembly and when he went to the New York State Constitutional Convention he was fairly free.

Elihu Root, chairman of the convention, declared that Smith knew the government of New York State more intelligently than any other delegate.[8] It was then that he began to command attention from his political opponents. He was the tough-brained, hard-headed, fact-seeking, ever-ready, hard-working realist that is called "able." Naturally Senator Elihu Root took a liking to him. The Republican *New York Tribune* spoke well of Smith. He grew in power and stature politically.

---

7. William Barnes (1866–1930), Thomas Platt (1833–1910), William Ward (1856–1933), and Louis Payn (1835–1923) were all prominent politicians in the New York Republican Party in the late nineteenth and early twentieth centuries. William Devery (1854–1919), New York City's Chief of Police and later co-owner of the New York Yankees baseball team. Augustus Van Wyck (1850–1922) served as a justice for the Supreme Court of Brooklyn, New York, from 1884 to 1896. He ran for governor of New York. William Gaynor (1849–1913) was mayor of New York City from 1910 until his death in 1913.

8. Elihu Root (1845–1937) was a Republican politician who served in the cabinets of Presidents William McKinley (1843–1901) and Theodore Roosevelt (1858–1919).

First Consul of the Back Alley

He had those qualities of heart and mind which make men leaders. He made money easily. He had that indefinable quality we know as charm. As sheriff and then president of the Board of Aldermen he was honest, hard-working, good-natured, painstaking, and at base, for all his happy Tammany regularity, he was becoming a free man.

He had met in the legislature during his decade and a half of service the acutest minds of the state: leaders or lobbyists. He formed many friendships across party lines, being essentially a friendly man, with a lust for the affection of his kind. He is the kind who loves the good company, a good cigar, a good story and good song after a good drink and is not ashamed of it. He is a man's man.

The primrose path never has lured him. He rose in the councils of his party upon his social graces. But he rose in popular esteem upon his intellectual qualities. His brain wins his adversaries. His heart holds his friends. It is a rare combination—the Al Smith composite. He attended the national conventions of his party and met, incidentally, leaders from other regions. He absorbed politics.

Smith makes no pretense of erudition, but no one can deny his wisdom. The wisdom of the back alley is just as impregnable as the wisdom of the back-woods, and possibly from now on back-alley statesmen may crowd the back-woods statesmen into second place.

Smith himself may not rise to a major place in American politics, but he may be the forerunner of a new type which shall rise to important and possibly triumphant leadership. For the backwoods are cleared. From the muck of the cities, as from the pioneer's rude cabin, are coming leaders of the new industrial democracy.

Al Smith must rise or fall in our national life, if ever he should enter it, as our first urbanite. Sometimes our cities have brought statesmen into our national life, as, for instance, New York brought Chester A. Arthur and Theodore Roosevelt, each a president by right of another man's death.

Our urban life has put a certain veneer upon the few statesman it has produced—a certain sophistication, a certain debonair contract with men which passes for urbanity, but neither Roosevelt, who was born in the city, nor Arthur, who came from Vermont to the city, was purely urbanite. Roosevelt's mother was from a Southern plantation. Roosevelt's formative youth after he left Harvard was hardened in the Dakotas. His following was never from the great cities.

But Al Smith is city-born, city-bred, "city-broke," city-minded, and city-hearted. He has exactly the same attitude toward the farmer that Coolidge has toward the city man, an intense desire to know him, a curious feeling that he is real; but Smith and Coolidge have a baffling sense of futility in trying to get the other man's viewpoint. This division, partly spiritual and partly material, this difference between the city man and the country man, is as old as civilization.

The city and the country do make different kinds of men externally. And the externals of men do make different attitudes and contacts. As experiences differ, great issues are formed.

Symbol of a Mighty Challenge

We may be facing new issues in our politics, based for the first time upon the conflicting interests, the conflicting morals, the conflicting aspirations of a rural civilization as those interests, morals, and aspirations clash in a nation which is rapidly becoming industrialized and urban. Hence Al Smith—with his pink-and-white skin, his pink-and-crimson tie and the scarlet border of his handkerchief, his silk socks and conventional gray trousers—becomes something more than a sporadic figure in our politics. He becomes the symbol of a mighty challenge to our American traditions, a challenge which, if it wins in the struggle which may ensue, will bring deep changes into our American life.

In early July, 1924, after the National Democratic Convention had wrangled through the longest session ever held by a major party in America and nominated a compromise candidate for the Presidency on the 103rd ballot, Al Smith appeared after the nomination of John W. Davis had been made.[9] had been made. During the long, bitter sessions of the convention Smith had appeared as a presidential candidate, for days a formidable candidate, always the candidate of a militant minority in the convention. His following had come

9. John Davis (1873–1955) was a politician who served in the cabinet of President Woodrow Wilson (1856–1924) and ran as the Democratic candidate for president in 1924.

from the Atlantic seaboard and from the states where the Democratic organization is dominated by large cities.

The apparent issue upon which Smith rallied his strength was a distaste for the law prohibiting the sale and manufacture of liquor. And certainly the opposition to Smith rallied around the presumption that Smith is a "Wet."

As a corollary to his wetness came the fact that he is a Catholic, and that fact gained and lost delegates for him in the convention. His strongest opponent, Mr. McAdoo, typified the opposing view of life.[10]

Mr. McAdoo unquestionably had the support of the Ku Klux Klan, an organization which at the moment was strong in the South and West, where belief in prohibition prevails and where the Klan organized what may be called the lower forces of Puritanism around Puritan vices. The struggle in the convention, therefore, was between the hard, ascetic morality of Puritanism and the lighter, brighter, happier philosophy of Catholicism.

Supporting the harsher, sterner view of life was the rural civilization in the states south of the Mason and Dixon Line and, broadly speaking, west of the Mississippi.

There was conflict deep and decimating between the two ideals in the states east of the Mississippi, north of the Ohio and west of the Alleghenies. There, in those Middle States, the change has not come definitely from the rural to the urban civilization.

Only a Local Figure—Yet

In the East agriculture as it was known in America forty years ago has been forced into the hinterland. In Ohio, Indiana, Illinois, parts of Michigan, and Wisconsin this is but a decade or two away.

The end of that convention was a meaningless compromise, a truce for breath, and there, as the convention panted in its impotence, stood Al Smith that night, delivering a speech to the delegates pledging his loyalty to the ticket that had been nominated. It was his first national appearance.

When he appeared the cheers of his supporters raged in fanatic fury. But

10. William McAdoo (1863–1941) was a Progressive Democrat who unsuccessfully sought the presidential nomination in the 1920 and 1924 elections.

he made a bad fist of his speech. As he stood, slamming his arms about, bellowing fiercely, wagging his head, sweating like a horse, he did not measure up to the occasion. He disillusioned his friends and justified the contention of his enemies that he was merely a local figure: just a popular New York man functioning as a local hero in the national limelight.

Al Smith *is* of national size mentally and spiritually, but he does not comprehend his nation nor think in national terms. He is a borough leader now, and no amount of advertising, no amount of propaganda in his behalf, will expand him into a national figure until he finds some stage whereon he may dramatize himself in terms of the national statement of his cause, which means that he must study national politics, know the truth about national issues, and by his stand upon those issues win a national following. He has only a local, indeed a most provincial, following now. But he has ability and strength for national leadership if he will take it.

What changes have come into American life which give this new kind of statesman the power of a hero? In two words: blood and iron, but the blood in this instance is the changing blood of the American nation, the iron is the vast framework of wires and tubes and beams and stringers, girders, and reenforcing upon which the new urban structure of the material life of America is rising—new blood and new iron.

Perhaps it wasn't the old blood of New England and the colonial blood of the South, now slowly mixing with new blood, so much as tradition and environment. But, at any rate, the America of the last quarter of the nineteenth century was essentially an agricultural nation. Our cities beyond the seaboard were agricultural towns. The English blood, or Teutonic blood if you will, naturally takes to agriculture, and we were of one blood as we were of one tongue. The farmer ruled us either actually by his votes, which made powerful minorities, or by his interests and traditions.

Our national leaders thought rurally. Our national policies were such policies as an intelligent, upright, altruistic American farmer might formulate in an eminently respectable world in which each man earned all he got and in which every man got all he earned by the grace of God and by such amendments to the Constitution as were necessary to establish the grace of God.

Our American story has been somewhat the record of those moral yearnings of the farmer and his fireside.

And now comes the clash.

The Democratic party naturally would be the custodian of these new urban issues, and out of the Democratic party the new kind of candidate probably will come. For the Democratic party has two curiously different branches—its Southern branch and its urban branch. The Democratic party is impregnable to-day in the South, in the aristocracies of Virginia, Louisiana, and Mississippi; in the South of the hill-billies of Georgia and Tennessee and in the South of the newly awakened industrial areas of the Carolinas, Alabama and Texas.

The other branch of the Democracy thrives in the cities. Tammany is its perfect example. Whenever the population of a city mounts to a half-million there the urban Democracy is intrenched. This Democracy controls the Democratic state organizations in New England, the Middle Atlantic States of Pennsylvania, New Jersey, and Delaware; in the Lake States of Ohio, Indiana, Michigan and Wisconsin, and exerts a powerful influence in the Democratic councils of Minnesota, Montana and the Pacific Coast States. As urban life predominates over rural life in America the Democracy led by Tammany will challenge the Democracy led by the Southern aristocracy and the hill-billies, and sooner or later Tammany and its kind must control the Democratic party. And in 1928 Al Smith will be the herald of a new order. He may be its champion. As governor of New York he has made a splendid state record, but his record has not attracted national attention because his state issues are not national issues.

His state record is good as that of governors go, perhaps extraordinarily good. He forced through a popular referendum and then through the legislature a number of major measures in state administration which loom large in the American metropolis but dwindle after one crosses the Alleghenies.

He secured what is colloquially known in politics as the short ballot, eliminating several elective offices and consolidating state departments. He conducted the propaganda for enlarging state institutions like a statesman and has been spending money like an engineer.

A Town-Lot Sir Galahad

He recognizes the folly of cramping public opinion—even treasonable public opinion—in a democracy, and by pardoning political prisoners convicted in wartime hysteria, and by vetoing repressive measures he has made a democratic record for free speech which might be more than a local record if there was much real sentiment in America in favor of justice when it threatens the basswood gods of reactionary fear.

Governor Smith's chief victory probably was the law providing for better housing in the larger cities, his only failure his attempt to put the state electric power under state regulation.

Al Smith, like most of the statesmen and probably a considerable majority of the people east of the Alleghenies and north of the Mason-Dixon line, has opposed prohibition because it has never come to the East as it has come to the rest of the country after a slow process of education, experiment, trail and failure, theory and practice. West—beyond the Alleghenies—prohibition was an accomplished fact from ten to forty years before national prohibition.

So even as an antiprohibition leader, while he picks up some followers in the larger cities of the hinterland, Al Smith still is a local leader dealing in local issues—urban issues all: prohibition, electric power, housing, the centralization of Democratic power, improvement of conditions for defectives.

Governor Al Smith could go to the United States Senate if he chose. His reasons for not going are excuses. Probably deep down in his underconsciousness he halts before tackling the larger economic issues of America in the Senate.

There is not, in American public life today, a clearer, stronger, more accurately working brain in any man's head than Al Smith's brain. His process of thought are logical, and he has the courage to defend them. But he cannot think clearly about matters of which he knows little.

To educate himself on these matters would take ten years. He would blunder in the Senate while he was learning that lesson. Hence he backs off from a senatorial career.

If Republican blundering should shunt Smith into the White House in '28 or '32, he would know where to get advisers on whom to call for expert and administrative wisdom. He would furnish the administrative talent and courage, but in the Senate one must act quickly on one's own immediate resources—which must come from experience or education. Smith has no such resources.

Here is a most human, affectionate, wise and brave man whose sincerity is never seriously questioned, whose courage is proverbial, whose humanity holds friends with steel rods. Yet he is at this moment a provincial statesman not because he has no national qualities of leadership. He has striking qualities of leadership. No other statesman in America has such powers of leadership as he, and yet he is provincial, not geographically but because he has not projected himself into the wider range of American issues, and unless the one issue in which he is national—that is, prohibition—should become more widely acute than it is now, Smith's greater qualities of leadership would languish. And he might remain in history, for all his high qualities, a town-lot Sir Galahad who never fared afield.

The Country Town Issue

(*The Emporia Gazette*, October 9, 1928)

When the great cities of America swinging their states with them rolled into a menacing column in the democratic convention, and overthrew the rural democracy of the South and West, a new issue entered American politics. It was the domination of all the American Tammanies in all the American cities, the rule of the big city against the old American order.

Herbert Hoover has met the challenge in a characteristic way.[1]

In his speech at Elizabethton, Tennessee, last week, he paid his tribute of admiration and respect to the American country town, the town between the village of three thousand and the big town of a quarter of a million. In that area lies the American country town, the town where men still have human touch with one another.

These American country towns of farmers, or villagers, people who still hold the old American ideals, the ideals of wholesome thrift, conscientious, neighborly relations, the call of duties before the demand for rights, the deep belief in a moral government of the universe, and a wholesome respect for public opinion of one's neighbors. Upon these customs and aspirations America has travelled for the last three hundred years to its success. The great cities scoff at what they call this country town "stuff," this respect for the public opinion of one's neighbors, this urge to put duty ahead of rights, this belief in the destiny of mankind and this ancient joy of neighboring.

Al Smith represents the new order, the carefree, Devil-take-the-hindermost belief that anything you can get away with goes. He was nominated by that kind of vote. If he is elected he will make that kind of president. His philosophy is the philosophy of the urbanite. And there is the chief fundamental issue in American politics. We call it Tammany, but it is deeper than Tammany. It is the philosophy of life, the opposition of the old rural America with

---

1. Herbert Hoover (1874–1964), Republican presidential candidate in 1928.

a biting conscience standing over against this new philosophy of pleasure at any price, motion for the sake of moving, joy for its own sake. It is a sign of decay when it strikes a state. It has not captured America but it menaces and the menace is incarnate in that gay smile through a cocktail.

The Country Editor Speaks

(*The Nation*, June 12, 1929)

For ten or a dozen years Sherwood Anderson has been a major figure in what for want of a better word we may call American letters.[1] He has been a writer with a vogue. His following has been among those who were low in spirits, down on their luck, grouched at the world—which has included in these years, speaking broadly, pretty nearly everyone in Christendom. Men in the mass probably get their philosophy from their conduct, and when they have been mean they are cynical. They think everybody has been mean. After the Western world has gone through the Great War, killing, lying, murdering, stealing, and everything, greatly to its own discredit, the Western world lost every sort of belief in the nobility of man; and having given up that, we lost faith in God, whatever He may be. We saw that man was a rattling good machine, that if you punched him here he would react there, and in a general way that accounted for everything that we could see in our philosophy—a philosophy like Horatio's which took stock only of "things in heaven and earth."[2] We took a chance when we should have taken council. We read the stars and wept. And having nothing else to do we turned to Sherwood Anderson and psyched ourselves into his way of thinking; or perhaps he, being an artist, took the color of his environment. At least his mental slant conformed to our general idea about the cosmos, which was a low opinion due to the low-down character of our own behavior.

---

1. Sherwood Anderson (1876–1941) was a novelist and writer best known for his 1919 short story collection *Winesburg, Ohio*, which focused on the repression and isolation of living in a small Midwestern town. White was a long-standing critic of Anderson, whom he associated with the pessimistic turn in the American literary scene of the 1920s.
2. From *Hamlet* by William Shakespeare.

So out came one book after another from Mr. Anderson, exhibiting man as a mechanism about seven cuts below the angels, and we bought his books like hot-cakes. But man is funny. One of the semi-precious blessings of God is man's high-powered forgetter. And we began to forget how ornery and dirty and beastly we were in the war; indeed, as the decade grew old, we began to esteem ourselves a little. The bounce in man must be the despair of all the devils in hell and all the misanthropic philosophers on earth. For pretty soon, after man has done his dirtiest, he forgets how bad he was and begins to think about how good he should be. Pretty soon he says: "Well, I'm not so rotten. Man after all walks on two feet. What's the matter with God anyway? Life's a grand game. God's in his heaven, all's right with the world. Let's go . . . "

So at the end of the first decade after the war, humanity is beginning to perk up and is not so sure that Sherwood Anderson has established an important school of thought. Men are beginning to say: "Now you take that guy that was all the time talking about slimy conduct and writing books out of a maggoty mind. Nothing is in it. This Sherwood Anderson has got to quit kicking *homo sapiens* around, or thumbs down for S. A." So off goes Sherwood Anderson to a little town down in Virginia and gets into the country-newspaper business. And now he comes back with a book that is pretty well tinctured with the philosophic doctrine that man, the proud biped who has sloughed off his tail, when you get right down to cases, is a good bet. His book, "Hello Towns," reveals Sherwood Anderson upholding the Western man's recrudescent philosophy. Soon Sherwood Anderson, mellowed in the woods, may be hitting the sawdust trail.

"Hello Towns," is a book made up of clippings from his country newspaper. These clippings might have been taken from any of a hundred American country newspapers. Kansas is full of newspapers that write their local items with this gaudy super-simple pose. When we can get a reporter on the *Gazette* who does it he is double starred. Ed Howe has had the same style for fifty years, and in the end it is the style which attracts the scissor-snippers of the great city papers who are filling that little column on the editorial page called Our Country Neighbors. Country-town people like to be gently guyed in this style, and country editors know it. Sherwood Anderson has done the job beautifully. But his work has no great distinction compared with that of many of his American fellow-editors in the little towns of the hinterland.

Apparently Mr. Anderson is a Kiwanian, or possibly a Lion. It would seem as though the Rotarians did not get down into his town. Probably his town is a shade small for Rotary.[3] It would be comforting to see him sitting at the Kiwanian luncheon table singing "The more we get together the happier we'll be."[4] But if he likes to sing he will enjoy it. The book indicates that he is lapping up life as a country editor and that he is getting closer to folks than he used to be and finding that they average up pretty well. Through the pages of his book move these kindly decent people of the country neighborhood. Some of the folks are successful. Some of the folks are subject to a discount of ninety and five and then are a loss when you have them on your hands. Some of the folks in "Hello Towns" are good outside and rotten within and others are rotten outside and good within. But the run of the mill is pretty good.

Mr. Anderson leaves the impression that he is a gay old dog, but probably he is not. Mostly when men pretend to be gay old dogs they are exhibiting their wishes rather than their deeds. Sheep-killing dogs don't carry much wool on their teeth. He says in the book one should never doubt the immortality of an author, but so long as he speaks of it, a reasonable doubt arises in his case. Maybe he's just bragging. Anyway this "Hello Towns" is a good enough book to go into a Sunday-school library. It is beautifully written, for certainly Sherwood Anderson jabs a mean typewriter keyboard. But the book as a book is wholesome with "nothing in it to offend the taste of the most fastidious," as the old minstrel bills used to say.[5]

As America comes out of her decade of dirty and disillusion, this Dostoevsky of Winesburg, Ohio, this mid-American Chekhov suffers a sea change into something rich and strange. He emerges puffing and snorting out of the vasty deep with as gay and glad and good a book as Pollyanna ever read.[6]

---

3. Kiwanian: a member of Kiwanis International, a volunteer service club founded in 1915. Lions and Rotarians refer to members of Lions Clubs International and Rotary International, two service clubs organized in 1917 and 1905 respectively.

4. From the song "The More We Get Together" by Jimmy Campbell (1903–1967) and Reg Connelly (1895–1963).

5. "Nothing in it to offend": a phrase used by traveling tent shows to advertise family-friendly entertainment.

6. The main character of Eleanor H. Porter's (1868–1920) 1913 novel *Pollyanna*, known for her cheerful naivete.

If I Were a Dictator

(*The Nation*, December 2, 1931)

My first experience in politics was as a boy of eighteen riding beside the driver on the high seat of my country town's one public hack, rounding up voters on election day forty-five years ago. Since then I have been at various times, my party's precinct committeeman, county committeeman, member of the State Central Committee, member of the National Committee—all offices without emolument but carrying a certain amount of power. Yet for a generation I secretly cherished one political ambition: to be benevolent despot of some political unit—a city, or county, or State. But, alas, as I grew out of my fifties I made a disillusioning discovery. Despots are never benevolent. Power breeds arrogance; arrogance corrupts the understanding heart. The more power a man has, the bigger fool he is, whether power is generated in politics or with money or with fame. So I know now that if I could be dictator of this land my failure would be measured by the extent of my power.

Therefore, if suddenly, after a rubbing of the magic ring, a company of nimble genii should rise and offer me a kingdom of the earth, first of all I should say to the lads from the magic power-house as I picked up the scepter of my dictatorship:

"Most esteemed and worshipful slaves of the ring, accept my salaams and let the political government of this land go hang. It so happens that as those things go, Washington isn't half bad. It never has been half-bad, and never will be. It represents about the intelligence, the courage, and the honesty of the folks. The people get what they deserve in the way of government."

Then, continuing my deceptive attitude of humility, I should roll my eyes and plead:

"Give me, the most unworthy of men, no clanking hardware of rank and power, no sidearms, no gold braid, no ribbons, no rooster feathers. Just let me have for a while authority over the invisible government. Give me secret power to control and coerce those salaried ladies and gentlemen employed by the various organizations of America—the Bankers' Association, the Federation of Labor, the League of Women Voters, the Y.M.C.A, the Knights of Columbus, the bar associations, the Navy League, the medical societies, the Farm Bureau, the Grange, the publishers' various organizations, the Associated Press and its rivals, the various affiliations of churches, Protestant and Catholic, the bootleggers' alliances, the scientific societies, the organized college presidents, the National Chamber of Commerce, the American Legion, all those happy little soviets in American life that form public opinion and hold Congress in leash—those subterranean forces that make executives dance on the various hot grids."

Then, after the palavering amenities, I should get down to business. For with power over those who dominate these societies, associations, organizations, and amalgamated groups, I could snap my fingers at the vote-greedy statesmen of the responsible governments of the land—all of them, in cities, States, and in Washington. Quickly, however, I should call a small conference of politicians, not because politicians are particularly wise, but because they have the previous power of getting along with people, doing team work, making programs, getting the day's work done. I should probably put in charge as my lieutenant commander none other than Alfred Emanuel Smith, or failing to get him, Calvin Coolidge—politicians and men of their type and kind.[1] I should say, having them all pleasantly lined up in my cabinet room:

"Now, ladies and gents, I have one job for you, one desire in my heart, and you can do what I require. I give you two decades to do the work I shall cut out for you. Here is the little, not impossible miracle I demand. To wit: Produce a social and economic status in this land which shall guarantee to men and women who are employed the same status for their lives that a dollar has when it is well invested in a bond or mortgage. Remove the fear motive from industry so that a man who works for others may know reasonably well that he is secure in his job or his wages. And don't forget this incidental detail—his

---

    1. Al Smith (1873–1944): Democratic president candidate in 1928; Calvin Coolidge (1872–1933): Republican president of the United States (1923–1929).
    2. G.P.U.: Acronym for the Soviet Union's secret police during the early 1920s.

wages must be sufficient to guarantee him a certain minimum standard of living. For your further instructions let me add that when I say a decent standard of living I mean a standard upon which he can live in a decent house, enjoying the mechanical comforts and luxuries of this modern civilization, eating clean, wholesome food, wearing decent and beautiful clothes, educating his children until they are at least twenty-one. The workers must be insured against the financial evils that come with sickness, accident, and old age. Moreover—here is something most important—with all his common heritage the worker must still have the priceless boon of liberty. I do not mean the right to desert his wife and children, to drive his own car at his own speed, to sell dirty milk or watered stock. I am not talking of those questionable individual rights which absolve a man from his duties under organized government based upon majority opinion definitely expressed. What I am driving at, as your fellow-dictator or fellow-tyrant, is the freedom to rise as high as any citizen will, by reason of any exceptional qualities he may have, so long as he remains honest and does not, through his own rise, cramp or curtail the freedom and well-being of his fellows. In other words, ladies and gents, let's define liberty as a man's royal American right to go as far as he will honestly above the mass, if in rising he contributes something valuable to society."

It would hardly be my job to say how this should be done, but a man who came up from the lower rounds of politics honestly and successfully would know how to begin if he had before him as tools the implements that make for public sentiment and the force and energy and protection of the organized groups in American business and social life above listed. Having given my lieutenants their orders I should let them alone and not nag them, assuming their honesty, their intelligence, their courage, in short, their patriotism. If one failed me I should chop off his head and perhaps put it on a pike and let it drip all over the first page of the newspapers for a week, to terrify others. What I should do with my own time is this: I should organize a secret police,

3. Heywood Broun (1888–1939) was a prominent sports writer, theater critic, and syndicated columnist for the *New York Tribune,* and the *New York World.* Broun also published a regular column for *The Nation,* "It Seems to Heywood Broun." Frank R. Adams (1883–1963) began his career as a journalist, but by the 1920s was a popular novelist, composer, dramatist, and composer of musicals. Will Rogers (1879–1935) began his career in vaudeville, but by the 1920s was a prominent film actor, staring in silent films and "talkies" through the

my G.P.U., under some such general title as Society for the Seduction of the Supercilious.[2] I should call into this council only men who could laugh—and laugh not maliciously but tolerantly. Perhaps I should make Heywood Broun, or Frank Adams, or Will Rogers, or Marc Connelly my Chief of Staff.[3] And I should say to this noble band of jesters:

"Boys, the besetting sin of our beloved country is vain and carnal pride. We're a lot of strutters, and the more money we get the worse we are; indeed, in reality the richer we seem the poorer we are. What we need is humility. America will only grow strong and wax fat in truth with the strength of the humble. Therefore it is your job to go into every rich state, city, town, and village, diligently spy out there the supercilious leadership, and seduce it. Boys, humble its pride not by taking away its power, but by letting these self-sufficient sinners know their own weaknesses and realize that 'we are all poor critters and that everything goes contrary-wise.'[4] Catch the town banker tapping his till for pennies not dollars. Slip Russian gold into the purses of the D.A.R.[5] Effect an exchange of pulpits between bishops of the true faith and the Methodist Church South. Set an Episcopalian bishop over the United Brethren, and a United Brethren bishop in Bishop's Manning's place; even stand up Billy Sunday in a Unitarian pulpit in Boston.[6] If you could give a lover to

---

late 1920s. He was best known for his popular portrayal of plain-spokeness and humor, often while portraying a cowboy. Rogers also wrote a popular syndicated column entitled "Slipping the Lariat Over" starting in the 1920s. Marc Connelly (1890–1980), a member of the Algonquin Roundtable of prominent writers and critics in New York City, was a playwright. He was awarded the Pulitzer Prize in 1930.

4. "We are all poor critters": A loose quote from Charles Dickens's *David Copperfield*, "'No. It had better be done by somebody else, Dan'l,' said Mrs. Gummidge. 'I'm a lone lorn creetur' myself, and everythink that reminds me of creetur's that ain't lone and lorn, goes contrary with me.'" White also used this quote in an editorial in *The Emporia Gazette*, from May 19, 1927.

5. "Russian" gold is a gold-copper alloy, known for its reddish color. The alloy is worth less than purer gold by weight. The Daughters of the American Revolution (DAR) was an organizaton founded in 1889 for female descendants of participants in the American Revolution. It is traditionally known for its exclusivity and White means to imply as much here.

6. The United Brethren was an evangelical denomination now part of the United Methodist Church; here, it represents a middlebrow US denomination. William T. Manning (1866–1949), episcopalian bishop of New York City, here represents a more exclusive and wealthy denominations in the United States. Billy Sunday (1862–1935) was a prominent

some of our leading ladies of one of the various anti leagues it would help a lot. And flash the white light of self-revelation upon certain pillars of purity across the land. Don't understand that I wish to topple men down in public disgrace and humiliation, not at all. That isn't your job. What we are trying to do is to teach tolerance to the haughty through a healing knowledge of their own weaknesses. But hold on now, get this straight whatever you do. Don't make them cynics, boys; make them penitents. Don't disillusion them into thinking that all men are bad because they are suddenly taken in sin. But do let them know, dearly beloved, that man can be noble even though he fails and falls and fails again. Put comic strips upon the whitened walls of the charnel-house of our institutional life. The boys across the hall who are saving democracy by cherishing economic liberty have a big job and you can help it, most gay and irreverent seigniors, by mellowing the times. So hop to it with a will."

Sooner or later one of those political adjutants from the uplift across the hall—maybe Al Smith or Gifford Pinchot or, say, Carter Glass—is going to come out and point a finger of scorn at me and say: "What about prohibition?"[7] And I'm going to be ready for him with this answer:

"For one hundred years and more, maybe a thousand, there will be a liquor problem in America. The conflict between the individual's liberty to drink what he pleases and society's dictum that the individual's drinking shall not depress the general welfare may not be settled in a decade or even a generation. Abolish prohibition and the problem is still here. Modify prohibition and the problem remains. Alcohol is a habit-forming drug. It must be distributed so that the salesmen will not find it profitable to oversell the customer and thereby increase the liquor habit, which menaces a highly organized social structure. It is not the content of liquor, whether 2 per cent or 98 per cent, that

---

evangelist popular in the 1920s. Here, he is contrasted with the more highbrow, cerebral Unitarians.

Unitarians reject the theological arguments for the Trinity, as well as Jesus Christ's divine nature. While Unitarianism has its origins in Europe, White places them in Boston to imply a cerebral theology in contrast to Billy Sunday's passionate evangelism. Ralph Waldo Emerson began his career as a New England Unitarian minister.

7. Gifford Pinchot (1865–1946) was a prominent progressive Republican who helped found the US Forest Service under President Theodore Roosevelt. Carter Glass (1858–1946) was a journalist, editor and prominent Democratic politician.

makes the problem. It is the distribution of liquor so that it shall not create addicts which makes the problem.

"Now then, gentlemen, here is a great opportunity for liberals. Under the prohibitory amendment and the Volstead Act we find a restless, determined, fairly well-organized minority that which think it's a majority of the people. This minority is chafing under what it regards as an unjust restraint. Some way should be found to give a considerable minority which thinks it is a majority the right to prove its case, to present its case formally and legally, and demand a count of noses. The need of this right, which is now demonstrated by the prohibitory law, may come up in the future. Someday the lack of this right affecting a more vital issue than prohibition might shatter the Republic. Prohibition offers liberals their great opportunity. Let them organize for a constitutional amendment which will make it possible at any time for any considerable restless minority which thinks itself unjustly restrained to call under the Constitution for a vote. Therefore, gentlemen of the council, as your dictator I hereby demand that you present to the American people a constitutional amendment which shall provide that when half of the States, through a majority of each house in their legislatures with the governor concurring, shall demand a national referendum upon any given subject, whether of statute or a constitutional enactment, then Congress shall submit the proposition to a direct vote of the people of the States. Or when two-fifths of the legislatures in States having two-thirds' majority of all the population of the United States shall submit such a proposition to two-thirds' majority of each house of each legislature with the governor concurring, a similar nation-wide popular vote may be had. And, further, the proposed amendment I have in mind shall prevail when it has been adopted by a majority vote in two-thirds of the States, provided the eighteen States shall contain two-thirds of the population of the United States; and that this majority shall be a majority of all votes cast upon the proposed question; and further, it shall be provided that in this popular vote majorities shall always be defined as majority voting upon the proposition.

"Here prohibition has coined the golden hour for a real reform. If the wets are too conservative to accept it they need not palaver about their high patriotism. If they are unwilling to grant to any minority that feels oppressed by government the same right which the wets today demand for themselves, all this talk about their rights may be safely ignored. If the Constitution of the

United States were liberalized by such an amendment as has been outlined above, no minority, no section, no class could ever rule this country against the wishes and the will of the majority of the people."

And at the close of the perfect day as dictator, I should go back to my G.P.U., my secret police, the men and women who could laugh and say this:

"Finally, dearly beloved, hunt down the gloom spreaders—those sad, solemn, disillusioned, baffled, doubting ladies and gents who have no faith in God or man, who believe that this is a mechanical self-winding universe, a machine that has lost its key or never had one. I mean that vinegar bunch which is all mixed up and low in its mind, sure only that its own raging melancholy is the wrath of God. Teach that outfit, O my most giggliferous pest-eradicators, that it really makes little differences about these sad theories. This gloomy philosophy gets men nowhere. The gloom-peddlers can't prove that nothing matters because matter is a phantasm; any more than the cheerful idiots can prove the moral government of the universe. But this much is finally certain: the job of a man is to live happily and usefully and to be kind and brave and as wise as he can, and after that, with God be the rest if there is a God, and if not, be kind and brave and wise anyway and charge it up to profit and loss."

And there is the plan. If I were dictator I should embody it in a few well-chosen words of general order, proclamation, and ukase, then hide myself in conference through the decades when it was working out, knowing full well that if I found my general orders obeyed, my proclamations considered, my ukases working, I should become vain and arrogant, mad probably. And so through tinkering with the machinery I had established, I should wreck it in calamity.

Acknowledgments

This book would not have been possible without the support of family, friends, colleagues, and students. Special thanks go to Jon Lauck and Patricia Oman for their helpful recommendations on the proposal, to the editorial team at the University Press of Kansas for their insightful recommendations and hard work, and to Jessica Guldner for her expert indexing skills.

Jason Stacy thanks his research assistants, Jamie Derousse, Zachary Ozirsky, Christopher Parks, and Taylor Thomas, whose determined efforts and hard work brought the draft to fruition. Thanks, also, go to his colleagues at Southern Illinois University Edwardsville, who offered good cheer and helpful suggestions, especially Jeff Manuel, who withstood many misbegotten arguments on their weekly bike rides. Jason is also grateful for Michelle, Abigail, and Margaret Stacy, who fill his days with delight.

Charles Delgadillo thanks Nelson Lichtenstein for his continued advice, support, and friendship, long after his official duties as committee chairman had been fulfilled.

Index

Iowa (tribe), 4
isolationism, 29
isolationist, 8, 20, 29

Jackson, Andrew, 179, 223–224
Jefferson, Thomas, 194n8
jocose spirit, 65
Johnson, Andrew, 223
journalism, 1, 5, 18
journalist(s), 6, 18, 141n3, 241n3, 243n7
judge(s), 63, 87, 220, 226
Jumbo the Elephant, 222
justice (fairness), 123–124, 152, 161, 176, 178, 183, 207, 212, 232
justice (judge), 118n1, 190, 226n7

Kansas City, 14, 44, 47, 99, 104, 108, 144, 177, 191, 215n3
Kansas City Journal, The, 6
Kansas City Star, The, 5–6
Kaw (tribe), 4, 47
Kentucky, 2, 223n3
Kickapoo (tribe), 4
kindness, 27, 100, 117, 123–124, 130, 152, 186, 207
king(s), 126, 128
Kipling, Rudyard, 150n4, 151n7, 208n3
Ku Klux Klan, 8, 25–26, 209–218, 229

labor, 5, 12, 19, 21, 24, 29, 64, 78, 115, 121, 132n10, 142
    activist(s), 25, 154n13
    child, 200, 217n1
    crowd, 166–167
    movement, 216
    See also enslaved labor
La Follette, Robert Sr., 202
land, 8–9, 35–36, 46, 57, 140, 143, 165, 171, 210, 217, 239–240, 243
    of opportunity, 176
    ownership, 132n10
    promised, 120
    speculators, 150
lawyer(s), 63, 80, 116, 175, 189, 190n5, 191, 194, 197, 201, 202n7, 210n6
leadership, 29, 110, 167, 200, 213, 222, 226–227, 230, 232–233, 242
League of Nations, 19–21, 146, 206n1
legislature, 27, 46, 76, 90, 189, 194, 199, 203, 227, 231, 244
Lewis, Sinclair, 23, 151n6, 152n11, 155n1, 156, 161

liberal, 24, 30, 216, 218
liberalism, 24, 28
library, 23, 34, 61, 78–79, 157, 238
Lincoln, Abraham, 4, 179, 223–224
liquor, 74, 157, 229, 243. *See also* alcohol
literature, 22, 60, 154, 162, 217
loan(s), 6, 35, 193
local (newspaper), 5, 159, 173
Longfellow, Henry Wadsworth, 180
Lord, 16, 44, 91, 118, 133, 149n1. *See also* God
Louisiana Purchase, 4
Lowden, Frank, 223
Lyon, Nathaniel, 220

Main Street (concept), 2–3, 10, 151
Main Street (novel), 22–23, 151n6, 155–156, 161, 163–164, 170
Manifest Destiny, 165, 196
Manitou (Colorado), 75–77, 81, 88
manufactured goods, 187, 196, 204
married, 13, 42, 59, 73, 84, 97, 99, 102, 192, 225
masculinity, 17
Mason, Walt, 1
Mason-Dixon Line, 229, 232
Masters, Edgar Lee, 22, 152
materialism, 18, 22, 150
materialist, 164
McClure, Samuel, 150
McClure's Magazine, 7, 12, 150
McKinley, William, 7, 225, 226n8
Mencken, Henry Louis, 152–154
Methodist(s), 60, 102, 242
Michigan, 5, 229, 231
middle-class (economy), 10, 17–19, 28, 197, 200–201, 204
middle-class (people), 9–10, 15, 25, 139, 168, 200
Midwest, 3–5, 8n10, 9–11, 21, 23, 163n9, 209n1
Midwestern, 2–12, 14–17, 19, 23–27, 149, 236n1
Ministerial Alliance (of Emporia), 103
minorities (political), 25, 178, 189, 192, 203–204, 230
minority (political), 27, 63, 117, 176–179, 201, 204, 208, 216, 228, 243–244
Missouri, 72, 190n3
Missouri Compromise, 4
modernism, 8, 22
money. *See* capital (money)
morality, 19, 124, 182, 229
Morgan, J. P., 12, 116, 144
moron, 174, 176–178, 183

www.ingramcontent.com/pod-product-compliance
Lightning Source LLC
Chambersburg PA
CBHW020338100426

42812CB00029B/3171/J